ALL THE TIME
IN THE WORLD

ALL THE TIME
IN THE WORLD

Hugo Williams

The Akadine Press
1997

All the Time in the World

A Common Reader Edition published 1997
by The Akadine Press, Inc., by arrangement with the author.

A Common Reader Edition and fountain colophon are trademarks
of The Akadine Press, Inc.

ISBN 1-888173-19-X

10   9   8   7   6   5   4   3   2   1

Contents

I – MIDDLE EAST

Beginning to go

Venice was cold and dark. I arrived at the station at about midnight with two heavy suitcases and a piece of paper saying 'Communist Bicycling Hostel, Isle of Iudecca'. Outside it was snowing, pattering down into the Grand Canal and settling on the gondolas. Even on this December midnight there were still a few shivering hotel touts waiting by motor boats for the odd honeymooner, but that was all. When they were sure I was sold to the hostel, they told me which vaporetto to catch for the Iudecca.

I stood outside on the deck, snow on my raincoat, warm and shivering with excitement.

When I got there, it was unlit and deserted and when I found the Communist Bicycling Asylum down a pitch-dark, mile-long quay, it was boarded up. I remember thinking perhaps I could creep off to a hotel and forget this madness, but there weren't any hotels and my suitcases anchored me to the spot. It is no good carrying dressing-gown, slippers, dinner jacket, type-writer, if you can't even get into a youth hostel. A week later I sent them home anyway. 'Hostello Iuventu?' I asked someone hurrying by.

'You're in luck, boy. I'm the manager. I was just going home. Let's see your card.'

'I haven't got a card. I'm not a member.'

'You're not a member? Why not?'

9

'Perhaps I could become a member?' Any minute he was going to accuse me of not being a bicyclist either.

'You could. But if you did you couldn't sleep here tonight. Memberships take 48 hours to come through. At least that. Members only. I'm sorry.'

'Why don't I just sleep here tonight, as a guest, and join up in the morning?'

'You could do that, I suppose.' He unlocked the door. 'Do you have a sheet, or do you want to hire one?'

'I'd like to hire one.' He handed me a strip of material.

'Toilet paper? . . . Two lira.'

'Thank you. Where's my room?'

'ROOM?' he ejaculated. 'You come here, not a member, make me open up for you. . . . The dormitory's across the yard and up that ladder.'

I put the sheet under my arm and carried my suitcases up the ladder, holding on with my knees. Inside was a naked man reading a map under a bulb.

'You find those cases stop cars?' he asked.

'I don't know. I haven't tried yet.' The room seemed full of people.

'We got turned off the Autostrada this morning. Bloody . . . ' Just then the bulb went out and I wondered if he had been about to say 'Capitalists'. I stood there trying to remember where there was an empty bunk.

Next morning I went on board my ship for Haifa.

Venice to Athens I shared a cabin with an Athenian jockey, returning from a working holiday in Europe. I found him in the morning sitting on the edge of the lower bunk, glumly looking through the photographs he'd taken. He passed one sadly up to me of a girl in Munich. Munich had the most beautiful girls in the world, he said. No, he hadn't spoken to her. He knew no German. Here was one of his little son. I took it from him and saw it was folded down the middle with only a single protective arm betraying the presence of his wife. When I handed it back he showed me the other half as an after-thought. She was far more beautiful than the Munich girl. But the sight of her seemed to fill him with dread and he drew his finger across his throat at the thought of facing her. His holiday had been ruined, he said. He'd planned to race in every town he came to, but in Naples a suitcase containing his racing boots, training boots and breeches had been stolen and he'd had to come home. 'When she finds out what's happened she'll be putting on the spurs, I daresay,' he said gloomily. But he brightened up at a snap of himself winning a race in Rome and got to his feet to demonstrate how he'd scraped through with his boot on the rails at the last minute. If ever I wanted a tip in Athens I was to look him up, he said. He'd put me in the paddock and see I won.

It was New Year's Eve and there was to be a party on board. The unfamiliar figure '1963' was pinned up behind the band-stand and by six o'clock the ship's photographer had behaved badly in the dark-room with a young Jewess from Brighton. I danced with her later and she told me he'd tried to make her pose in the nude *in* the dark-room. She said she hadn't at all liked Venice. Everything was so depressing and dull. Even the gondolas were painted black and everything had been shut up for the winter. Why couldn't they paint the river-boats yellow or something? When I met her parents they said they felt the same. They owned a tobacconist shop in Brighton's East Street which I'd often been into. The father called me 'Williams' and the mother brought me a piece of cake out of the first-class diner because she thought I looked thin. We started talking about Israel and I said something about the Jews in Israel having almost forgotten they were Jews in their eagerness to be Israelites. I danced with the girl again and she said: 'You mustn't speak like that about the Jews to Mum and Dad.

They're very sensitive.'

'What did I say?'

'I don't know.' Later on the trip someone who was sitting at their table told me the whole family thought I was anti-Semitic and might easily be a spy.

From Piraeus to Haifa I was very seasick and remember only a fat Armenian looking into my bunk and plucking at my hair and making scissor movements with his fingers. Seeing I was past his stupid advice, he must have walked off with my only drip-dry shirt.

'If You Will It Is No Fable', said the inscription on a statue of a young Israelite, welcoming me with outstretched arms to the Haifa Customs Shed. Outside the same gesture came to life. The streets were like some giant club. People seemed to touch and rebound in a way they never do in England. There was a common impetus and a common style. The cult of the Kibbutz must in its hey-day have started a fashion for work clothes, for everyone seemed to be hurrying about some semi-military mission in faded khaki shorts or dungarees. Especially the girls, who were in uniform to a woman, the thin beige skirts shamelessly hand-tailored, the breast-pockets of their blouses tight-stretched.

There were leaders and followers, that was all, and so little time to spare they were even eating and drinking at stalls on the pavement. There was not a restaurant to be found, and nothing at all of the old Mediterranean 'manyana manyana' about the place. Yet it was not Oriental. It is probably more like America than Europe.

I had no plans for staying in Haifa, so I set out round the Haifa shipping offices on the chance of getting work on a boat leaving within a couple of months. I didn't care in which direction I went, as any voyage would have taken me on my way, but I thought I would rather go east than west.

No ships it seemed were going in either direction. Especially east, because of the Egyptian boycott. I waited in a dozen different queues, claimed to be able to cut hair, cook, paint, wait, and in the end got an unpaid job on a ship going back to Venice, the only place in the world I wasn't prepared to go to, so I gave it up. I have tried often since to travel free on ships, but never with any success. I shall always be full of admiration for travellers who speak casually about 'getting work on a little freighter going to Rio', or 'hitch-hiking by sea'. The reality is the usual vicious circle protecting professionals and natives from amateurs and freebooters: no job without papers, no papers without job.

Anyway, my immediate objective was Jerusalem, so I took an express bus to the city. The Israeli hit parade was on the radio and the driver turned up the volume till the loudspeakers filled the bus with Helen Shapiro and Jerry Lee Lewis, pushed in strident Hebrew. By that time only one Beatle number, *From Me to You*, had been issued.

We stopped once, on a barren stretch of country with not a house for miles, and a robed Arab got in out of nowhere and sat down on the floor. He looked much like everyone else on the bus, except me. I hadn't yet seen anyone I thought looked Jewish.

We came through the stretch of desert and the countryside turned almost English, with downs and hedges and poplars in fields. Something you couldn't find on the opposite coast of the Mediterranean. Here the bulldozers and irrigation pipes and combine harvesters come with their green fingers right down to the beaches. Only the occasional 'saabra' – the cactus which the new Israelites call themselves after because of its prickly skin, but soft heart – proclaims the true climate of the land.

We passed through an orange plantation and the bus filled with the sensual taste of blossom, which we bore away into the mountains of Jerusalem.

The first view of the city was from above. The Israeli sector is served, supplied and kept alive now by a single mountain

13

corridor through enemy territory. This hairpins up into lovely, red-cliffed hills until it tops a last ridge near an overturned tank. Then below us was the sun impaling itself on the cypresses of Jerusalem and I saw no more of the city till the morning.

Jerusalem landladies prefer the colour of your money to that of your passport. Israel, in fact, is the new Foreign Legion. The date and place of your birth is a matter of indifference to them, so long as you pay up before sleeping. (On the Sabbath you do so by placing your four Israeli pounds between the pages of a proffered book, which closes religiously upon them till the morrow.) Here are some of the old Yiddish-speaking Jerusalem Jews, originally from eastern Europe, but lodged in the city long before Israel was born. They are not as orthodox as some, not quite resenting the new state, but nevertheless not part of this hurtling new people so unlike them.

I opened my window in the morning and caught a first glimpse of the low, sand-coloured villas of some, I knew not what, Jerusalem suburb, behind the long, ash-grey leaves of a eucalypt. The eucalypt had been sent there all the way from Australia on Independence Day.

Outside it was colder than Haifa, almost another climate, and the people dressed more sedately. 'Haifa works, Tel Aviv dances, Jerusalem prays.' Hurrying by in their long, double-breasted coats were the Orthodox Jews, their pale faces turned away from the street, fair ringlets drooping under high, round hats.

I went into the YMCA and up the tower in the lift to see across the wall into Arab territory. Beneath my feet was No-Man's Land, like a dried-up moat, obviously used as a rubbish dump by both sides. It looked as if long ago the water had receded to reveal these old hulks of Austins, barbed wire, piles of rags with stinging nettles on them, chickens and old guns and some corrugated iron lean-to's lived in by those past mortal danger. Children too were playing there in an over-turned armoured car. To them it was a mysterious, exciting place where grown-ups were not allowed.

Next door at the American Express was a letter from an old friend, Michael Brett. It had been forwarded from home, but posted not a mile away on the other side of the Gate in Jordan. My only plan on leaving had been to meet him there for my 21st, just before his job at the American School of Oriental Research ended and he returned home, leaving me to voyage eastward. 'Where are you? and when are you arriving?' it said. 'I have a whole sack of birthday cards for you, sent, needless to say, to the right city but the wrong country, and brought through the Gate for you by the United Nations in one of their white station wagons. If you are coming, do be careful. In case you didn't know, Israel and Jordan are at war, and Jerusalem is partitioned like Berlin. Several people have been shot in No-Man's Land recently, so do me a favour and don't go stumbling across in broad daylight or at any other time. You are the most likely candidate for a pot shot I can think of. There is a gate. Make enquiries and go through it. Michael.'

I went to the Consulate and was told I might not be able to go through the Gate for a week. All the Arab officials were away for the fast of Ramadan, which depended for its termina-tion on the visibility of the moon.

Three days later I set out in the rain to cross this strange frontier.

The Mandelbaum Gate is an uninhabited, bombed-out street with bullet screens and tank blocks at each end. It is one more East-West turnstile at which the twain are destined not to meet. If you want to walk down it into the other world at the end, you have to have at least two passports, a certificate of baptism, a permit from both governments, a visa, which may have expired before this comes through, and a name which isn't Cohen or Mohammed waiting for you at both border controls.

What happens is this. At the Israeli border you bring out your extra passport, valid for Israel only, and they put their exit stamp in it. Then you put that one in your back pocket, pick up your suitcase and walk about a thousand miles east and a hundred years back in time. Actually it is only a few hundred yards, but the transition is instant. Suddenly you look up and see an Arab in a red check burnous levelling his eyebrows down a rifle at you from a sand-bagged window. You wonder on what detail of your appearance your life hinges. It's like a game of grandmother's footsteps, with a sort of mental rush for cover at the finish.

Once across No-Man's Land you bring out your ordinary passport. Someone once produced his Israeli passport and the border official threw it straight over his shoulder into a furnace. By a curious process of doublethink they are able to let you enter their country from Israel, providing they don't see an Israeli stamp in your passport. Officially speaking you drop straight down into No-Man's Land from outer space.

At the far end of the street and soaking wet, I put down my suitcase and typewriter and handed over the correct passport. The official began to look through the list of people due to cross that day. After a minute he said:

'Your name isn't on the list.'

'But it must be. I applied. . . . I was told I could go today. . . .'

'Well, I'm afraid you'll have to go back for today.'

'Could you look at the list again, please. I can't understand it.'

'Williams, Williams, Williams, and you're coming from Israel into Jordan, you say?'

'Yes.'

A long silence, during which something seemed to come to light.

'Well, it says here you're going from Jordan into Israel. Are you sure which way you're going?'

'Quite sure.'

'One minute, please.' He went away and had a conference

with his colleague. Then he came back saying that there must
have been a mistake and that I'd better enter. 'You realize you
can't re-enter Israel, don't you?' he said, as he handed me back
my passport. But I think there was doubt in his voice that I had
ever been there.

QUEEN'S COSY CELLAR
JERUSALEM JORDAN

Cosy Bar, European Restaurant,
Tea Room, Pastries and Stimulants,
For All Tourists and Visitors
        Welcome
One Visit to Queen's Bar, Tea Room,
Restaurant, Oriental and European
Pastries and Foods Will Make a
Remarkable Feeling & Remembrance
Of Your Life's Visit & Will Be a
Boast To Your Friends and Associates.
Try it Once and You Will Be Reassured Of it.
Moderate Prices. Most Welcomed

Three days late for my 21st, Michael and I sat in this rather
ambiguous joint, absorbing stimulants like mad and feeling on
the whole reassured of it.

When I arrived at the American School I found him brown
and crew cut, quietly eating his lunch of meat and two veg in
the refectory. I felt like the mountaineer who finds a small
party of Girl Guides picnicking on the summit of the mountain
he has just conquered. He was so domesticated. Yet he was as
homesick as I was travel-struck. He had been there six months,
yet had no idea what it was like on the other side of the wall, or
how much greener the grass. Here there were no pretty girls, in
or out of uniform. Only long-robed Bedouin soldiers, usually
holding hands, travel agents offering tours in the footsteps of

Christ, American cars full of dark-spectacled Arabs like jokes out of *Punch* and an after-dark curfew. He was even on a committee to get some kind of club started for the young people in the city, as yet still on paper. 'I know there's a brothel somewhere down that street,' he said to me one evening, 'but I've never been able to find it.' Typical.

Sitting in Queen's Cosy Cellar, I began opening my birthday cards.

One in particular from Michael's brother Guy reminded me of what I had left behind. 'How I envy you far from this foul winter,' he said, 'knowing nothing of beer, baked beans, shillings in the meter and damp elastic-sided boots.'

In Jerusalem it was warm and sunny like the best kind of English June. The priests were already wearing their summer cassocks, which, according to Michael, was as reliable a seasonal indicator as what the typists wear in London.

The hotels were crowded, but in the end I managed to get into a very old, crumbling, carefree one called The Jerusalem. This hotel was famous for its hot-water system. Whenever you wanted a bath, a bonfire had to be lit in the garden and burning logs hurried indoors between tongs and stuffed into a vast, cast-iron boiler, which extinguished them almost instantly.

Before I had been there long a charabanc of students from Aleppo turned up and I was asked if I would mind moving down the road to the management's A-class hotel, the Ritz, for the same tariff, as my room was needed.

I was rather sorry to leave as I had grown rather fond of the flaming logs, high ceilings and well-mannered chaos of The Jerusalem. But one of the students very kindly packed up my things for me and then insisted on escorting me to my new room. He told me on the way that American planes had recently been dropping photographs of President Nasser over Syria to turn the people against the Ba'at Government. He was very talkative and anti-American and he asked me to go to

Bethlehem with him and the other students in a couple of days' time.

Meanwhile I met Michael for lunch, and in the evenings we walked through the cavernous underworld of the Old City, searching for presents for his family. Here in the fabulous Via Dolorosa the flagging life of Arab Jerusalem had its pulse.

Donkeys and bicycles bumped over the cobbles and down shallow stairs. Above, square awnings like sails held off the sun in patches of dirty colour. Barbarous butchers hacked at carcasses in dark cells. Sheep pelts hung up to dry. Beggars. Treasure. Sacks of spice. Yet it was not completely strange. There are very few locations in the world left by the cinema and journalism still intact and undreamt. Without knowing it one has built up from a thousand sources, mostly unconsciously, a fairly accurate visual picture round themes such as 'Outback', 'Corrida', 'Kasbah', even, who knows, 'Outer Space'. The picture is a lurid parody of the reality, but it is the exaggeration which the mind so easily modifies and stores.

What Cinemascope and colour supplements can never communicate is the condition of being there. Loneliness, frustration and tiredness for instance, usually help reality rather than blur it. One journey therefore, however short, can teach one this gap in the experience of description, and perhaps fill it with experience of somewhere else.

Once we left the Old City and walked round the embankment outside the city wall. We passed through a little desecrated Jewish graveyard with the Hebrew headstones lying smashed and defaced by Arabs. Then a chicken-scratch encampment of refugee bedouins from Israel, quite different from the city Arabs. These were fine-looking, dark-skinned and gaudily bejewelled. The unveiled women even looked strangely sensual against their barren background. Though their lives must have been long past vanity. They ran after us, begging without a word of English, pulling at our sleeves, slyly smiling, weeping.

Two mornings later I met the Syrian students. They came round in their bus to my hotel and picked me up to go to Bethlehem. There were thirty of them, all newly released from the hardships of Ramadan and each keen to infect me with his gaiety. They took turns to sit next to me to try out their English above the deafening discord of a drum and accordion with which I was being serenaded. It was not very like a pilgrimage. One little woman was telling me about a dream she had had of the Virgin Mary helping her with her exams, another wanted me to do the twist for them in the aisle. Then they all wanted me to do the twist. 'William Twist, William Twist,' they chanted. I tried to concentrate on the dream. I knew I would have to get over feeling like a performing monkey wherever I went. It would get me nowhere. Travel is an exchange, but already I was resenting my side of the bargain.

The bus dropped down through the powder-coloured hills of Jerusalem, crossed the muddy little Jordan and climbed up towards Bethlehem. It was about a two-hour journey.

The small town looked Mediterranean. All whitewash, cobblestones and churches. There was less of the East about it than Jerusalem. At first it was almost what one had expected from childhood images. Except that now one saw in crisp sun-light what had always been in darkness.

Of course there were variations. We visited the Grotto of Milk, where some of the milk from Mary's heavy breast is said to have spilled on to the marble, staining it white, while she was hiding from Herod's executioners. Women who are barren go there now to pray. Inside was a gaudy plaster cast of the Flight to Egypt. 'This is Mary and Jesus,' said the little lady who had told me her dream. She was like a newly-wed showing me round her new house. 'And that is a friend who was looking after them,' she said, showing me Joseph. I asked her whether she was Christian and she said no, but that she believed Jesus was a prophet. Did she believe he was the Son of God, or the son of the friend who was with them? 'Not Son of God, only messenger, like Mahomet,' said another girl student. A third disagreed with them both and said she believed completely in the Virgin Birth. Allah was bigger than everything, she said, and whatever he wanted on earth, took place. Moses and Mohammed both had human fathers, but God had wanted Jesus to be 'clean and fresh and clear', so he had put his own life into Mary's body. It seemed that Bethlehem was common ground for Muslim and Christian alike. In a strange way these girls were both Christian and Moslem. I even heard from them a story about the Nativity which I don't remember reading in the Bible. It tells how Herod's executioners eventually caught up with Mary where she was hiding from them. They wanted to kill the babe, but Mary told them her child was not Joseph's but God's. They did not believe her, so she told them to ask the infant for themselves. When they did so, the child opened his mouth and said 'I am the Son of God.' The men were then so frightened they spared the child and fled.

After the Milk Grotto we walked into the middle of the town to Manger Square, where the rambling Greek Orthodox Church stands on the site of Christ's birthplace. Facing the church across the square was the Christ Child Café and the Nativity Store. I bought a little card with petals pasted to it, called 'Flowers from the Holy Land'. From every doorway touts tried to flog luminous Virgin Mary's and bakelite cribs.

We went into the ancient, abbey-like church and all was quiet. Brass chandeliers from Russia hung from the ceiling. Drapes from the East shrouded innumerable little shrines, each with its host of candles burning.

A few at a time, we went into the crypt, where the actual birthplace is said to be. It was very dark and crowded and heavy with incense. I hung back on the steps and one of the students said he didn't believe I was a Christian because I didn't *like* the place. I suppose the imagery of thatch and woody inn had held out to the last. The ponderous superfluities of Greek Orthodox: drapes and doilies, hangings and coverings and little lights in pots on chains seemed somehow obsequious. I thought of Chartres' clear authority and wanted to run up into the thin air.

On the way back in the bus there were more high jinks. The band paraded up and down the aisle and the congregation sang out: 'Am-Man, Am-man, Am-man.' They were fed up with curfewed Jerusalem and wanted a bit of fun in the capital.

When I met Michael in the evening he told me what Bethlehem had been like on Christmas Eve. First of all the Ministry of Tourism had laid on various diversions. There was carol singing in one of the three official 'Shepherd's Fields'. Everyone queued up to get inside a kind of wire compound strung with fairy lights and public address systems, rather like Belsen on liberation day. Later there was midnight mass at the Church of the Nativity. Outside in the square, taxi drivers were seeing who could mow down the largest number of pilgrims, who were scuttling about like frightened chickens squawking in every language you can think of, while venerable Greek patriarchs in flowing beards bolted for the doors of churches. The crowds were so great that the High Priest had to have four peons going ahead of him keeping back the people with tennis racquets.

Inside the church several thousand people were attending mass and watching a kind of firework display, with Roman candles and neon lights going on and off saying 'Gloria In Excelsis Deo' and illuminated boxes being carried about on poles containing life-size models of the Christ Child in swaddling clothes. The Roman patriarch who was officiating kept undressing and dressing up again in different clothes, while groups of surpliced acolytes drifted about bearing relics on sticks.

A few days later it was time for Michael to fly home and for me to go eastwards, for I had decided to go overland to India.

Allah giveth and Allah taketh away

There was a big diesel truck standing in the oily sawdust of the depot in Amman. For a week I had been manoeuvring for a lift in one out of Jordan, across Saudi Arabia. 'Come back first thing tomorrow,' they had said each day. 'There'll be someone leaving then.'

At ten a trucky arrived in a taxi, carrying a huge branch of bananas, bread, tins of condensed milk, a primus stove, blankets and wearing dark glasses. I went up to him and said I'd been told he could take me to Kuwait.

'Who said?' he scowled at me.

'A man in the office.'

'Who driving this truck? Me. You ask me. I work for myself.'

'I have to get to Kuwait. May I come with you?'

'OK.'

Just before we left some friends of his came to the depot to see him off. They were all dressed in their best suits and one of them had a bunch of blue flowers which he pushed through the window of the truck. I'd forgotten it was a holiday. The day before was the birthday of Mohammed. Nobody likes working on Boxing Day. It explained the trucky's scowl.

His friends gave him some brandy and peaches. Then everyone was embraced and we set out.

The truck was much bigger than any you see in England. It was a magnificent great Mercedes like a rhinoceros, with coloured lights round the outside of the cabin and green tape twisted round everything inside. There was even a piece of Persian carpet on the floor.

Suddenly the driver asked me:

'You know King Hussein?'

'No, I don't know him.'

'You see he is the King of Jordan.'

'I know.'

'You like kings?'

What should I say? It might be important.

'No.'

'King no bloody good. No fucking good. You see that house? King gave house to Arab woman. He have girl here, girl there, but really he likes his mother best. Why he marry to English girl? English girl not Musselman. King like Arab woman best.'

'I'm English.'

'You like Arab girl?'

'I never see Arab girl. They stay at home. They don't come out.'

'Hah ha ha. My name Ghazi. How do you do. Tomorrow you tell me all about English girls. Ha ha ha.'

'My name's Hugo. How do you do.'

'Ucho?'

'Yes.'

'No other name?'

'Williams.'

'OK William, my name Ghazi. OK?'

'OK.'

We had left the town and were going through scrubland. I sat back and enjoyed the vibration of the wheels riding up through my bones. This was the first step east. The first assault.

At H4, the final checkpoint in Jordan, we left the Baghdad road and turned south into Saudi Arabia along a rough wheel track which was to be our road from now on. Regular black oil-stained boulders stretched as far as the eye could see, with the occasional chassis of a yellow American car riding spectrally over them into eternity. You could even see jerrycans and tank tracks left over from the war, which had not even begun to rust yet. There is nowhere for such things to go in the desert. They simply become part of the skyline for ever.

The rock and rubble and strange salvage continued all day. Then the conventional desert began and the sun went down, catching the side of each ripple with its last rays, till the sand took on its own tiny, chiselled world of shadows and glinting specks of mineral. In the desert the sun seems to set almost below the level of your feet, lighting the land from the side and revealing its texture.

At night it was hard to see the way and Ghazi kept putting his head out the window to get his bearing from the stars. We went pitching up the sides of sand dunes and through floods, and once we hit a little hut, which just turned round a bit like a summer-house. Ghazi told me to try to get some sleep, so I wedged myself into a corner. He himself stayed awake by sticking matchsticks up his nose to make himself sneeze, or by cricking his neck to one side. Then suddenly the truck stopped and there was a man waving to us in the headlights. He got up on to the running board and started speaking to Ghazi like a man explaining an accident to a policeman, occasionally glancing over at me as if I was the third party. He wanted to go to Kuwait and he seemed to be getting his way. Ghazi asked me if I'd mind sitting on the other side of him, next to the window and I realized there must be others coming who had sensibly stayed out of sight until the initial negotiations had been made. I looked out the window and there beside the road a whole tribe had materialized. The man had with him his wife, his three children, his brother, his brother's wife, their three children and a great mound of rotten-looking baggages. There was also a suitcase made out of old Pepsi Cola tins.

I saw that the game was up for me inside the cabin, so I got up on to the roof and into a sort of luggage cradle. The women and babies got inside, then the baggage was passed up on to the roof in endless damp eiderdowns and made into nests for the other children.

I shall never know why Ghazi took them on. Whether there was an understanding about the women, promise of remuneration in heaven, or whether he simply liked having them running round him, looking after him and making tea whenever he wanted it, and he wanted it a great deal. He was the sort of man who takes four days to reach Spain from Calais and travels with a collapsible table and china plates. Every two hours we stopped, put up a little aluminium windscreen on the running board and lit up the primus. There were only two glasses and Ghazi and I had at least four each before Unis, the gypsy, was allowed any. Then he and his brother had all they wanted and poured the drainings from the teapot into a bowl which they handed up to their women for them to dip their terrible pieces of old, dry bread into. I never saw them eating anything else and they always offered me some if they caught my eye. The men thought they had a better deal. They occasionally fumbled inside their robes and brought out little pieces of dried goat's cheese like stones.

All the first night we kept moving, then stopped at about five and slept for a few hours. I had no sleeping bag so I climbed under the tarpaulins on the roof. The gypsies spread themselves out in the desert and Ghazi occupied the cabin. I had never slept out before in my life, but it wasn't difficult. Looking up into the extraordinary desert night, painted like the Court of Star Chamber with big golden, silver and green stars, mysteriously underneath one, like the seabed, was to be already dreaming.

In the morning there was a wind blowing. We drove for a while, then stopped at a little teahouse, bobbing like a lightship among the dunes. There was sand lapping and spraying at its foundations and inside it was cool and dark like the hold of a ship.

Sitting all round, silently, were the bedu, with their long, dry hair plaited in blue ribbons down their backs and rifles leaning against chairs beside them. There was black paint on their eyes and they stared at me, or very near me, with the passive, feline gaze of young girls. Their eyes were like reflections of eyes in pools. I ate some stew and they followed the spoon to and from my mouth, wondering perhaps how I could stomach the grubs and dragons it was probably made of.

Ghazi seemed to live on curds and bananas and he shared everything with me. He said if I gave him a pound in Kuwait he would pay for what we ate along the way, though in fact it was all put down on the slate. I never once saw any Saudi currency. I set out without currency or supplies. But not entirely by accident. I prefer it that way. I hate landscaping my life as far as the eye can see. I like arrival to be something more than the result of my calculations. I like it to be a kind of bonus satisfaction, like coming out of a film at the beginning of the holidays and suddenly remembering that it's not the film which is over, but the holidays which have begun.

We finished eating and drank some green sherbet. Outside the sky was leathern and the surface sand was shifting in its tracks as if there were snakes underneath it. We had a timetable to stick to, so we set out and were soon in a sandstorm. The sand swung back and forth like a heavy curtain against the windscreen and eventually shut out visibility. We stopped and the gypsies got down into it and somehow existed under their eiderdowns. Ghazi stretched out on the seat and I lay down among the pedals on the floor.

It was a bad storm and I can still taste the sand, where it whistled through the floorboards, and feel it clotting my eyelashes. It lasted for the rest of the day and half the night. In the middle of the night it began to rain and the rain weighted the sand down and we could breathe again. The gypsies emerged from the darkness, looking rather refreshed and we had a chilly breakfast of mashed-up beans and split peas doused in lemon.

27

Then we sang *Mustapha*, a tune they never tired of, clapped hands and pushed on.

It had stopped raining now and the desert was sparkling like new sandpaper. Here and there we encountered floods like silver cloaks laid down in the mud for us, and oddly enough we had to go through them. Wherever there is water you're safe from quicksand. Elsewhere the land seldom recognized our wheels with much respect. A kind of grudging support from the undersoil was the best we received.

Soon we began to follow a huge pipeline taking oil to the Mediterranean from Kuwait. It was about ten feet high and sometimes the track crossed underneath it. Beyond we sometimes saw the old red Thames Traders of the bedouins, shunning even the wheel marks we were following, and sometimes their black goatskin tents, tied up at the sides to catch the air.

Otherwise there was only the white horizon and the smooth desert circling us like a ring of Saturn. I lay on top of the truck, watching the imprint of the tyres running out behind and the little dotted racks of clouds, proving the immense amplitude of the sky. In towns, walls limit our sight and we are obliged to close our eyes. I think we would never be tired if we could always see far enough.

Driving here was easy and Ghazi let me drive awhile so he could sleep. I hung on to the top of the big wheel. We passed a man in a green turban. At nightfall we reached a village where Ghazi's father lived. We had dinner with him, lying on string cots outside his petrol station, and he told me in English how he remembered the Australians coming there in the first war. He said the Australians were very gentlemen men. Was I by any chance Australian? Yes, half Australian.

'You are not half Jew-boy?'

'No.'

'Then you are a friend of mine. Do you like the Jews?'

'They're not my enemies.'

'Yes. Good. OK. They are my enemies, you see.'

Six hundred miles from Israel this man felt hate.

'Why do you hate them?'

'They steal our land, they rape our women. Here we obey the law of the Koran. If a man steals, we cut off his hand. If a man rapes, we bury him to the waist in sand, cover him with curds and set the hungry dogs on him.'

At this village we took on two soldiers on leave from the Saudi army. One of them had a magnificent transistor with a six-foot aerial and whenever we stopped for tea he sat down a little way off, his wireless between his knees and began to flick the needle over the continents with a bubbling staccato music which seemed to please him. Being a bedouin, I think he preferred to feel the distances roll under his thumb than to settle for any one station.

It was the third day now. Very early that morning one of the soldiers, who came from a bedouin family, said he knew a short cut to Kuwait, so we turned sharp left and headed out across another equally featureless piece of land. He seemed confident and kept looking up at the fading night sky as if he had divined his route in the cosmos. Two hours later we were up to the axles in soft mud and five of us had to push for an hour to get us out. The result was a cruel loss of face for the soldiers, who thereafter remained completely silent except to sing strange curdling rounds to one another, which seemed to come from a long way off.

The journey was almost finished and the sand beginning to roughen into something more homely. We joined a road and the truck bounced about again on its rigid suspension system. Once my suitcase broke loose and nearly slithered off the roof. Luckily Unis managed to get to it just before it fell, but as he was making it fast some pages from his Koran began blowing out of his pocket and back down the road in the wind. I thought he would be upset, but he just finished tying up the suitcase, lifted up his shoulders and said what must have been 'Allah giveth and Allah taketh away.'

Two miles outside the Kuwait border we stopped for a last cup of tea and something happened which I couldn't understand. Unis was reading palms when suddenly he seemed to lose his temper and started shouting at his wife, then at one of the soldiers, then at Allah, and finally at me. Then everyone started shouting at Allah and Unis's wife took off one of her shoes and hit her husband a terrific blow on the head with it. Ghazi said something rather quietly and the two women began throwing down their bedding into the road. I kept asking Ghazi what was going on and eventually he said that the gypsies would probably not be allowed to enter Kuwait as they had no passports. He said he had told Unis he might as well start walking back to Turkey.

Just then another lorry came trundling out of its sleep upon the horizon, its tarpaulins billowing in the wind like the sails of a galleon and as soon as it got near us Unis began running after it, praying and begging it to stop for him and take him home. The lorry did stop and Unis did get in, but after a minute he got down and started walking gloomily back towards us.

Unis, Unis, sad, lovable scum of the earth, what are you going to do now? Nothing. That's better. Sit down in the mud about a hundred yards off, light up one of your terrible fags and fill the desert air with the smoke of your injustice.

Meanwhile Ghazi was like a man at his son's school play, resigned to something he had set in motion and yet had no control over. Water was fetched from a wheel rut and we had sweet, sandy tea again. Then Ghazi took a glass over to Unis like a white flag and peace was made.

But he had been right. At the frontier they were impounded and told they'd be repatriated, or more properly expatriated, the following week. The last I saw of them the children were splashing in some oily puddles near the quarantine shed and the women were hunched near their eiderdowns like poor snails.

Smugglers

Kuwait is not yet flattered by a tourist industry, but those that do come approach by sea or air. If they came at it from the desert, they would pass as we did through a stinking shanty town of aliens. This is the inevitable detention camp for all the flies of Arabia who have been drawn towards the country's legendary riches.

As we drove through this square mile of lean-to's I saw a man carrying a sheet of corrugated iron on his back, looking for somewhere to set down his house. Dogs were everywhere. Women scrubbed clothes round a little water stagnating in some wheel-tracks. There was a yellowish pall over the scene.

The actual inhabitants of Kuwait are of three kinds: rich Kuwaitis, foreign technicians and a few aliens. The aliens, like Unis, my gypsy-cum-bedouin travelling companion from Turkey, are usually prevented at the last from seeing that the streets of Kuwait are not paved with gold. They are herded into these twilight encampments and left to rot.

We left Unis beside the road, surrounded by his enormous family, talking to a uniformed official. He looked like the last remnant of a tribe condemned to extinction. He had come 900 miles with us in the truck across Saudi Arabia. Soon he would have to retrace his hard-won tracks.

As a British subject, I didn't need a visa, only a few injections.

Probably of oil. Ghazi already had his transit visa, so we proceeded into the town.

We pulled up finally in a depot near the harbour. Being neither alien-Arab, Kuwaiti, or white-collared, I was immediately surrounded by seventeen young boys. They watched but did not beg for money. Feeling suddenly tired, I began to heave my suitcase down from the roof of the lorry. Just then a customs official spotted me and strolled towards me out of a little Pepsi-Cola transport café. 'Open.' I unlocked my case and there beside the truck, with thirty-four eyes watching, it was thoroughly raped and left to adjust its clothing as best it might.

Ghazi took me to his office and I had coffee and cigarettes on an empty stomach, which made me feel rather drunk. Then I rang up the British Embassy and started telling the Second Consul how I'd just arrived from Jordan in a lorry and needed somewhere to clean up. The Embassy could provide no accommodation, he told me. The Embassy was not a travel agent or a youth hostel. It was there to protect the rights of residents, etc. I should have known better. All over the world British Embassies have the air of royal palaces which have been swept through by Republicans about twenty-five years previously and everyone is very sensitive about it. Embassy officials always think they are being got at in some way, rather like skilled craftsmen who think the machines are after them. If you say 'Is this the British Embassy?' they usually say 'No' out of sheer nerves. This one told me, amazingly, that the Ambassador was about the cheapest hotel, if that was what I wanted. So there I went.

At the Ambassador, the doorman held the door very wide for me to enter. In a mirror above the reception desk I saw a dark-skinned fanatical face, overtopped with matted hair. A man approached. Could I be helped? A room for tonight? £4 10s. Four days travelling, food included, from Amman in Jordan had cost me £2, so I wasn't in the mood for that kind of fun. I asked if I could use the lavatory and spent half an hour there washing and shaving.

Two hours later I was in a dhow heading towards the Tigris-Euphrates delta. On top of clip-joint prices, Kuwait was expecting a sandstorm – not expecting one so much as awaiting its arrival, for you could see it in the distance. So I decided to go straight on towards Isfahan, Iran.

I think I must have paid more, about 30s, than the other three passengers on the boat, for one of the crew had made me a kind of throne out of cushions near the stern. Here I reclined, photographing the pantalooned sailors as they hauled sails and smoked hubble-bubbles.

To my amazement, as soon as we were out of Kuwait waters, they took out piles of new shirts and trousers from a locker and proceeded to put them all on, one after the other. Each of them put on three pairs of jeans, six check shirts and a suede jacket. I realized they must be smuggling and had to have the stuff looking worn before Abadan. Even the oldest member of the crew, a gnome in striped pantaloons, was going about like a bulging American teenager. He also had a tape recorder and two transistors, both of which he played on different stations, while recording them on the tape.

The dhow turned out to be a converted pearler and for several hours we moved along a vague coastline, scooping a little wind off the surface with a huge patched sail.

We arrived at the river mouth too late at night to sail up to Abadan, so we anchored and prepared to spend the night.

The little man in striped pantaloons soon produced from his pocket a little pellet of hashish, wrapped up in silver paper. He made a cigarette and offered me a smoke. I pretended to know how to do it and sucked the tobacco through my clenched fist. This made me very popular and the cigarette kept being passed back to me till I could feel the drug in my scalp, seething about under my hair. Then it settled down and I was able to enjoy the warm night, the fireflies like lovely fat stupid virgins giving themselves away to the night birds, the bobbing, luminous floats of the fisher boats, the shooting stars between the masts, the laughs in a strange language. For the first time I noticed how very far I was getting from home and experienced almost physical pleasure at the thought. I saw the map of England, as on the L-plates of the British School of Motoring, driving itself and its steering wheel away in the opposite direction and I couldn't have cared less.

There was drinking and songs, and I had to sing a song so I sang what anyone would have sung: *Over the Sea to Skye* and *The Road to the Isles*. There was only one drawback. Since quite early on in the trip, all I'd really wanted to do was pee. After eight hours still nobody seemed to have done it over the side. I waited and waited and when the gaiety subsided, had the best pee of my life into the ancient twin rivers. Then I slept.

In the morning the river was like a well-worn stair-carpet being shaken out against our bows. It was thick brown water, the same colour as the beaches and the same colour as the mud houses like mole-hills on them. Fishing canoes, chugging pearlers, sailing dhows, BP tankers passed us by. We saw the flaming refineries of Abadan. Then beneath them a game of cricket being played on a mud-flat, the fluttering white shirts like rare insects pinned to a specimen sheet by the steel sun.

The rose garden

From Abadan I caught the Teheran Express to Aznow where the buses leave for Isfahan. It was easier than I'd thought. People imagine the obstacles mounting as you get further from home, but the hardest country of all to travel in must be England, where everyone thinks you're barmy if you don't speak English in the local dialect. Persia has had caravans of foreigners going through it for centuries and its manners have developed accordingly. Less English is spoken here than in most Eastern countries, but if you can stand the aggressive interest they take, there'll always be someone willing to explain.

And, of course, others equally willing to rob you.

I slept for a few hours in the train, stretched out on a bench. There was a man asleep on the bench opposite, another asleep on the floor and two more in the luggage racks. Suddenly in the middle of the night I woke up feeling in my hip pocket for my wallet. It had gone. I switched on the light and everyone woke up and looked at me except the man on the floor, who just moved over a bit till I could see the wallet sticking out from under him. Everything was intact. It was a neat security measure on his part. Like the tie tidied away under the drawer paper till the client has left the hotel.

By the morning we had left the hot plain and were among green mountains and poplars. Bright leaves hung down over smart little stations dotted with roses. They have trees in

Kuwait, but they are dust-coated municipal weeds. They grow out of concrete in long lines and the fine for driving into one is the cost of the water it took to grow: £150.

There is something cool and fabulous about the word 'Persia'. But I knew that it was an out-dated word and had been ready to find a more prosaic countryside, more like the word 'Iran'. I was soon proved wrong.

At Aznow I got down and someone came hurrying up to ask me in French if I needed a car to Isfahan. I said I would go by bus if there was one and the man said:

'Voudriez-vous du thé?'

'Oui,' I said and we went into a dark tea-room and sat on a raised platform covered with carpet, with a gangway down the middle for the waiter. The tea came in glasses and with it large flat pieces of bread like elephant ears. We ate and drank for a while, then the man said 'Vous ne portez pas des chausettes?'

I looked down at the sockless feet crossed before me and told him I must have forgotten to put them on when I left hot Abadan. This seemed to decide him. He said he was going to Isfahan anyway and I could go with him if I wanted to. When we had finished the bread and tea we set out in his Citroën.

A few days before I had been making delighted desert similes. Now I was glad to be out of it. Man needs a human landscape in which to live. Distance is necessary for the health of the eye, yet we must have something to focus on. A desert presents only the sky, which is why its inhabitants are itinerant. All they can do is journey onwards towards the blue they see ahead of them, searching for an object, a lake or a hill against which to scale themselves and find their dignity. It is the dignity they find without these things which fascinates the Northerner.

Beside the road the rich valleys were almost untouched. Huts like little ovens were folded in their contours, seemingly overpowered by them.

We approached Isfahan through long, perfumed orchards.

Far away, where the walls of the orchards met in the distance, a green porcelain onion was all I could see of the city.

Then we were in the Chahar Bagh, a tree'd dual carriageway, flanked with wooden arcades and crowded with bicycles. In the centre was a wide promenade bordered by two cycle lanes, but every inch of the street, including the pavements, seemed legitimate thoroughfare for bicycles. They were threading the oncoming traffic or window-shopping at will.

My friend had to pick up something and go straight back to Aznow. He dropped me at the top of the avenue and I went into the first hotel I could see. This was the three-star *Isfahan*. I left my bags there and started to walk down the avenue and down through the stars to the unrecognized *Golestan*, Farsi for a rose garden.

In the rose garden were some boys painting a banner in the lovely Farsi script. Two of them were kneeling holding it tight while another put the red characters on with long twisting brushstrokes. I tried to ask them what they were doing and they looked up with beaming faces and said 'Gina. Gina Lollo.' Was Lollobrigida coming to Isfahan? I couldn't understand the rest, so I made sleeping mimes and one of the boys unlocked a door giving on to the garden. The room was 7s a day.

I was flaked out, but more than a sleep I wanted a bath. Bath mimes however were too much for the boys and an old woman was sent for who spoke French. Instead of showing me the shower, she gave me an address and drew a little map of how to get there. I asked her about the banner and she shrugged her shoulders and said she believed Gina Lollobrigida was flying down from Tehran in a week's time for some kind of charity garden party. The banner was for her. 'Welcome to Isfahan, Gina.'

The public baths were about half a mile away. Two or three men were drinking Pepsi under sunshades outside. I paid half a crown and was given two red cloths. I took off my shoes and they were taken away to be cleaned. The bathroom was divided in two. A wet and steaming shower room and a drying room with a couch spread with another red cloth.

'When you are finished, ring the bell,' said a man.

I bathed and rang the bell. In came another man wearing only a red cloth round his waist. He pointed to the couch and made massaging movements with his fingers. This man wanted to massage me. I knew that, but I didn't know whether I wanted to be. I repeated the two gestures stupidly, playing for time. He nodded delightedly. The way he stood in the doorway, flexing his knucklebones, I had a momentary impression of a torturer. I wanted to tell him that nothing like this had happened to me before and could I go away, please. But I lay down.

My impression of my masseur as a torturer was not far off. Grunting involuntarily, he began to pick up bits of my sparse flesh and to hit them with the side of his other hand. When he had hit me all over, he got hold of my head and started moving it about till suddenly he cricked my neck to one side, making me see stars. He did the same to my ears and nose and even my fingers. There, luckily, it ended.

With my new rubber body I walked back to my hotel and slept.

In the morning I hired a bicycle and joined the circus. I had come in for a lot of staring in the last few days and I was keen to join the majority. It's something you notice much more when you're tired or looking for your way. Your blink rate increases and you see eyes everywhere. I was beginning to feel unnecessarily tall and doll-like. It was great to be up on a bike and out from under the microscope. Even if I didn't know where I was, at least I could go somewhere and be lost on my own. The bike gave me a kind of citizenship.

The city itself was more demure.

Beyond the Chahar Bagh the streets were windowless

ravines. I heard sounds of life from inner courtyards, but the people in the streets were quiet and anonymous, inward-facing like the windows of their houses. Sometimes a garden was glimpsed through a half-open doorway, but it always seemed out of reach, sunnier than the street. The town seemed veiled from sight like its tender, shadowy womenfolk.

I was mystified by the studied privacy of the place. But by riding fast round it on a bicycle I was at least able to see it objectively enough to understand that I was really there. Freed from the crowded sidewalk and anchoring suitcase, I could look at the place without needing it.

Travel is almost impossible to accept today because transport is instantaneous, yet foreign countries are still strange places to us. I heard of an elderly Canadian couple not long ago who were completely disorientated by it. They arrived in London at night on the last stop of a world tour. A car picked them up at the airport and took them straight to the Savoy. In the morning a tour of London had been laid on. But when the couple were ensconced in their limousine they gave the driver their address in Ottawa. The driver got out and went and asked reception what the game was. Reception hurried to assure the couple that this was London. But to no avail. They agreed to go on the tour, but were not convinced. Buckingham Palace, Tower Bridge, Piccadilly, these were parts of Ottawa they hadn't seen before. Or else had gone up since they'd been away. It was not until a psychiatrist had been called in that time and place were restored to them.

On the bike I was catching up. The town was coming to meet me. I began to notice its strange contrasts. Rough mud walls would suddenly give forth the eggshell delicacy of minarets like Limoges porcelain, narrow wickets reveal the dome of a mosque, traced with fantastic serpentine patterns in blue and yellow. Even the fluttering ankle-length veils of the women sometimes blew aside from twin-sets and stilettos – a clue to life over the inscrutable walls.

But the best place was the bazaar – another whole town of alleys and passages such as modern town planners must dream about in their sterile dormitory suburbs. I only found it after I had been in Isfahan three days. It was evening and musicians were drumming down the sun from the Drum House above the bazaar's main entrance. Inside was a cavernous underworld of high-ceilinged arcades and a smell of food and spice the West has long since shut up in tins. Further on came the crash of hammers from the coppersmiths, the copper catching the last sunbeams which veer all day from holes in the roof. In another quarter were the carpet-makers, young girls from five to sixteen who work twelve hours a day in this half-light. One carpet may take nine child-years to finish and may cost a girl her eyes. In a courtyard a blindfolded camel was turning an 800-year-old cottonseed oil press.

The strangest things were the shops, like little shelves in the alley walls, the vendors crouched among their merchandise like idols among offerings. And with hardly more activity. There were so many more shops than buyers that running one seemed to be more a kind of faith than a business proposition.

Nebuchadnezzar, the Assyrian Emperor, sent a tribe of Jews here in 700 BC, but their descendants have little chance to display their traditional talents. I noticed the condescension of the shoppers, the pessimism of the shopkeepers. It was strange to see the merchant at such a disadvantage. If he wanted to sell something he really had to work at it. In the West his advertising and marketing troubles are taken care of for him, so he doesn't give a damn.

Here every deal was fought like a game of liar dice. How much could they take for how little? With the result that they only took it once. You were wiser next time. They seemed to tend towards their poet Omar Khayam: 'Ah, take the cash in hand and waive the rest.'

One day I went to the street of jewellers to buy a ring. I had been wondering for a week what Persian word to have engraved on it and in the end decided simply to have the date. But it wasn't simple.

When I had chosen a ring, walked out on its price, gone elsewhere, walked out, been called back and finally settled, my day had only just begun. First the engraver was sent for. He would do it while I waited I was told. Ten minutes later he arrived and took the ring off to his shop. To pass the time while he was away I showed the jeweller a postcard I was sending my grandmother. He turned it over and read her Christian name: Ruby. This was the signal for some old-fashioned sales-talk. 'Ruby very beautiful name sir, very good sir, very beautiful sir. You like Ruby sir? Look sir, ruby ring from old times, for you sir, for your Ruby. You like?'

Just for fun I put the ring on and said nothing.

Another ten minutes and the engraver returned with the ring coated in white paste for the jeweller to mark in it what I wanted engraved. Which date did I want, Persian or E-U-R-O-P-E? He spelt it out on a piece of paper. There is a different calendar in Persia, about twenty-one years behind ours. We were in the year of my birth, but I said I would like the European date. At this he began to scratch an unhappy 23.5.63 into the paste. Persia doesn't use Latin numerals and nor, obviously, did the jeweller. Anyway I wanted it in Persian. I explained and this time he tried to write both the Persian and European dates in Latin numerals. There was paste everywhere and the poor man's hand was beginning to shake. Once again the ring was wiped clean, fresh paste applied, and the job thrown open to the floor. 'What did I want then?' said the jeweller. 'Why didn't I do it myself?' I tried. The engraver tried. A hopeless, hamfisted goliath tried, and finally I decided I didn't want the ring any more. I began to buy some cuff-links.

Here the engraver decided to take his revenge, for it was he whose time had been wasted. He pinched the skin on my arm and said something to the jeweller to translate. 'You are "faible"' he says,' said the jeweller. I nodded warmly. 'Faible,' he said again. Then he looked the word up in a dictionary and underneath EUROPE, wrote the word WEAK. I rolled up my sleeve and told the engraver to put his elbow on the counter. For some reason everyone fancies himself at this game and I was no exception. For a minute and a half we quivered, then I slowly crumbled. 'Weak,' said the engraver, but everyone was delighted with me now. I had done something human.

The next day – I say the next day as one says 'Once upon a time'. One has to begin somewhere – I was in a shop getting my camera mended. The watchmaker spoke English. He had been a student in Brighton and when he heard I came from near there he said he would shut up his shop and show me Isfahan. I must see the 'shaking minarets' he said. He would pick up his friend who had a car and we would have dinner on the old bridge.

Unfortunately his friend had a car but no English, so talk was mostly in Farsi. We drove several miles out of Isfahan to a little mosque in an orchard. Inside the mosque I was invited to climb up a spiral stair to the minaret. It was so narrow I could hardly get my shoulders in. At the top I poked my head out of a hole and the watchmaker shouted up to me to shake the minaret. I moved around a bit and the whole little turret began swaying like a grass in the wind. I thought it was going to break off and crash down, but a boy in the other one seemed to be rocking even more. Everyone, including my guidebook, was agreed that Allah was responsible for this magic. But it must have been due in some way to the four crossed beams which went through the minaret near where it joined the mosque, acting as a kind of hinge. But why?

We left the shaking minarets and drove down a dried-up river to the old Khajoo Bridge. It was no more used as a bridge, but was still a meeting place, place of prayer and even a market. It was six o'clock and the bridge was crowded with young men in low-cut waistcoats and knocked-out trilbys, walking along with their arms round one another's necks. Some of the old men had beards dyed red with henna to restore their youth.

Under the thoroughfare were two storeys of cloisters. The lower had flat buttresses jutting out on each side into the river-bed, and on these were one or two kebab stalls with chairs and tables. Here we sat eating the little pieces of kidney and liver with spring onions and Pepsi Cola, and listening to men singing prayers in the upper cloister. This was a famous meeting place for lovers they told me, though lovers were always married ones in Isfahan.

Later they took me back to the hotel.

It was about ten o'clock. I'm not sure whether it was that night or the following one. I had begun to write a letter, when suddenly there came a lot of knocking on my door. Outside were some uniformed men and one saying in English that I should pay my hotel bill. I shut the door and went on writing. More knocking. Then nothing. So I went to ask the old woman what was going on. Why the police? She said they were not the police, only some soldiers who were staying at the hotel and had offered to speak to me. It seemed that in Isfahan it was the custom to pay for your room every few days. I gave her some money and went to see the soldiers who were all in one big room. I said I was sorry, I had thought they were the police, that I didn't know I was expected to pay, etc. etc. I was immediately enclosed by dozens of names, hands, cigarettes, addresses. Tea was sent for like champagne and a party begun. 'I will imitate the animals,' said one soldier sitting very near me, and looking into my eyes he miaowed, bleeted, barked and cried like a baby, to the huge enjoyment of his friends who obviously knew his tricks well.

They had only knocked on my door to talk to me, they explained. They had heard about me from the old woman and wanted to know why I was travelling, why I was alone, whether I was lonely. They were questions I had been asking myself

43

recently, but I had an unreasonable longing to brag and romanticize. For the first time ever I mentioned a journey round the world and basked in the glory of it like the Playboy of the Western World. I know now that it's no good waiting till you get home to tell of your travels. They simply aren't interested. The best audiences are along the way, for you yourself, not your experiences. In Persia, for instance, related families live together, relying completely on one another for accommodation, counsel and company. It is from this that they get their sense of hospitality, something we have forgotten about in our race for status. They are wide-eyed at the independence of Westerners, who always think that their curiosity is backed by some ulterior motive. Very often it is. The man has a shop and would like to show you his gold. You feel encroached upon, taken advantage of. But much of the time all he wants is for you to sit in his front room, a kind of status symbol yourself, and drink a cup of multilateral tea.

If I had been able to learn this early on it would have saved me a lot of trouble. With these soldiers, for instance. Even after we had made friends I couldn't forget my old standards of criticism, and relax. Conversation seemed to be an endless series of questions and answers which I longed to escape from. If only I had remembered that talk at home is seldom more than that. But I was expecting too much and at the same time, through a growing loneliness, beginning to idealize home.

I suppose shopping was one of the distractions from loneliness. I enjoyed the familiar ritual, the formal exchanges, the escapes. I remember the beginning of term being bearable if I had a few new things to take back, or some comics. Today's comics were novels, cigarettes, antique shops, sleep.

While you are on the move, you are in a sense also returning, so nothing seems to matter. Isfahan was my first real stopping place and the halt had given me time for home-sickness and to realize that I was still heading in the opposite direction.

I spent a lot of time in my room writing poems and letters

44

Once I went to the Post Office and got an English-speaking letter-writer to write a letter in Farsi to a girl-friend. I must have said something inane like 'If I had wings I would fly to you' for the letter-writer corrected me: 'You mean "If I had the money I would fly to you" don't you?' he said. 'Anyway, it is she who should fly to you.'

I would sit in the hotel watching the old woman hanging out washing and cutting roses. Once she came into my room with her grand-daughter and gave me a big bunch of roses and a hug.

I rather enjoyed the hotel, and when I could describe it, I enjoyed the loneliness. Bicycling round like Don Quixote was all very well, but I wanted a Sancho Panza to share it with. Or a girl to show it to. A girl with a stupid little high voice, such as you don't hear in Isfahan.

A girl was probably all I wanted, in fact, but I seldom saw a girl's face very clearly and I could certainly not speak with one. They were always hurrying along in the shadow of walls or of their menfolk. Short, voluptuous creatures in long, black-flowered 'chaderis' which fluttered across their faces and about their ankles, sheathing them in ambiguity against the looks of men. You could see them, but they were not really there. They seemed to be only half sketched in, fleeting impressions of extreme femininity, like veiled statues, or the mourners in *L'enterrement à Ornans* by Courbet.

A generation ago they would not have been seen at all. Mohammed fixed womanhood in a position of divinely decreed inferiority, from which evolution was almost impossible. Even today the Pakistani poet Iqbal can write 'The chaste fatimah is harvest of the field of submission.' But more and more chaste fatimahs seem to be going to school, and each year the harvest is less submissive.

But you still don't see much of them. The question is no longer whether they may go out, but rather how much of themselves should they show when they do. For the Persians the question is agonizing, for their attitude towards their women is so touchingly subjective. It ranges from tender over-protectiveness for their own womenfolk to a distrust and contempt for other women.

What did they think about Gina, for instance? 'Welcome to Isfahan' wrote the boys in my hotel. Others I met called her 'Lulu', a flesh-eating fury they frighten their children with. Through her films she was familiar to them. Yet they felt on the defensive, for she was not one of them. It was sad that in the end she never turned up, being too tired, and the banners had to be taken down.

Girls national and international seemed equally elusive. It was that which finally made me want to go on to Shiraz. In the face of such a city, a single memory and pair of eyes seemed powerless to remember it all. It was all too communicable. Too gracious and incredible.

You hear people in 'Entertainment' talking about 'Consumers', but you can't consume beauty any more than you can entertainment. If anything's consumed it's the spectator. Or that's how I was feeling. It was like a short circuit. I felt numb because I could not feel the current of my reactions flow through me into someone else and back again.

But after all it was a small price to pay, and one you can pay at home just as easily, with nothing in return. Here the returns were ample. It was even a pleasure to know that nothing was keeping me, that I could go when I liked. In a way it even kept me there longer. There is nothing so exhilarating as sitting in your room, knowing that at any moment you can walk out and catch a bus to another country. You sit in the bus, waiting for it to go, knowing that where it stops will be infinitely far away and mysterious and that you are free to stay or leave there too, as briefly as you came, a free agent in an anchored world.

The cup bearer

All the way from Isfahan to Shiraz the Bactiori mountains stand guard, sometimes like teeth, sometimes like whales. Steely first, then ashen. But they do not guard the coachloads of travellers running across the plain. They guard the million Kurdish tribesmen who live in them and partly off the coachloads.

Recently there was an English girl on board. The bandits slipped out of the darkness from the steep hills beside the road and entered the bus with guns. When they came to the English girl she held out her British passport and they bowed and left her alone. When the bus came to Shiraz mysterious hands began to make life easy for her. Bills were paid, trips arranged, friends made.

On the bus I got my passport down out of my suitcase and put it in my pocket. I was talking to someone who had no illusions about the romantic bandits. 'Gypsies' he would have called them. He'd lost some money already and didn't want it to happen again. He actually asked me to keep about £15 for him.

Then the bus broke down.

The sun was setting and there was one bedouin in the bus whom everyone thought might give the signal at any minute. Several people got out and started praying into the setting sun. We were in for a wait, so everyone was wandering about looking for something to do. Some honeymooners went off for a walk and started to sing. Someone else was picking rock flowers. Others were squatting behind lumps of heather, and one got hit by a stone someone had thrown without knowing he was there.

An hour later we were off. I had half hoped the bandits would call.

In one village there was a procession of children going through the dusk chanting mournfully and symbolically lashing themselves with chains like cats-o'-nine-tails. They were lamenting the death of Mohammed's grandsons, Hassan and Hussein, who were starved and slaughtered in their house by the unfaithful.

The scene was an eerie foreshadowing of something less symbolical I was to see in Tehran a few weeks later.

Shiraz is 200 miles south of Isfahan and has the traditional southern personality: easy-going, sensuous, artistic. Men here are inclined to walk about with roses, which they hand to people in the street. The 'ruby-lipped damsels', demurely advertised in the tourist brochure, are unveiled and swagger the long Khiaband Zand like starch-frocked young Mediterranean girls during the paseo. I remember an Englishman telling me an extraordinary story about one of them. He had picked her up in the street and been invited to come to her house later that night. He arrived there and a man showed him straight through the house into a dark garden. In the garden the girl was lying almost naked on a string cot. The man then left them together and walked away into the garden, disappearing among some trees. The visitor went up to the girl, but was still aware of the man moving about behind the trees. He became frightened and went back into the house and out into the street.

But Shiraz is not really like that – or wasn't for me. And looking back I don't think I believe the story. It sounds more like one of my own dreams.

The first morning in Shiraz I went straight to the hospital

48

for a cholera and typhoid jab. I told the doctor where I had been and the first thing he did was to ring up the British Council to say he was bringing me round for a drink before lunch.

The British Councillor was a charming man called Mr Gotch and the British Council was a beautiful, verandahed villa at the end of a long, chestnut-crowded drive off the Khiaband Zand. We entered through vast gates and walked for four minutes before seeing the house among the trees. The British Council had come to Shiraz hot on the heels of the departing Foreign Office and just in time to move straight into the old Consulate. I swam in their pool and sat in the garden drinking with them, enjoying every minute. In the distance a gazelle was wandering about and the Gotches told me they had four dogs, a dumb sheep, rabbits, two ring doves and sometimes a brilliant blue bee-eater in the pink chestnuts.

In the evening I met them again and we went to the Iran America Society to see a film called *Mark Twain's America*. It was in a garden and a woman kept putting insecticide on the lighted screen. The film was a clever montage of stills from Twain's life which the camera almost seemed to animate. 'And this is a time the world will never see the like of again', the commentator kept repeating. But the shots of Twain fooling about on the Sphinx were intriguing proof that the American disease of Tourism is congenital.

What a joy one's own culture is when it greets one on alien ground! As I sat there loving Twain's old Mississippi riverboat, I knew how easy and agreeable it would be to slip into the expatriate's weird snobberies and affiliations. Expatriates are so splendidly biased. They know nothing of the native's indifference because they are not subjected to the same barrage of cancelling opinions from mass media.

I sat there in my deck chair feeling on home ground and at peace with the world. It was great to know I was going back afterwards to have dinner inside someone's house. It might have been America I was in and Persia that was flickering away on the screen. As I sat there the silver moon came up and hung a screen of its own in the sky, anchoring me in Shiraz, but bridging the gap with its chinless smile.

After dinner, to my delight, Mr Gotch declared himself a Jazz fan and produced a library of New Orleans and a gramophone which played into the garden.

We sat out there and an owl came and perched on the swimming bath tap with his back to us. We were listening to Woody Herman and Billie Holliday, the music sighing with an extra pathos in the foreign air, as if there were ears in the darkness which rejected it – as doubtless there were.

I saw the Gotches a couple of times more and they arranged for me to go to Persepolis with some people called Tuffnell. I was to go to their bungalow to meet them at 4.30. I dressed up and went round, but there was no one there. I knocked and knocked, walked round the house tapping on the windows, then knocked again and eventually a man came to the door in his dressing gown. He had grey, normally smooth hair and a short moustache. I began to apologize and he said: 'No-no. All is well, all is well,' – so that I knew that he had been asleep and that it wasn't. But he asked me in and said that he was sorry, but his wife and daughter were at the bazaar. I think he made some tea and when I had explained my presence in Shiraz, he explained his. Unbelievably, he was a policeman, a member of the vice-squad, there to attend a symposium on drug addiction. 'Just be careful while you're here not to get bribed into helping anyone who peddles the stuff,' he said, then proceeded to tell me about two young tourists who were now serving five-year terms in Tehran for doing so. One had been on his way from England, east through India to Australia. In Madras he met an American going in the opposite direction, who persuaded him to retrace his steps to earn some money selling opium. The Englishman was broke, so he agreed. Opium is easily bought in

Afghanistan, so they bought several kilos and took it across the border into Persia, hoping to sell it to one of the flourishing heroin laboratories. Just inside Persia, in Meched, they began to make enquiries. A contact was made and they soon found themselves talking to a plain-clothes policeman. They had been in prison for sixteen months. The consuls had done what they could, but they were not sympathetic and the boys would probably have to serve at least another year. I decided I would go and see them in Tehran, but when I tried, the unsympathetic vice-consul made it impossible and I gave up.

The conversation returned to Shiraz and I learnt that he wouldn't be able to take me to Persepolis as he had to fly suddenly to Tehran the next day. He would, however, see that I was looked after. Mrs and Miss Tuffnell would take me to the tombs of two poets, Hafiz and Saadi.

Shiraz's reputation as a centre of Farsi culture is based on the fame of these two men and their prestige is cherished by the Department of Tourism. 'Hafiz, with his delicate and beautiful *ghazals*, is the acknowledged master of lyricism, mysticism and ERFAN and some scholars go so far as to give him the title of "the greatest poet of the world",' says the guide, while 'no other poet in the world is so versatile as Saadi', who 'lived to be a hundred, travelled much and saw the world of his time. He was taken prisoner by the Crusaders, enslaved and set to digging in Tripoli, saw India, Africa and Asia Minor.'

Plenty is known about the introverted Hafiz who made only one trip abroad, which he regretted, and the adventurous Saadi. But what they were like as poets is hard to know as they have not yet been translated by anyone good. 'It is difficult for anyone not acquainted with Persian literature to follow the lines of Hafiz and Saadi, for when they speak of wine, love, the cupbearer and the music, they are not talking of the things that are usually understood by such things, but the essence, the nectar and the spirit which flows through life.'

That may be, but it is impossible to believe the translators were aware of it in the verses the guide gives for examples. Hafiz:

> 'O Cupbearer fill the goblet and hand it
> Around to us all,
> For love that seemed easy at first,
> These unfortunate troubles befall.'

And Saadi:

> 'O! erring sufi in pain for fame
> And bound by the chains of shining name,
> Thou shalt not be relieved of this pain
> If the wine to dregs dost not thou drain.'

The translator seems to have been affected by the same brain drain. But there must be more to them than we know of, for them to have survived in such splendour. In the garden of Hafiz is an Islamic pavilion, shaded with evergreen oaks and cypresses and on his tomb lies a volume of his poetry. When we arrived a man was reading aloud from it in a sing-song voice that was all appreciation. But he had a way of crash-landing with great glee on the rhyme-words, as if there was nothing to the poem between them. I longed to find out what the poem meant to him, but he spoke no English.

On the tomb of Saadi there was no book, but a vase of roses – perhaps the best translation he could hope for.

In the evening the Tuffnells took me to a cocktail party. Shiraz was having its 'season' and anyone who spoke English was part of it. Most of the people were from the huge American hospital – the largest in the Middle East.

The excited homesickness I had felt was being lulled asleep by familiarity and I almost resented it. But it was soon awoken by an old doctor who became very interested in my journey and suggested I go through Tibet and China to Hong Kong. That way I would miss the Indian heat and the Monsoon. He said I could get a Chinese visa at Rawalpindi. 'Then you can write a book about the trip,' he said brightly. 'I'd like to know if you make it,' and he wrote out his address. Later I met an English writer called Bernard Newman who was in Shiraz to get material for a course of school lectures. He had overheard the doctor and told me it was quite impossible. They hadn't let anyone through for nine years, there certainly weren't any buses and anyway the Chinese were poised all over Tibet. A month later he was proved right when they attacked India.

The cherry tree

Wherever I go, towns black out for Independence Day, or a religious holiday, or – as here – religious holiday plus riots. There were whole streets of shuttered stores, barricaded cinemas and people in black hurrying away on visits. Take away a town's shopfronts and it closes its eyes like a corpse.

Tehran is a sweltering pocket under huge Alps which tower at the end of every street, too close for their height. Snow peaks rise incredibly out of a heat haze. I was at the lowest, hottest corner of the pocket. As always, there had been someone helpful on the bus and he found me this hotel in the bus station for 6s a night.

The first morning there I needed a swim. I don't think it matters what you do to get the hang of a place so long as you don't go to the Embassy or the Tourist Office, who will both be needing you to practise their public relations on. The best thing to do is get lost, or into some utterly ridiculous situation which will break down people's reserves as they rescue you from it.

This I looked like doing admirably by attempting to go swimming.

The first person I asked where I could go conjured briefly with childhood images and came up with a lake called Anjadié. I got him to write it down and was just about to jump in a taxi when someone else came up who had overheard the conversation and told me that there was no water in that lake at the moment. In a way I almost wished he hadn't told me. It would have made such a perfect parody of my adventures: arrival in bathing kit at a dried-up lake with perhaps a few Muslims praying or flaying themselves on its banks.

Looking back, the whole thing seems so mad I really believe I was in a daze half the time I was abroad and that I'm very lucky to have got back alive. In fact it was only after I did get back that I began to realize where on earth I'd been and what travelling was really like. At the time I was its zombie, always trying to get comfortable and feel homesick.

For instance, about my first night in Tehran I thought I would have some caviar – not that it would have awoken any fond nostalgia in me, for I'd never tasted it. But I knew there were sturgeon in the Caspian and that caviar was cheap there. So at about 7.30 I set out for a restaurant called 'Leons'.

Everything was very quiet and when I arrived the restaurant was just closing down. At first I wasn't surprised as I very often get the time wrong by about four or five hours – my watch sometimes runs down in the middle of the night and I have a habit of winding it up in my sleep. But then a waiter came out of the restaurant and told me to go home immediately. He said there was a curfew in the city and no one was allowed out after 8 o'clock. I could hardly believe it, but on my way back to the bus station I saw a patrol of five enormous tanks ploughing up the soft tar of one of the main avenues and a squad of soldiers shouting 'Huh, huh, huh,' as they marched. Then a car drew up beside me and the driver told me to get in and he'd take me to my hotel. He said there was a mob collecting in the bazaar and it wasn't safe on the streets.

Next day I went into an English bookshop to see if there was anything about it in the papers. There it was: Riots threatened over Shah's replacement and imprisonment of a religious leader opposed to his land reforms. If I'd flown into Tehran airport I'd at least have known something was wrong from a

55

newspaper or taxi driver, but arriving by bus and sleeping for 6s, I was blissfully oblivious in traditional man-on-the-spot style. People talk a lot of rot about 'seeing the country the hard way' – which I don't claim to have done – and 'really getting to know what makes it tick'. You may learn all about the local enthusiasm for Western culture – and grow to hate it, but in order not to miss useful snippets of information like news of the outbreak of war, or the Black Death, or the fact that the area you are in is cordoned off by blood-mad rebels, you had best make the conventional coach tour from the airport.

In the bookshop I met a young Persian called Shouroush, who had just hitch-hiked home from England. He'd been at school in America for five years, then two years at Swansea University studying the life of Dylan Thomas. He'd read every book I picked up and had seen all sorts of new films and plays in London I'd never heard of, and seemed almost desperate to talk about them. I had to leave to go and get an Afghan visa, but he asked me to come to dinner at his father's house that evening.

The Afghan Embassy proved a real wild goose. First of all it had just moved. That's nothing new. Embassies flutter about like merry widows most of the time. But nobody seemed to know where this one had gone to. Someone told me a wrong tram to get on and I walked miles round the urban foothills of Tehran's upper, mercifully cooler reaches till I thought I would go mad. I believe one person I asked actually directed me to the railway station where the trains left for the Afghan border. I foolishly thought it would be quicker to find the Embassy.

Eventually I found it, manned by a powerful woman who made my day by saying that if I was going to Pakistan I couldn't go through Afghanistan because the border between the two was closed diplomatically to all except those with private cars. She was one of those smiling head-shakers who so love working for governments. Why is it one either meets pessimists or lunatic optimists in such jobs? And why is it that whatever they say one always believes? In order not to waste the entire day, I said I had a car and the woman left me with a pile of forms to duplicate and went off to lunch. I sat and stared at them. Should I go through Afghanistan and risk, as she said, having to fly from Kabul to Delhi? Or should I change plans and go south over the Persia-Pakistan border? I ached for someone to argue it out with. Someone to take the braver course against. In the end I decided not to decide. I didn't fancy leaving my passport with this distant Embassy in case I wanted to leave suddenly, and I knew you could always get a visa at the border if it came to that.

Why do I put in all this red tape? Because that is what occupied me and that is what travelling comes down to and what has to be fought against, like sleeping sickness, or the big woman in the Embassy.

One of the best antidotes is reading. I had bought *The Outsider* by Camus, so I stumbled down the hill and read it straight through sitting in a restaurant. I found the daring self-dependence of the existentialist cheered me up no end. It stood so clearly for confidence and belief in consciousness. 'That happiness is consciousness and consciousness is one that all its manifestations are sacred.' It is the philosophy of the individual, whose *raison d'être* is the perfect working order of his own perceptions. I saw that life itself was too good to be depressed by any of its setbacks, which are all only coincidences anyway. Or failures to understand that they are.

At 6 o'clock I went back to the bookshop. Shouroush was waiting in a car outside and he drove me far up against the mountain again to where his house stood in a terraced garden. The garden had cherries and apricots and figs and roses and sweet smelling shrubs 'which don't grow in England'. The boughs of the cherry trees were laden down to the ground with unwanted fruit.

Inside the house I met his mother, whose hair, he said, had turned white through all her children leaving her – one to be a fellow at Cambridge. At dinner we drank her home-made wine and, after the meat and rice, everyone helped himself to a spoonful of jam.

Talk was mostly about Persia, in a rather helpless, detached tone of voice, as if they were barely more involved with the country than I was. They made me feel one of them more by disowning it than drawing me into it.

Shouroush, fresh from England, was particularly rough. He told me he had just had a car stolen from outside the house, a brand new Mercedes. When he told the police about it they said nothing had turned up, but would he like a Cadillac they had found abandoned nearby. He said it was a good example of Persian logic. Persia had suffered from never having had the nursing hand of one of the Western empires – only their thieving hands on its oil. He said his family were fond of using the cherry trees in the garden as a parable of it. There were far too many cherries for them to eat themselves, so one year they had asked people in from the street to come and pick what they wanted. At the end of the day the garden was ruined and the trees broken. The rich had so much, yet the poor were not yet ready to take it. Oil was another cherry tree. Vast reserves and a country on the brink of starvation. Shouroush said the Government was struggling to de-feudalize the country, but the priests, who wielded most influence on the people, were against it, as they were the largest landowners and stood only to lose by it.

Fifteen years before, the Shah had begun to break up his own properties and to sell them to the people. He received his payment from the agricultural bank. Recently the Land Reforms had been enforced throughout the country and all the big landowners had suffered, either because the Government bought their properties for the exact sum they themselves had entered on their yearly tax declarations, i.e. a fraction of its true worth, or because the landowners were left to extract payment from the new farmers themselves, an impossible task as the farmers had no experience of such responsibility.

Shouroush said the Shah had made one vital error. He had been so intent on de-feudalizing his country he had overlooked its effect on the peasants themselves. He had tried to give them hope before they knew what to hope for, symbols before they knew the meaning of status. He had tried to create a middle class by forgetting a 90 per cent illiteracy rate.

The result was that they all now hated him and were putty in the hands of the priests who posed as their protectors. The riots going on in the town were the direct result of propaganda put out by the powerful shrines, twisting the Government's motives. If the Government made each man responsible for his own plot of land, they said, who would look after them in a bad year? Who would clean out their wells for them? The Government was forcing the shrines to sell their property in order to profit by splitting it up into small holdings.

The following day Shouroush and I saw the fruition of this poisoned message. We were walking towards the bazaar when a man came running up to us and told us not to go any further. The mob had set light to a car and were trying to fire a building. If they saw my camera anything could happen. I put the camera inside my shirt and we walked on a bit more to see what was happening. A hundred yards further on the road was blocked with old cars, one of them in flames. In front of the barricades were strewn rocks and bricks which had been thrown at the police. The riot had obviously died down a bit, for the barricade was no longer manned. But there were large crowds hanging about like cinders waiting for the next little breeze of violence to come upon them. Here and there in the crowd were the black-shirted, barefooted mourners I'd seen on the way to Shiraz. Shouroush said it was still the fast of Hassan and Hussein and the priests had taken advantage of the emotional tension attending it to stir up hatred of the Shah and his Government. He seemed disgusted and ashamed. He kept picking up bits of information which he wouldn't translate to me. Suddenly we heard a kind of moaning and a procession of black-shirted, dark-faced fanatics came slowly down the street, chanting something. The panels in the backs of their shirts were unbuttoned and this time they were really lashing themselves. The jingle and clank of the iron whips made a chilling accompaniment to their words. They stopped and one of them got up on a box and started shrieking something at the crowd. Shouroush told me he was preaching against votes for women – another religious *bête noire*. But the invective was obviously versatile. There were no women present, but a coach was coming down the road and in a flash he had everyone picking up rocks and stoning it. All the windows were broken and the driver was hit by a rock coming through the window. He turned round as best he could and went back the way he had come.

Anything with the stamp of officialdom on it was legitimate prey and we soon heard that a plain-clothes policeman had been unmasked and decapitated. Later we actually saw the bloody board on which his body had lain being carried head-high through the streets. I felt fairly safe in the crowd, yet dared not take out my camera for a second. There was no distinct line between rioters and onlookers, yet sparks were flying everywhere, taking fire here, being dampened elsewhere. Every now and then a spectator would catch the venom and go running about with the stupid mob-light in his eye, yelling parrot-wise at everyone. We saw one of these jump on the bonnet of a Landrover with two foreign girls in it and be driven, yelling, all round the main square until he was taken prisoner by a posse of soldiers.

In one corner of the main square tanks and infantry were amassing with a great noise but not much movement. Their task was perhaps impossible because the rioters were protected by the crowd.

Altogether thirty people were killed that day.

Looking back it seems hard to imagine how I had time for anything else in that wracked city, let alone caviar and existentialism. But the fact is that cities themselves minimize their own news headlines. Contrary to the impression a journalist seeks to give, there is always something else going on in some other part of town, unconnected to whatever misery is occupying his pen at the time.

So it was that the next day Shouroush and I went to the British Embassy to get permission to see the two European boys in prison for carrying drugs – but we didn't get much encouragement. The consuls both thought they'd been lucky to get only five years. 'And you see the original length of the sentence was fifty years,' said a watery grey one, as if that proved to him the actual gravity of the crime. When I asked to see them I was told they already had their full quota of visitors. American ladies went twice a week, etc. I said I was surprised someone hadn't paid their fine and given them a chance to work to repay it. But the consuls were not surprised. They both had better things to do with their money. I wished I had known then what Shouroush told me outside: that it was a relation of the Queen who ran the country's drug racket and she who trapped rivals and made examples out of them to prove her virtue. Even the Health Minister was in her pay, he said. Once this man had brought a lot of heroin through the customs on the very night a warning had gone round and when they found it on him they simply thought he must be testing their dragnet.

To prolong Shouroush's parable, it seemed that the cherry tree itself was rotten and due for a fall.

At 5 a.m. the next morning I was outside my hotel waiting for a bus to Pakistan. There was another Englishman there on his way home from India. He said he had come through Pakistan and Afghanistan, 'living with the people in the villages'. So I asked about the Afghan-Pak border and he said it may have been closed diplomatically, but that didn't stop you walking

61

the odd hundred yards across it if you wanted to. Anyway, I shouldn't miss going through the Khyber Pass. That decided me. Just before the bus left I was on the roof getting my suitcase out from under the tarpaulin. Going south had been a compromise and I was delighted to give it up.

Now all I had to do was get the money back on my bus ticket and take the train to Meched, last Persian town before the Afghan border.

At the station there were guards with fixed bayonets, and I had to show my passport before I was allowed inside. Russian spies were rumoured to be aiding the rebels. Nobody at all was popular in Tehran at that time.

America loves Afghanistan,
so does Russia

The train was eighteen hours across the desert. I had an ancient student card from the Sorbonne which got me a wooden seat in a Pilgrim class compartment for 15s. Around me were the pilgrims, some very old, journeying to Meched in order to die near the shrine of Imman Shah, the poor man's Mecca; others quite young, loudly chanting the Koran or reciting Hafiz:

> God counts our tears and knows our misery;
> Ah, weep not . . . take thy Koran and recite
> Litanies infinite, and weep no more.

I managed to get one of them to belt up by trying to teach him chess. But it was a lengthy business as we only had a few words in common, and they were in French. There was a lot of 'Si vous faîtes comme ça par exemple, moi, je peux faire comme ça'. Then whenever the train stopped everyone would tumble out and into the prayer halls on the platforms – one for men and one for women – and the board would go flying. I would put my head under the station fountain and stock up with Coca Cola. Then the whistle would blow and everyone would scramble for his seat again.

It was a long ride. During the night I sat by my window, dizzily watching the stars coming out of the horizon and the distant lightning shimmering like the light of battle. Late the next day we reached Meched.

The Bakhtur Hotel was full of English and Americans, either recovering from or preparing to invade the map of Afghanistan. I met a man called Clutter, from an Outward Bound school in Kenya, and his wife, a nurse: the cause and the cure so to speak. And a Fulbright professor called Broadwell, who had decided to travel home overland with his wife and child from a post in Tehran. He too was going through Afghanistan towards the Monsoon, so we told each other we had mistimed our trips on purpose and that we *wanted* to see the rain. After all, why not? But first of all, how? Afghanistan had an airline, but no buses or trains. Neither of us had cars, so we were going to have to hitch hike. The other Americans turned out to be U S Aid men stationed in the Afghan desert. They had all been collecting their cars from the Persian Gulf, so, theoretically, there was plenty of space.

The night before they were due to leave they threw a party at the Coca Cola factory. It was there that we met Mr Henty from Texas, who agreed to take us all in his Buick.

The factory had a glass wall and the machinery was lit up so you could see the bottles coming off the production line. This was the nearest thing Meched had to a cabaret and there was a little café-night-spot in the field beside it, where we sat late into the night, drinking illicit American beer and watching Persia's favourite beverage tumbling out of the sky above our heads.

At the Afghan Embassy next morning there were two very happy men. One said: 'We are human beings and when one human meets another he should be happy.' At which, meeting me, he burst into laughter.

We set out for the border in a convoy of five cars. Before we had gone a mile one of them hit a little boy who ran into the road. He wasn't hurt, but the driver had to stay behind with our one interpreter to sort out allegations with an angry crowd and the US Consul. That was the first little nigger boy. Four cars remained.

Around lunch time we reached the border and more trouble. The head customs official had recently been insulted by an American and in his zeal to avenge the blow he discovered that two of the cars had wrong licence numbers copied into their triptiques. Four hours we waited while decisions, telephone calls and tea were taken in a back room. Out in the courtyard we were at the mercy of heat and flies and a gang of small boys who descended on us like jackdaws, fiercely rubbing clean a small patch on the dusty Buick with one hand, while holding out the other for money. Eventually the official emerged with his verdict. We would have to return to Meched and sort it out with the Afghan Consul there. We were livid. But with the slight smugness of parasites, the Broadwells and I lifted our bags from one of the doomed cars into a healthy one.

That night we were in Herat, a beautiful oasis with palm trees and clay-coloured houses which seemed to turn their backs on the broad streets in favour of invisible courtyards. At any rate there were no windows or women to be seen. Only tall, angular men in bright, loosely-tied turbans, embroidered green waistcoats and flowing pantaloons, caught at the waist with a dagger. We spent the night at a huge candle-lit hotel rather like a cricket pavilion. We were the only guests, but we all had to sleep in the same room on string cots. On the wall was a picture of a Russian tzar. Before we had been there five minutes boiled eggs were brought by a servant, who then lay down outside our door and went to sleep.

At 6 a.m. we woke him up and sent him off to boil more eggs. Then we filled up with petrol from the hand pump outside and set out to catch the cool of the morning – already disappearing.

South of Herat on my locally-bought map called Map Roads is a dotted line across the Desert of Death. This represents a kind of dotted road through the most extraordinary landscape I've ever seen. To the right the red desert stretches away towards the sky. On the left, mountains like stalagmites rise sharply out of the dust like fangs afflicted with various colours of decay. The effect is no more realistic than a backdrop for a pantomime of Ali Baba. In fact if you saw it in Cinemascope you'd spot the designer's work immediately. It must be one of a film maker's problems, how to make his locations look as real as his studio sets. Once the track took us clear over a field of dried-out geysers. The scene was as corny and fabulous as Dan Dare's Venus.

We were soon to discover what the breaks in the dotted line meant. They were deep gulleys left behind by annual floods, with steep banks and soft beds which made each one a subject of interest to the vultures which came and sat nearby to watch as the car crept upwards over the creaking sand, only to slip back again like a dying turtle. Once a jet of red water began to spout out of the bonnet which must have encouraged them. But though it wasn't blood, it could have been worse. The cooling system had cracked – as well it might. We needed wire. Everyone was sent prowling about the desert and I found an old piece of rope and an inner tube and with these we bound up the broken pipe and proceeded. But it still leaked and little by little we had to pour in our enormous supply of drinking water. The temperature was 108° – but very dry, which made it tolerable. But we had to keep the windows up because of the clouds of locusts, each four inches long and blue, which occasionally battered against the car. In fact it was so hot that even my cucumbers gave up the battle. To eat we had tins of hot spam and boxes of warm biscuits, washed down with a thermos cup of hot water, which the Americans insisted on flavouring with iodine. In the afternoon we came to a garden in the desert and a house which used to belong to a king. We drove up and an old man brought us piping hot tea.

Towards evening we reached Lashkargah, an oasis laid

out in the desert by America, to challenge, without actually recognizing, Russian prestige in this crucially-positioned country.

After a night in the staff guest house, we learnt from a young secretary that the Russians had been taking advantage of the selfless campaign against drought which the Americans were waging in the desert. They had gained cheap publicity by 'flinging a strip of macadam' through nearby Kandahar. But they had got what they deserved, he said, when the tar curled up in the heat, sealing fast the town's entire complement of hansoms. It would teach them to use second-rate material. But then everything Russia used was second-rate. 'Most of the petrol comes from Russia,' he said, 'but it's such low octane stuff it soon fouls American motors.'

The two countries were like jealous suitors for the hand of a poor maiden, who, one couldn't help thinking, must be laughing up her sleeve.

As part of the American suit, Lashkargah was quite convincing. Here were privet hedges, cherry trees, garden paths to air-conditioned bungalows, tennis courts and swimming pools – all for Aid personnel. It was true to the old idea of Civil Lines. And perhaps inevitably, what lay behind the façade was less miraculous. At the far end of Lashkargah was Lashkar, the old village and bazaar – still in existence like a scab. Here were shanties kicked together out of rusty corrugated iron and sacking, stores selling pots and pans patiently hammered out of old coke tins.

Instead of having shop-windows and doors, the shops themselves were no more than shelves, with the shopkeepers on display with their goods. I wanted to buy a red neckerchief so Carolyn Broadwell asked the man if the colour was 'fast'. He took the cloth and rubbed it against his white robe, leaving a big red mark on it. 'Yes, yes, fast, very fast,' he said, and indeed it had Fast Colour printed across it in blue letters. I bought one.

Flanked on three sides by the scabrous bazaar was the new American hospital, like a dressing on the wound.

For one day the Broadwells and I sat in the Staff House getting air-conditioned and caloried-up on steak and pumpkin pie. Then we got a lift to Kandahar in the weekly provisions van.

In the Kandahar Hotel there was only one room with three beds. So I assumed the Broadwells would take it. They had a son of 7. But Chris said he had to sleep on the floor because of his back and I could share it with them if I felt like it. It was exactly what I felt like. For the moment I had had enough of the endless numbered rooms – unapproached privacy from nothing in particular. And so had the Broadwells. They said if they'd been born ten years later they'd probably have been beatniks. As it was they transmitted exactly the right mixture of security and enthusiasm for the least detail of their sur-roundings – the strange showcase in the hotel lobby containing bars of chocolate, tins of peaches, jars of Horlicks, symbols from another world (not for sale) of the kind of hotel this was intended to be, or the price tags in shop windows, with one price in Persian figures and another – twice as great for the more unobservant traveller – in the more usual numerals. Even the grapeseller who washed his delicious grapes in the open drain over which he chose to set up shop, fascinated them. They were ideal companions and as they had to hurry on to Kabul by air, I decided to fly with them.

From Kandahar I wrote to a girl in London: 'It is 120° but dry and the air is full of sweet, dusty, flower smells. I am quite well. I think about you in the bazaars. They are full of your trappings. It takes a day to arrange a parcel, or I'd send you some junk to sell. Did you get a letter from Isfahan? I couldn't resist getting an English-speaking scribe who used to sit outside the post office, to write you a letter in Farsi. He was full of fine ideas. "Fly to me like a nightingale, or a sparrow," he suggested. Then "or in an aeroplane," as if the first two were impractical.

O God I have so much to tell you. But I will never tell you. For a while we will talk about the countries with the best names and then we will go to the cinema. Bundling along these ghastly roads has been wonderfully peaceful. The rhythm strokes the metabolism. It removes any reason for pleasing someone – even yourself. There's no longer any reason to panic about creating something. It's out of the question. The future unrolls of its own accord with the road. The present is a moveable holiday, sometimes in the past, with you, sometimes in the future. Sometimes part of both forever. Moments and faces from the past can be held steady and lived almost like a drug, or dismissed completely for a new life. I miss you and them in a romantic way and would not bring them closer for worlds.

'Kandahar was founded by Alexander. There's an Acropolis on a hill at the back. We prance about in little jingling horse carriages called tongas. Tomorrow we go to Kabul, then through the Khyber towards the Monsoon.'

In the green-painted Afghan Air DC4 I had my usual tension-prevention. I could do nothing but sit breathing hard with my eyes closed, thinking, as I have been told to, of nails, nails I suppose being the exact opposite of vomit. There was an Indian sitting beside me who apparently didn't like my colour, for he leant over and poked my face with a finger to make sure I was still alive. I discovered later that I still was, but that I had missed seeing the cratered ranges of the Hindu Kush where Kabul is situated. In fact I had no more than an air traveller's view of the city even after landing. The Broadwells were still anxious to push on and I was still anxious to stay with them. I remember the huge American cafeteria, 'The Khyber', parked in the middle of the town like an American Embassy where the town hall should have been, or a theatre. And I remember entering it with glee as if I'd been crawling across the wilderness for months with pancakes and a milkshake in a bubble above my head. We stayed in some hotel, but The Khyber was our base. From there we explored yet another bazaar.

The shops for yellow yakskin jackets and red leather poufs, were three steps up from the road and under them, like prompt boxes, were little gutter basements selling chains and shoes made of old tyres. I never saw anyone wearing tyre shoes though, or even turned-up Afghan slippers: most people seemed to prefer pointed Italian moccasins with the heels trampled down.

But one couldn't linger indefinitely in these streets. Lavatories seemed to have been installed all right, but without the usual pipes. So at the backs of the houses the excrement just ran down the walls into the street, where it waited perhaps a week for the 'honey-carts'. I think it was this which started Carolyn disinfecting things. She became very nostalgic for hygienic Oakland, California, with all its 'facilities'. She bought a bottle of Dettol and, I believe, sprinkled herself and her husband with it liberally. Even in restaurants, fruit had to be washed in Tide, water iodized, spoons sterilized and not put down *anywhere*. Chris, thank God, remained calm and, below deck, made jokes about her. But she seemed to have grown perceptibly taller than him suddenly.

Early the next morning we were in a bus hoping it to be the one for the Pakistan border. For a long time it didn't move and Carolyn told me I should take advantage of the delay to take notes on my surroundings. We were in a muddy bus depot and there was plenty to note. Boys were lighting up big hubble-bubbles and hiring them out for a few pesas a drag. Another lay sprawled on a bank, asleep, the colour of the earth. There was a man in mustard-coloured robes and a black turban. Men were flocking round the bus with trays of brown cigarettes and sticky white sweets. Their faces appeared at the windows like Ali Baba's thieves looking out of their urns. By a wall a man was cooking lumps of liver on a stick. Someone else had set up a drink stall. There were all different shapes and sizes of bottles filled up with bright green and pink liquids, none of them with tops on.

Three hours later we were in Jalalabad, 50 miles short of the border, discovering that that was as far as the bus went. But a van with four rows of seats would go on to Turkham when and if it filled up. We got in and our example seemed to encourage everyone in the neighbourhood to do the same: first class inside, second class on the roof. No standing on the roof.

On the way we saw little cone-shaped houses with goats' horns coming out of the top. These showed where old or great men had died. Graves in Afghanistan are honoured with a holly tree or a piece of string hung between two goat horns. When the string breaks it is a sign that the man's spirit has risen to heaven. We stopped at a little hermitage beside the road and a religious man came out and began to break off bits of thread from a reel. When he had three, he tied them together in three places, kissing the knots (three vows?). Then he handed it through the window to one of the passengers, who paid him and placed it carefully in his wallet.

At Turkham we got down to walk the 400 yards into Pakistan. Before we had gone 10 yards we made out half a dozen minute figures racing towards us from the other side. They arrived breathless, even smaller, pleading to be allowed to carry our huge suitcases. We had no rupees, but we gave them all chocolate for escorting us into their country.

There is a certain kind of cinema which delights in showing a man in an overcoat driving alone in a car, stopping, getting out of his car, crossing a pavement, ringing a bell, entering a house, mounting a staircase, knocking on a door and finally, if you're lucky, shooting the place up. The film is often of an African leader calling at No. 10 Downing Street, though in this case the subsequent shoot-up is always censored. In France they call it Cinema de Papa. And in a sense all travel writing is

Cinema de Papa because the journey to the door, the knocking, the climb, etc., is its subject and plot combined. It is the some-times laborious step-taking of the man in the overcoat, leading you with luck from one shoot-up to the next.

Nobody is more sensitive about how many steps he may take between shoot-ups than the man in the overcoat himself. But steps he must take.

'Commonwealth or Alien?' said a fat, white-robed official. He was the first fat man I'd seen for weeks and he symbolized the obvious differences between these two countries: suddenly there were trees and flowerbeds and a tarred road through a fertile plain.

'Commonwealth!' I said and was ushered through Immigra-tion while the Broadwells filled in questionnaires.

But it wasn't as simple as that. Customs, they said, was a currency formality. It wouldn't take a minute. In the shed there were two Australian hitch-hikers. I signed something for the official and turned to talk to them. But the signature was the commencement of something not the settlement. I had turned away too soon. I was ordered to sit down.

Something in the man's eyes had begun to sulk and my string of no's to his questions got on his nerves. He kept asking me if I had any gold and he clearly didn't believe me. Suddenly he said I was to get my suitcase – already loaded into a bus. I brought it back and began to be sarcastic. By this time he was absolutely livid. He kept saying 'come on, open up, come on,' and his servants dug their hands into my dirty clothes and lifted them out on to the floor. 'Times have changed since the British were here,' he said. 'Times have changed.'

'I'm afraid it's all horribly familiar.'

'We do not give a fig for you Britishers,' he spat. 'Every Britisher who passes through here is the same. You think you can give us orders. But we do not give a fig for you.'

'Well, isn't that nice? Such a nice welcome.'

'You are just a cheeky boy. You know nothing. You think

because you are British you can . . . Ah, what is this? Pornography!'

A magazine called *Sexology* had been unearthed. The atmosphere was charged. The Broadwells became more interested than impatient. But they needn't have bothered. A list of banned books was eagerly scanned but found wanting. Miserable, the official ordered me to re-count my travellers' cheques in front of him. I lost some face here, for my hands were shaking and I made it £10 more than I had declared. Now he had me. Everything could be confiscated, he said. 'You realize I could take all your money?' 'Yes.' 'But I will not. I will teach you a lesson in manners. Because of this man – this gentleman – you are with, I will let you keep it. Now get out of here.' Before leaving, I apologized to the man. It is a whimsical compulsion I have always to apologize. But the wind had dropped. It was not a dramatic move and the man accepted it as nothing short of his due.

II–INDIA

Hill stations

The sun was setting behind us as we started down the Khyber Pass and the hills were exercising their fierce muscles under the shadows. The pass is a gigantic chasm twisting between greenish mountains with farms like toys in the fertile valleys below. The road hairpins round its shoulders and only occasionally one sees the valleys linked in a single system, stretching away to the fort of the Khyber Rifles in the distance.

At the far end is Landikotal, official outlet for the illegal firearms manufactured by the Pathans. These men live very poor tribal lives in the mountains and the Government lets them go on smuggling their hardware in the hope that rupees will tempt them to become law-abiding citizens. But the Pathans have their own laws – or lore – bravery in warfare, the avenging of insults, hospitality to strangers even though they be enemies. They even carry guns with them wherever they go and shoot on sight. We saw plenty of the powerful, Oriental-looking warriors hanging about with an imitation Webley or two stuck into a cartridge belt. They make them by hand out of old bicycle frames and the barrels are said to melt and droop if they are used too much. In a bazaar like a cave under the road there were pistols for £5.

At Landikotal we got into another bus, an old Thames Trader loaded with locally-built buswork and painted like a circus. On it Mrs Broadwell was handed an enormous ball of rather dusty white toffee, which she sat holding like something her child had found on the beach, smiling gratefully for it, all the way to Peshawar.

Peshawar was like a summer evening in Cheltenham. What did I expect? Not Lady Grifiths Government High School for Girls, situated boldly in Station Road. After Persia's remote deserts, not chestnuts, white railings and enamel advertisements for Tetley Teabags. After colourful Afghans, not portly gentlemen like characters from old cricketing prints. But the greatest surprise of all was at the Dak Bungalow where we stayed the night. 'Have you heard about the scandal?' said the Pickwickian proprietor. 'No. What scandal?' 'Your war minister, Profumo, is tied up with a vice ring. Parliament is in a great rumpus. Wait while I fetch the paper. Everyone is talking about it here,' and he scuttled off excitedly. I can't remember what the paper said, except that it was delighted to the point of incoherence and continued to be so with daily Christine Keeler pages until President Ayub Khan's name entered the case, when it became libellous to the point of hysteria. Months later the following bizarre passage appeared in India's *Blitz*:

> Even the tightest society of the Palace, it seems, could not withstand the assault of Dr Ward and his tarts. Half of the Royal family has evidently sat for portraits by a person whom the Tory Government has prosecuted on charges of high class pimping and sent to suicide. Even during the trial of the osteopath-artist, a mysterious personage showed up to remove from an exhibition every image of British Royalty put on canvas by Dr Ward. All of which has made Royal patronage of this odd practitioner of the black arts of sex somewhat suspicious.

Later I met a party of students from Karachi also staying at the Dak. They came and stood in the door of our room, watching us burning ourselves on curry. I went out into the garden where they were preparing to sleep and they bombarded me with questions. Where was I going? How old was I? Were those people my Mummy and Daddy? Surely I was not alone? By a marvellous chance they were going next morning to the Kingdom of Swat and they asked me to go with them. As the bus set off, the Broadwells stood sweetly yelling instructions on how to find their house in Oakland, California. I was going to miss the family life we had led.

On the bus I met Amin, Ajas and Masood. Amin was an extraordinary student with a moustache and a walking stick and a way of enquiring if I understood what he was saying by lifting his voice and saying 'clear?' at the end of each sentence. 'Punjab equals "land of five rivers", clear? Punj equals five. Ab equals water. Clear? Recently the Indians have diverted two of these rivers from their rightful courses. So we have been obliged to construct the artificial waterfall you see over there to overcome our lack of hydro-electric power. Clear?'

But the noise from the engine was so great that most of what he said was very unclear and I wanted to look out of the window all the time. Suddenly the landscape seemed so crowded with life and colour. Fields, turbans, lorries, flowers, birds, blazed in the hot sunlight. But nothing seemed to move. At the speed we were going even the flick of an ox's tail couldn't blur the photograph. Life simply plodded through the rich soil in its infinitely ponderous footsteps.

It was not until the evening, when we stopped at a roadside hostel in the Swat village of Mingorra, that the stills came alive. From the verandah I could see a white rivulet twisting down from a range of hills and rippling over stones on the other side of the road. Little boys were splashing naked in it and some of our group were washing themselves by squatting on stones in mid-stream and discreetly soaping inside their underclothes.

By the road sat old men in white, their reddened beards glowing. Here and there someone was asleep or praying.

Between the stream and the road was a spring and people kept coming for their water. Round the spring were some old string cots in case someone felt tired. From a telephone wire above the road, long black swallows called quails were dive-bombing dogs. Later, some boys catapulted one and were trying to get it to fly again by throwing it into the air.

That night we all slept on the verandah and Amin said I could stay with the expedition as long as I liked because they were going all over the north of Pakistan.

In the morning the bus came round and bore us upwards to Bahrain, a village high under the clouds at the junction of two mountain rivers. One sometimes wonders what a resort looked like before it was developed. This was it. The fresh-minted water ran unchecked down paths, through houses and privies, under bridges, over waterfalls in rainbows. There was a constant clatter of it, changing its tune wherever you walked – perfect for a honeymoon. It was like a bird's nest on a creeper behind a falls. Light filtered pearly and dim through the clouds. Rain fell in petals. Water washed away talk. We had stew at the inn and afterwards I lay on a cot and stared at a rockstrewn hillside till I fell asleep.

The bus tottered back to Mingorra and I could hardly keep my eyes open. Between snappings of my head I was vaguely aware of intimate, terraced valleys, lime green fields and blossom. My head kept colliding with Amin's to the great amusement of everyone behind us. When we got back Amin said 'You have missed seeing the most beautiful scenery in Pakistan, clear?' And Ajas told me that Hindu students used to tie their single long locks of hair to a nail above their desks, so when they began to fall asleep, their heads would be jerked up by it.

Back at the hostel the younger students made curry. We sat on the verandah playing trumps till it came. After the meal, a masseur called a 'chompey' came up and rubbed oil into Amin and Masood and honey into their eyelids.

The first glimpse of Abbotobad – named after General Abbot – was a Norman spire rising from chestnuts. All round the old resort were faded and out-dated traces of Britain. Lady Cunningham's Child Welfare Centre, ancient Vauxhalls, chocolate éclairs, The Ovaltinis, rosebeds, deck chairs.

But our doss space at the hotel was less than Imperial – three tiny rooms, completely covered with bedding for thirty, on the axis of a stinking commode. Sharing our space was a Pathan brave, uneasily in town 'to defend his cousin in court over a piece of land'. He was a splendid looking chap with black stuff on his lower eyelids and a way of offering everyone within hearing a cigarette – especially me, whom he kept inviting to visit his tribe. He told Amin that he would very much like to prove to his people that he was friendly with foreigners and that if I visited him he would give me a pistol. I asked him how he had hurt his hand and he laughed and said a stove had fallen on it while he was breaking into a house. I took some strange, descriptive address, but in the end it was too far off and I cosily forgot about it.

There was nowhere to wash in the hotel so the first morning we followed a well-trodden path to a mosque over a spring. Under the mosque were bathrooms, each with an icy waterfall thundering through it, and people queueing. Outside was the pond the water flowed into for further use. Children were bathing under the spout, fish were swarming for breadcrumbs and farmers were driving in buffalo and horses for washing and watering. Nearby was an old canvas awning over a charcoal fire and a stall selling fried potatoes, chickpeas and onions. All the time people were coming and going, clean and dirty, rich and poor, waiting for their baths before praying and smoking. It was a kind of squalid purification typical of Islam – and not a woman in sight. In fact women weren't much in evidence any-where. Men served in the shops. Men bought tea. Men gave massages. Men held hands. Did men, I wondered, invite other men to meet their families – or tribes? It was something one noticed suddenly with a bout of prisoner's restlessness. In the sweeping, formal park for instance, there were tall hedges round the 'ladies corner' from which came only flashes of laughter and sari through the branches. You could see women's faces in the distance but long before you drew abreast they disappeared under veils, leaving you with only a silhouette and a sandalled foot to judge from. If it frustrated me, it seemed only to have made the menfolk smug and conceited, for they lacked the female's challenging edge about them.

Two days later a special old Bedford bus arrived to take us up the mountains like a funicular to the hill station of Nathiagali. The road up was so steep and narrow that it could take one-way traffic only and we had to wait at the bottom till the three 'down' hours were over. Across the windscreen of the bus were heady garlands of jasmine and wax roses. Every ten minutes we had to stop to pour water from streams over the steaming radiator. The valleys were beginning to open under us like holes in the floor of the sea. There was that green light from all the pines and the precipices falling from the roadside like dropped stones. Looking down from the ledge I could see eagles describing figures of eight above the mist and far away the horizons unfolding backwards into the sun.

Nathiagali too was perched upon a ledge, overlooking a relief map of redwoods. Above six shops, two narrow ramshackle hotels faced each other across the narrow street. Below them, the hillside fell through the vertical spikes of the redwoods to lower Nathiagali, two miles down. Best of all there was cool, fresh air.

All the students were delighted with the place and kept coming up to me to ask what I thought of it.

'Do you like the place, William?'

'Very much, do you?'

'Of course I like it. I am a Pakistani.'

I wondered how many high-school boys in England would

cherish the idea of a week without girls in a bedless hotel on a mountain side.

Actually, in this hotel I had a string cot half inside the kitchen, while the three others slept on the floor with their feet under it. But the mattress was mouldy as cheese and the thing that went over me was heavy with an unknown weight. I used to sleep with my clothes on and in the morning one of the boys would bring me tea and cake. I would lie in bed watching them come in one by one to dry-shave their moustaches with little coloured tin razor-blade holders in the good light from the back window and clean their teeth with a twig from some special tree. When I came to look in the mirror myself I thought I looked very strange. Not whiter, but more evil, with little pale eyes and a nose like a bone.

In fact less people stared at me up here, so I had more time to stare at them. From the balcony I could see up and down the road and into the hotel opposite which was open like the back of a doll's house. I remember a man having his head shaved in the 'barbar' shop and another picking up a tennis racquet from the floor of a little tea house and looking up straight into my face as he tested its strings on his hand. There were men in striped pyjamas strolling down the road, their fingers twined, one with a transistor to his ear and the high-pitched, childlike Urdu song drifting up to me with their talk. Dogs lay about everywhere. A chicken slid down a steep bank on its spurs into the street. I heard the triumphant slap of a winning card delivered next door, and downstairs the clacking of backgammon boards. Nobody was alone. Nobody, except me, was private, or wished to be, or thought it polite. They moved together in interlocking circles which spun clear of me. I felt like Dylan Thomas looking Under Milk Wood.

On the first afternoon Masood and I walked up to the Green Hotel. He needed a drink and wanted me to make some 'enquiries' for him about it. He said he was 'habitual' and would often drink alone. He told me he was married to a Christian

83

girl in India, but she was an only child and her parents wouldn't let her come to Pakistan. He had one daughter by her and another who died of smallpox. He said he had to get his degree, then he would see what he could do about getting her back. But though he loved her, he had no determination and seemed resigned to the power of his in-laws, drink and pathetic boasts about other girls in Karachi. At the Green Hotel I bought him some terrible Pak whisky and we sat in a little back drinking booth till we were driven out by two American children who said it was their club. On the way out I swiped a bottle of Worcestershire sauce and a pot of Marmite off a table in the dining room. They lasted me about three months.

A week later we moved on to Murree, Pakistan's summer capital and spa. Her Simla. The climb there was even more quixotic than the last. A road barely ledged to the precipice: anyone we met had to climb up the mountain to escape being crushed against it, red-bearded old gaffers with their retired hands loose over a rod across their shoulders, like little dead animals on a gibbet. We would see them wandering down the road or roosting like frightening old cockerels on a chair or a wall.

At the bus station we waited while Masood 'The Politician' found us somewhere to sleep. Then coolies with legs like rusty wire carried the huge bedding rolls up the steep lanes to a rancid barrack he had found. There was no floor or light, but it was free.

I hadn't lived so close to people since prep school and I sometimes found it hard to keep up the smiling. The boys had got over my strangeness and were always asking where I was going, what I was doing and why, without much interest in hearing.

I think it was about this time that I started to get unpopular. I was finding it impossible to write or sleep and things had crawled out of my bedding and bitten me all over the face. We were all sitting on the floor once, waiting for dahl to be served on leaves on a few pages of the *Pakistan Times*. I had taken off my shoes and was pulling my feet into a cross-legged position, when Ajas said 'You see we don't touch our feet when we're about to eat.' 'You're incredible,' I said. 'You might as well start scrubbing this earth floor if that's how you feel.'

'In this country we obey what we read in the Koran.'

'Mohammed must be laughing in his sleep.' They got up and left me. It was about then too that people started telling me things about Islam:

'You see we accept your prophets. Jesus was a great teacher. Moses was a prophet.'

'But the Jews and the Christians fell in God's sight. Moslems are the last of the chosen people.'

'Christianity fell because its gospel was twisted and changed and translated till the truth was lost.'

'How could God have a son or mother when He was everything? How could God suffer and die when He was almighty?'

'God would not submit to death. He would not even allow one of His prophets to be thus humiliated.'

'And since Jesus was a prophet, it must have been someone else who died on the cross – a martyr, yes. Or perhaps a bad man who had to die.'

'We do not believe in the confession and forgiveness. But perhaps we should do nowadays.'

'The Koran says that if a man rapes a girl he should be buried to the waist in sand, covered with curds and eaten by dogs while he is stoned. His sin is thus absolved in his pain and death. Today we think this barbaric and we do not practise it.'

'That is why chaos and evil is rife in the land.'

'There was a time – as you know from your bible – when a man would sacrifice his own son to the will of God. But God would not let Abraham kill his son Ishmael because Ishmael too was a prophet.'

'Did you say Ishmael?' I said.

'Yes.'

85

'But it was Isaac, his other son, who he was going to sacrifice.'

'No. You must be mistaken.'

'That's fascinating. In the bible Ishmael was the son of Hagar, Abraham's serving woman, and his wife Sarah was so jealous of her, Abraham had to send them away into the desert where Ishmael became the leader of a tribe of bowmen.'

'The Koran states quite definitely that it was Ishmael who . . .'

'That must be where Islam was born. It explains why the Koran allows a man more than one wife. In order to make Ishmael legitimate. I wonder which is the truth. What a marvellous plot it would make . . .'

'I think you have religious tendencies after all, Mr William.'

It was the Murree season and at six each day we sat on the steps of the Post Office or in Sam's Tea Rooms watching 'Pindi and Karachi society parading on the Mall, as the English must once have done. There were beautiful pale ladies in white silk pantaloons, nipped in at tiny up-turned slippers. Men in blazers and flannels, or tropical suits. Women hidden under black silk. Men in old pyjama suits. Here and there a blonde Embassy daughter in slacks or a print. Here and there a Hindu woman in a sari, her face unhidden showing her caste-mark, her reputation suspected by all. As they passed beneath me in all their coloured silks, the musky scent of their bodies and perfumes came drifting up on the evening breeze, the most sensuous, unattainable smell in the world.

In Sam's there were curtained booths for the women.

'We do not like to see a strange woman's face in public,' said Amin. 'It stirs up feelings which, if allowed to run loose, could lead to ugliness.' What about human moderation, tact, sensibility, even decency? Is beauty responsible for its own rape? I longed for those subtle antagonisms round a mixed dinner table. The defeats and victories. The clarity and doubt.

'Do you relish tea with milk now, Mister William?' said Ajas-sahib, with his serious beautiful eyes.

I think we got to Rawalpindi by bus. Then there was a long wait in the station for the train to Lahore. It was in 'Pindi I first noticed the heat – a kind of motionless sweating which brought me right down off my high horse and fighting for a place under the fan with everyone else. The station was crowded with beggars and cripples, families, schools and religious men. I remember an armless man who lay on the floor in a grey shroud. Others slept, but he was restless, uncomfortable. His shawl kept slipping off his shoulders and every now and then a thin curled finger appeared where his arm should have been to catch it back in place. It was like a little crab which quickly scuttled under its rock. Once he went and stood near the tea counter and I couldn't move to buy him a cup or help him. I can't understand it now, but I think I was afraid of his strange vitality and nervousness, afraid of making it worse. Being foreign makes subtle changes in one. I would have made any compromise to seem less strange. I felt sometimes like a cripple myself.

At Lahore I said goodbye to the students whose faces I knew so well. They were staying in the train for Karachi. I had been invited to stay in Lahore at the house of an engineer called Ferooqui, whom I'd met on the train. He had a scooter at the station and I followed him with the luggage in a motor rickshaw. His house was miles away in the Model Village. There was no one there. His wife had stayed in 'Pindi with toothache. I had a wonderful cold hip-bath and when I came out there was pink iced sherbet waiting. Ferooqui was rather a sad little man with the very un-Indian habit of not inserting the usual monosyllables of agreement and interest in a conversation, which made it rather hard going. He said he had once been rich and showed me where the telephone had been. But in 1951 he had exported flax to India without a credit note. There had been trouble between the two countries that year and the goods had stood untouched, ruining in a siding for five months. Nothing had been the same after that.

'Would you like a proper drink?' he asked. 'I'm afraid I like a drink occasionally.'

We got on his scooter and drove back into town where we met a friend of his who was a member of a club. He took us into a dark bar at the back of an hotel and we had a few priceless glasses of whisky and soda served with chicken curry and soft, guilty, Western music. Then we left for another club, Ferooqui and I on the scooter, his friend in a car. (Try to remember exactly what happened next, Mr Williams.) As we joined the main road at a roundabout a huge white Cadillac pulled up suddenly in front of us. Ferooqui lost balance but managed to wobble round it, and as we passed the driver's window I yelled 'Learn to drive, you bloody fool.' We wobbled on a bit more until I heard a heavy car door slam shut. I looked round and saw a huge figure in white flannels trumpeting down the road after us. For some reason Ferooqui couldn't accelerate. He seemed stuck in the highest gear and there was nothing I could do. It was like one of those dreams of running through mud. I dug in my spurs, but nothing happened. I felt a hand get hold of my collar and pull. I clung on to poor old Ferooqui and the heavy scooter keeled over like a drunken boat. I was yanked off it backwards and crashed down on to the base of my spine. I suppose thinking he had gone too far, the Indian had retreated momentarily. But when I got up and began hopping about in pain by the roadside, cursing him, he reappeared, shouting 'Do you know who you're talking to? Do you know who you're talking to.' I must have been smitten with a dying man's bravado or insanity, for I yelled back, 'Yes, you're the bloody fool who stopped in the middle of the roundabout.'

The next thing I knew I was scrambling to my feet again, seeing stars. It was quite dark and all I could make out was a crowd of white shirts. Somewhat to my dismay, I was still cursing him and soon received another open-handed blow which sent me down again like a tin soldier. By this time the man had thought better of asking me if I knew who I was speaking to, nervous perhaps that I should find out. Instead he hit upon 'You little white monkey, who do you think you are, you little white monkey?' Then I think he disappeared again. Brave as a lion, Ferooqui then helped me to my feet and told me I had been beaten up. He said if he had come to help me his scooter would have been stolen. I wanted to go after the man or get the police but he said it was illegal to drink without a permit in Pakistan and that he would be automatically in the wrong and guilty if it came out that we had been to a bar. He seemed thoroughly shifty to get away as if we had only received what was due to us.

So once again I behaved in a way which now seems unrecognizable to me, but which may in fact be a clue to the strange Jekyll-Hyde drug of travel.

I got on the back of the scooter and, with Ferooqui consoling me over his shoulder, beat a retreat.

The next day it was 110° F and 99% humidity, which should mean one was breathing water, but I didn't drown – or rather I only drowned in my own sweat. The worst thing is that sweat won't evaporate – so it can't cool you. The pores on the back of my hands were wide open, gasping for air, like little stars. They reminded me of the hands of an Indian I was at school with. He was called the Nawab of Pataudi and he sat next to me at tea, smelling strangely of what I thought of as 'musk', cricket bat oil, and something which excited the mothers as he brushed past them in his pink cricket colours on parents' day. I remember his hands very clearly because he'd be flicking a cricket ball round in his lap under the table and we'd keep asking him what the grip was for a 'Chinaman' or a 'Googly', mysterious devices from the East of which he alone, the Great Cricketer, knew the secret. What a long way this sweltering town from the visions of India started by his family's saris drifting across the cricket ground and his handsome face, which was for a while the only criterion of all other good looks in the school.

Lahore was the place where Rudyard Kipling edited *The Civil and Military Gazette* in the 1880's. The paper was still in existence, its offices suffering badly from Indianitis. The tall, pillared chambers might have been lost in nostalgic reverie for the days of Civil and Military Lines. But they were not. They were lost elsewhere.

'Mr Kipling believed we were a backward race,' the editor told me. 'But we cannot agree that India was the white man's burden. Rather the contrary.'

'But politics aside, is he loved for his literature?'

'He was a great craftsman, you see. But he wrote for his friends at home, who have been misguided about us ever since.'

'But he sat where you are sitting as the editor of a newspaper. He knew what was going on.'

'You see we are not sure in what capacity he worked. We have no files.'

'Is there no trace of him left at all then?' The editor got up from his wicker and wood chair. On every conceivable surface were bundles of paper tied with pink ribbon, ringed with coffee. He went to the mantelpiece and turned up an old photograph which was lying there face down.

'I believe this was taken while he was here.' He handed it to me and I propped it up in the middle of the mantelpiece. It was as if Kipling had left the paper the year before, under some kind of cloud which had been hushed up. But I dare say the photograph is still where I put it.

In the YMCA canteen I met an angry young Dane. He had just had £5 stolen by his travelling companion, a German who, three months later, was to steal my camera and that of a friend of mine in Madras. But he couldn't prove it and though we had disguised policemen waiting at the railway stations and the docks in Madras, we couldn't catch him either. He was an engaging, aggressive adventurer with a little hairy moustache and thick specs. He said he'd been in the Foreign Legion, lived with bedouins, climbed Everest, etc. And all on $1. He was the sort of smug little fellow who would creep back home with his adventures safely packed like a box of confidence tricks and quietly become an income tax inspector for the rest of his life. But the Dane was not only mad about his fiver. Like nearly every traveller I met who was not an American, he was full of spleen for the town he was in and its stupid, dishonest, dirty inhabitants. He even had a bayonet and a revolver to protect himself from them. He was eighteen and said he was going to join the Indian Army as a rifle maintenance instructor. Together we explored the Hindu quarter of Lahore. At last there were women again. Fat, fierce-looking, bawdy old hags jingling along in buggies like pearly queens, winking at us. And beside the road sat their emaciated menfolk, puffing hookahs, selling water-melon, lemon juice, mangoes, piles of powdered red paint for cast-marks and piles of any old iron for God knows what. In one corner Hindu holy men were doing weird leaping dances with drums and monkeys. They each had single long locks of hair falling from shaved scalps. They were almost naked and one had little bones and rags tied round his belt. India, it seemed, was not far away now.

Houseboats

At the Indian border I met two brothers from Portsmouth, one called Keith, and a German, and we decided to go to Kashmir together. We travelled fourth class in the train, but when we got to Pathankot that night the brothers rolled out their sleeping bags in the first-class waiting room – a quiet place with a fan, guarded by a Sikh for anyone, it seemed, who could distinguish himself from the crowds that slept on the platform. I had no bag, but there was a wicker settee with a big hole in it. So I put my suitcase under the hole and the doormat over it and slept with my head on my typewriter.

Next day, on to Jammu, where we called at the police station for permits to go on in trucks. They told us to come back the next day, so we found a room in the temple. It had an earth floor and tame chaffinches sitting on the table. From the window we could see the vast main temple with its rows of mitre-shaped spires, some covered with gold, others with gold emblems on the sandstone.

Outside in the courtyard gurus lectured their disciples. Empty string cots lay about in sunshine, or in the shadow of walls with the sick on them. On the train I'd seen a holy man dressed in a bit of fur, carrying a trident. He had string in his hair and in his long beard.

Keith was taking off his trousers. Suddenly three young Indians walked into the room.

'Good afternoon. I hope we are not disturbing you,' one said. 'What a fine view you have of the temple, have you not? May I ask if you have been inside, please?'

'No non-Hindus were allowed in,' I said.

'What? I can't believe it. This is disgraceful. You wished to enter the temple and were barred from entrance, is it?'

'Yes.'

'This is most humiliating. Come with me, please.'

The others weren't interested, so I followed the Indians across the courtyard and round behind the temple to the Principal's room. It was a dark, luxurious little booth with several servants squatting outside the door. Dogmas and doctrines darted above my head. The eyes of the young man gleamed for me. I was an educated man, what would I tell my countrymen when I returned? Indians were allowed into churches, why should a Christian not look into a temple? Ah, but I was a beef-eater. What proof had he that I was a beef-eater? None, but my presence would be offensive to devout men. Threats, addresses, promises of complaints: failure. It was all very British.

Back in our room I asked appreciative questions to make up. The young men were theology students.

'In Hinduism, there is no good or bad, right or wrong,' he began. 'It is all in the mind. And everything and everyone who is or was ever on earth is a part of Therma – that is a Sanskrit word meaning the eternal existence of things. . . .'

Just then, Keith, who had got his trousers on, but was still smarting from having been caught with them down by the 'wogs', said:

'Anyway, where's all the women got to in this town?'

'The nearest you will get to a woman in Jammu, my friend,' said this most un-obsequious of Indians, 'is at the cinema. I believe they are showing Ben Hur.'

He had to catch an aeroplane to Delhi, so that night I went with the others to see the film. It was open air. Stars circled the hazy screen. Later, lying on a cot under the temple walls, I watched the moon come up behind the gold spires. Everyone had moved their beds out of the little stables into the warm night air. You could see the sleeping families grouped together in the moonlight.

'They got no manners, these wogs,' said Keith, 'barging in without knocking like that.'

The police couldn't give us permits to hitch-hike but, having delayed us a day, decently gave us free passes on the bus.

One more night on the road, sleeping in rows on the floor of a dak bungalow, then at dawn we entered the Srinagar Valley. On either side shelf-like paddy fields full of water followed the contours of the hillsides in terraces down to the plain. There, the same unfamiliar weaving lines broke up the fields in ribbons, the water gleaming between the little spears of rice.

At the Srinagar bus station the houseboat touts danced round us like Red Indians. It was the off season, or I'm sure they wouldn't have bothered. Keith and the others got through to the YMCA, but I let myself be carried off in a trishaw to meet a houseboat owner.

Srinagar is more or less surrounded by the river Jelum and its tributary and every inch of their banks is crowded with cumbersome old houseboats, traditionally let to holiday-makers. The trishaw stopped and I was led over an embankment and down a little gangplank into a plush saloon. There sat the owner, an enormous, charming Muslim, president of the Houseboat Union.

'How long do you intend to stay?' he asked.

'Ten days.'

'Good. You can have the Annexe. Three rupees a day.' Moored beside his own was a tiny one-man boat with a bed, bath-tub and a table at a window on the river. It was 4s 6d a day.

For a week I enjoyed my hideout like a first room or a treehouse. At night it swayed slightly in the wash and frogs sang. Sometimes I woke to find my horizon totally changed by the rising tide or a new position at the mooring. Then a man would come wobbling down the gangplank with a tray of steaming kippers and coffee. It was legendary. I sat at my window pretending I was Shelley in long letters home, dreamily isolated even from my own idleness. The little boat was a time machine, floating clear of everyday life, yet not borne down by the timeless river. Instead it wheeled in limbo, like a lost day and night.

It was great fun, but it didn't last. Pirates soon bridged the time gap with their grappling hooks. The Red Indian touts had smelt me out and came in their war canoes to challenge my greed. The silent punts called 'shikarras' would sidle up and a tailor or jeweller leap aboard, spreading his wares at my feet as he did so. Or I would look up from my desk straight into a chemist, or fruit, or carpet shop which had materialized in my window. At first it was fun: walnuts, peaches, toothpaste, razor blades. I need never have left my seat. But it broke the spell. The whole point of staying so still had been to neutralize the present so I could catch up on the past in writing. But the shikarra wallahs serenaded me daily with their desperate salesmanship. They had three months of each year to sell a year's produce and no time for faint-hearted lovers. Their overtures were devilish. I found myself bargaining and gave up. I was soon on my way into town in search of company and the present.

Ray was manager of the night club. A London ice-cream-van driver, he'd left his wife and set off with £20 and an old army friend called Hobby, to see the world. He was 27, thin, fast-talking, witty, at home in pubs, cars, bedrooms, with the look of a regular soldier about him.

Hobby was very different: a West End type with all kinds of accents: Chelsea, disc-jockey, cockney, beat. More sophisticated and likeable than Ray, but less convincing. When he left the army, he'd married a Kashmiri girl and had two children by her. For four years he'd lived in Kashmir managing her estate above Srinagar. Then he'd got fed up and gone to fetch his old mate Ray for a last fling. He left Kashmir and hitched to London, where he stayed with Ray and helped him with the rounds. Ray's wife dreaded him. One day they both left her to it.

Now Ray was waiting on Hob in the night club and sleeping on one of the banquettes when it closed, while Hob stayed with his father-in-law and did nothing. It wasn't what he'd expected and now he'd got eczema and the Indians thought it was syphilis.

When I met them both they were shouting at each other across the street and seemed to welcome someone new to try their wits on. From then on I was the new boy who made them daredevils.

One morning we went swimming. Hob borrowed his father-in-law's shikarra and paddled us upstream to Negeen Lake where the swimming-boats lay. The waterway curled round the back of the city, under windows, under a Mogul bridge and past worshipful little temples crumbling down steps into the water, where naked children stood with arched backs, or swam out to us. We stopped at a river-level store and bought mangoes. The going was hard because there's a knack in using one paddle and only Hobby knew how to twist the boat back on to course at the end of each stroke. Once he held the boat in midstream and pointed under a tree down a backwater. There four naked girls were washing in the shallow water. They stood up and poured water over their white bodies. Hobby feigned boredom, but Ray and I watched fascinated till they saw us and got under the water, laughing. Hobby said you could quite easily buy a wife in north Kashmir if you wanted to, and for half an hour I dreamed of stepping ashore at Newhaven with a beautiful tribe girl on my arm – rather as one might consider a tattoo.

We had left the narrow channel through the town and come out into open, reeded water. Men in shikarras were towing floating allotments that passed us like little green stubble fields. On one a duck had nested and was glancing nervously round. Kashmir must be the only place in the world where land can be actually absconded with.

Negeen Lake is surrounded by green hills and then by snow-capped mountains. Round the edge are a few honeymooning houseboats, white and pink and yellow among the bullrushes. In the middle are the two swimming-boats like ancient Mississippi paddle steamers with cabins, bars and water-skiing. We approached them from the river which flows down to Srinagar but if you come by road you are prey once more to the shikarra wallahs – your only means of getting through the weeds which crowd the shallows out to the deep water round the swimming-boats. You've hardly got down from the bus than they are crowding you for custom. Their boats have names like 'The Cautious Amorist', 'Fanny', 'Mogul Emperor', 'Hot-Stuff', 'Never too Late', 'The Royal Family', 'Duckling', 'The Queen Mother', and have descriptive copy such as 'Big with lovely spring seats', 'Discretion is the soul of Virtue', and 'Go anywhere. Do anything', none of which apply. Hob and Ray had been caught in their monopoly before. As we sailed past, they yelled taunts at them. They were having a good time and that meant exercising every faculty – as in battle. They were good-time guys. Wherever they went something seemed to happen. They yelled at everything and everyone involving all. But I couldn't keep up. They were desperados. You couldn't tell them a thing. Their springy, cursing humour was their way of life, and a defence against my own, which meant staying, perhaps too solemnly, undefended against everything. I couldn't get used to saying everything that came into my head, or to the fact that a bad joke was better than none. But I was learning.

I looked up once and Hob did a fantastic stage fall from the roof of the swimming boat into the water. We fought on a floating plank, then took the shikarra into the leathery gramo-phone horns of the lotuses, looking for lotus nuts, but it was the wrong time of year.

It got dark very suddenly and Hob said he would take the shikarra back alone. Much later that night I met him in the street going to get some coffee and a blanket. He'd flaked out half way home and was going to sleep in the boat and take it on to his father-in-law in the morning. He said it would be stolen otherwise. He never once mentioned his wife while I knew him. I think she was in Bombay.

During the next couple of weeks I spent most of my time on the curious, good-for-nothing holiday Hob and Ray lived in. I was soon affected by their carelessness. I didn't mind hanging about for hours on end listening to their boasts, sun-bathing, fishing, smoking away the days. ('Scissors' cigarettes. Special Army Quality. Made in India by the successors to W. D. & H. O. Wills, Bristol and London.) I was the Wedding Guest, hypnotised by two Ancient Mariners. We used to sit beside the road eating baked cobs, or hitch up to the swimming-boats, or muck about in the shikarra. Once we looked for the naked girls again, but without success.

Hob and Ray said they might stay a month or two in Srinagar, but they didn't seem serious about either staying or leaving. Leaving was so hard anyway. Kashmir is miles away in the mountains and the temptation is always to go further, not to turn back. But we did neither.

There was a six-day pilgrimage setting out for the Great Ice Lingam in Ladakh. People said it would be a great experience to go on it, but about then Hobby got a job luring tourists into someone's woodwork shop. He used to go out to the airport and with his honest, Anglo-Saxon face, clip them straight off the runway. So the Great Ice Lingam melted without us and we stayed on in Srinagar.

I used to sit in my boat some of the time too. I was weeks behind with my diary and writing about the past instead of the present, which later proved less use than memory.

The shikarra wallahs always seemed to know when I was there and they went on plying me. I bought oranges and nuts and posted letters on the floating post office. 'You want sell your typewriter?' they would call, and I should have sold, because later it was stolen.

It was the fourth week.

Past the window went long barges full of bricks and timber; the giant vehicles slipping silently by as the old horse-barges and sailing ships must have. They were sent along by teams of punters, leaning on long wet poles. They would start at the bows, fingers interlocked over the ends of their poles as they walked over the bricks or timber, bare feet pressing till their bodies were almost face down over the water and they had to withdraw and march forward again.

I sat there and watched the strong brown god flow down. Across the river, I could sometimes hear a military band rehearsing *The Skye Boat Song* or *The Road to the Isles*. The weak pipe and the little drum. . . .

One day on the Bund – the promenade beside the river – I met an Anglo-Indian called Mr Wormer, who asked me to have tea with him. It was raining.

'I wonder are the weather forecasts as untrustworthy in UK as they are in India?' he said. 'You know my whole destiny was once affected by the weather. It was not long after Independence. I had met a charming English lady called Mrs Shaw. We became good friends. Real friends, you know. We used to sit talking in this very café. She used to take a mango squash and I would take tea. She was a very good person. She and I spent many happy hours together. But never alone, you understand. Then one day we planned an expedition. We were to climb the hill behind Srinagar. It would be necessary to start very early in the morning and take a picnic. It was a great moment for me as you can imagine, for it proved she trusted me. Everything depended on the weather. I remember listening intently to the forecast the night before. Set fine, they said. But in the morning it was raining and we had to call the whole thing off. I saw her once again after that. Then she returned to England. . . . Mrs Shaw, 35 Mallory Road, London. A very nice lady, lost to the weather. . . . There's nothing for me here any more. But I'm boring you. I apologize. The reason I asked you to have tea with me was that I hoped to interest you in establishing a branch of my firm in England. I have a small jewellery factory and . . . '

Just one more week, then I would go. All flights to Srinagar had been turned back because of the rains and Mr Wormer had told me that I'd better stay up there till the first flush of the Monsoon was over. So I did. Just one more week, I told myself. But I had the feeling that was how people decided to stay in places forever. The Christian graveyard was full of such people. 'Daisy Overton, Born Bath 1856, Laid to Rest in Her Beloved Kashmir, June 12th, 1927.' 'Jock Curl, 1873–1950. Professional at Srinagar Golf Club as his father before him.'

So the days slipped by like the river. Rain came and the houseboats rose among the trees. News of the Chinese invasion had frightened many tourists and the houseboats weren't filling up as expected. Ray lost his job at the night club on account of it, but he and Hob soon got another as houseboat agents. They had one to live in themselves and vaguely tried to flog me the one next door. I should have half the commission they said. But it was far too expensive.

Life seemed to be on credit for Hob and Ray. They wanted to know just how far they could push it and themselves before the reckoning. They had the splendid, desperate gaiety people seven years older than one sometimes seem to have for everything and nothing. They made no effort to sell houseboats, but sat all day fishing on their own one. The fish were numerous and every five minutes they swung one on to the deck. I remember there was a big blue kingfisher which acted as a kind of float. It sat on a branch over the water, then when a shoal came it would become a blue stone and enter the water without a splash. Up it would come with a little mirror carp speared on its long beak. Then it would work the fish off against the trunk, and sit happily on its branch, bobbing up and down every now and then to digest it.

A few days of that life and they were broke again. So Hobby went up to his old house in the hills and found some old pull-overs and a rifle to sell. They were both playing for time.

I had been there six weeks and suddenly the off season was officially over and we were all turned out of our houseboats. They had to be got ready for government officials and their families. Ray was friendly with the band at the night club, so we slept on the floor of their flat for a few days. I had no bedding, or blankets, but was rather amused to be able to reduce the night to such insignificance. I remembered the lover-like attentions I had lavished on it at home, the wasteful insomnia. It seemed ridiculous.

The last days in Srinagar were like hours in any other place. Or weeks. Hours on street corners, waiting for mealtimes. Hours in cafés, looking into the future.

At night the street was half-lit with bluish lamps, sticky with insects. Here and there, dogs scratched the mangy skin from their backs. Ray buzzed them with stones. Then the black and white cow would come mincing slowly down the deserted street, as to a life-long assignation: 11 p.m. at the Savoy every Thursday. Cows were banned in this Muslim town, so they were let out at night by their Hindu owners to forage for themselves. Driven off the streets, poor things. What could you expect?

A late tonga jingled by.

'Tonga sahib? Tonga sahib?'

'I'll tonga you, you naughty man,' said Ray.

One day we heard from a newcomer that there were **three** English spies loose in Srinagar, working for the Chinese. **After** that every movement had to be made suspiciously.

Time seemed to be what we made of it. You spent it either quickly, slowly, profitably or wastefully, like money. Time was how you used it. Time was yourself.

And slowly Ray and Hob gave in to it. Their plans for America slowly crumbled and they started looking homeward. Ray was trying to collect $30 for the return hitch. Hobby was thinking of going back to his wife and had ideas of being a planter in Assam for a few years. As always, I couldn't distinguish between their dreams and their plans, only their jokes were serious.

Monsoon diary

The bus from Srinagar to Jammu was thirteen hours down rutted, spiral roads and the base of my spine began to hurt again, five weeks after the beat-up in Lahore. I remember thinking I'd broken something. Far from making me more hardy and spiritual, as journeys are supposed to, so far it had made me more fussy and self-concerned, and half of what I wrote in my diary was about my bowels, or the heat, or 'don't eat fish during the Monsoon because they get washed up in the floods and people pick them off the roads'. In fact it's sometimes quite hard to root out facts from it on which to hang my memory. How will it be when facts and memory both have to be invented for fiction?

At the first stop a man asked me to stay with him in Jammu and I accepted immediately, as I wouldn't have done a month earlier. At least my craze for privacy was coming round. At another, the police wanted to see my passport and when I told them it was locked in my suitcase on the roof of the bus, they just looked through the register to see when I'd last passed and there was the entry, written exactly a month ago, but before so much that I suddenly felt older, seeing it. There is no time which seems so long looking back as that in which the rush of new sights and faces slides daily into a routine. That is why travelling goes so wonderfully slowly: the process is constantly repeating, the pace altering.

The man's house in Jammu had a flat roof with a fantastic view over the city. It was dusk and I could hear people talking as they sat out on their roofs, silhouetted against the pink and green sunset. Here and there a kite was in the air. Cranes flew by, or perched like fences on rooftops. Only the temple roofs were of stone, some of them sheathed in gold and crowned with sceptres of gold.

The man's name was Kapoor. 'If there is anything you require,' he must have said a hundred times, 'do not hesitate to ask for it, my friend.' His father had just died and when we went in his sister and mother were praying in front of a cup-board. Little plaintive, sing-song voices, both too loud and too soft to talk against. They were 'Catholic Hindus' Kapoor told me in a whisper. He himself was 'Westernized'.

Before dinner he said we would take a light stroll. This took two hours and was a series of exhausting courtesy calls on about nine different shopkeepers. He was late back from Kashmir, I gathered, and had to make his peace with them by grovelling a bit and getting me to finger their 'exceptionally fine' materials. Business in India is done through personal contacts and no one can afford to let one drop.

At dinner Kapoor's mother and sister served us with curry and returned to their singing. I had a cold and the night was hot and tears were soon streaming down my cheeks and sweat down my forehead, embarrassing everyone quite out of tune. Alone, I can usually eat curry without much trouble, but in people's houses, in the face of etiquette, my glands refuse.

Later we smoked aniseed cheroots and Kapoor told me how he had tried to start a pen-friend club with Europe. He had collected hundreds of addresses, had forms printed, sent out amusing statistics of how often different nations shaved per week, etc., but the thing had collapsed and, jilted by his beloved West, he had started collecting its stamps instead. Just as I thought there might be some chance of getting some sleep he got out his album and started flicking through the countries:

Portugal, Italy, Holland, Denmark. It was as if I was hearing their names for the first time. To him they were codewords for the exotic, as Persia, Tibet, or Siam are to us. I turned the word 'England' over in my sleepy head and it seemed to me as well like some Eldorado.

Next morning we had time for a visit to a garden between two canals before my bus left for Pathankot. The water in the canals was ice-cold from the hills, and there were beautiful little brown bodies leaping into it from trees and being borne down, battling with the torrent. I said to Kapoor we were unlucky not to be small and dark and naked on a day like this, but he said he would not like to be so dark. His mother had always taught him never to drink coffee for it affected the pigment of the skin. 'After all, we too are Aryans, you know.'

We had come to a walled section of the canal and Kapoor said that was where the women bathed. He looked at me uncertainly, then he made up his mind and told me that he had a collection of 2,000 photographs of nude girls from all over the world. It was the final declaration of his Westernization. To hell with the *Kama Sutra*, this was the real thing. But he was sorry he couldn't show them to me now. He had to keep them in his locker at the bank, for fear his mother or sister saw them – and today the banks were closed. For him Bank Holidays meant the stamp collection. He was about thirty, yet he didn't have a cupboard, let alone a room to call his own. For me to spend the night at his house his mother and sister had had to quit the one bed and sleep in cots on the terrace with him. No wonder his originality seemed forced.

On the way back from the gardens we met an old Sikh whom Kapoor said was an astrologer and we went into a shop to have tea with him. Kapoor asked him to tell me something about my future and past and I held out my palm. But he wasn't interested. He did miracles. He said the rose I'd picked in the garden and put in my shirt told him everything he wanted to know. But he was wrong there for a start. He took my pulse and said I had urinal trouble and that I had inherited faulty blood and had backaches. He said if I was interested he would cure me. He would send me a mixture which he would have to prepare and this I should bind to my arm in certain leaves before prayer. He said he'd probably see me in England anyway because he'd been invited to Buckingham Palace. He didn't want paying for his cure, but then he didn't send anything either.

Kapoor put me on the bus to Pathankot and before he left he asked me to send him a nude for his collection.

On the Delhi train at Pathankot there were no third-class seats. In fact you couldn't even open any of the doors it was so crowded. Eventually I had to push my suitcase through a window, wedge it into the people, then climb in after it. For an hour I stood, more or less vertical over it. Then I found a place on a luggage rack and in ten minutes had made enemies of twenty people getting up there. My feet hung down in the face of a Tibetan-looking man and he became very angry. 'What a strange man,' he kept saying, but no one took up his brief and realizing he couldn't beat me, he joined me on the rack and we both hung our feet over the edge and talked about Buddhism. He said most Indians had lost their energy and no longer had the power to understand their religions. Prayer was a meaning-less pantomime they grew accustomed to from childhood. It was due to a kind of malaise the sub-continent put upon all who had ever settled there. 'No one has ever lived happily in India,' he said. 'We are all homesick for previous, happier lives in far-off places. You see, we Buddhists believe in reincarna-tion, or transmigration, that humans are constantly dying, being changed and reborn. Every day we die in sleep and the only thing which connects our new existence to our old is memory, memory which may have one of a million influences on what we then become. Death is but another of these changes and it is the ultimate goal of every Buddhist to so improve his existence that in a future life he may become Buddha himself.'

I arrived in Delhi at 5 a.m. Five hours till the American Express opened, where three months' mail waited. The town seemed very fine. It is designed in a web, with an outer, middle and inner ring. Every curving avenue is lined with Empire-old limes and planes and the inner circus is so large you can only just make out the white pillars on the far side.

It was there the American Express stood. At nine it opened, but the mail counter didn't open till ten, so I had a wash in the Rest Room, changed and sat in the icy air-conditioning waiting for the grille to go up. Through the grille I could see the 'W' slot choc-full of air letters.

Half an hour later I was in an upstairs café with them piled in front of me beside a mango squash. The first one I opened was from Guy Brett, brother of the Michael who had been in Jerusalem. He was chucking up his job on *Apollo* magazine, he said, and coming to join me. My first reaction was to smile inanely round at everyone in the café. It was fantastic. He was the only possible travelling companion. It changed everything. Second: to write off telling him to bring a couple of pairs of Levis to Australia in October and we'd go and be bleeding cowboys together, and quoting a piece of Gide's *Immoralist* which I had with me: 'I have so little of it [property] that, as you see, nothing in this place is mine, not even – or rather especially not – the bed I sleep on. I have a horror of rest; possessions encourage one to indulge in it, and there's nothing like security for making one fall asleep. I like life well enough to want to live it awake, and so, in the very midst of my riches, I maintain the sensation of a state of precariousness, by which means I aggravate, or at any rate intensify, my life. I will not say I like danger, but I like life to be hazardous and I want it to demand at every moment the whole of my courage, my happiness, my health.' Writing that out made me feel very heroic. But as it turned out he didn't come.

I finished my letters and decided to look up my one contact

in Delhi—a friend's friend, Buddy Isenberg: hash smoker, hipster and sometime sidekick of Allen Ginsberg. 'If you like I'll connect you to New Delhi,' my friend had said. And sure enough, when I rang up, Buddy said he would pick me up at the YMCA at six. I found him reading a paper in the lobby and we took a motor trishaw across Delhi to Jor Barg.

Even before we arrived, I was the square. There is something about hip American which divides mankind instantly in two. If someone invites you to 'fall by some time with your sounds' you might as well accept defeat. You have been squared.

I had been two months in India, Buddy had been two years. He spoke Hindi, had hitched all over the sub-continent and Christmassed in the Taj Mahal with Allen Ginsberg. He had photographs to prove it. Every temple in India had a smoking room, he said, and all the holy men were permanently 'turned on'. He'd spent many happy hours smoking with them. They were all really cool cats – especially in Kashmir. Hashish grows wild up there apparently – 'really wild, man' – and you could buy the finished product in government stores.

Buddy's room belonged to his brother and there were some rules of tidiness addressed to him in mock-mother language on a scroll on the wall. Also a globe and a rack of Indian records. Bud politely offered me a reefer as he might have done a cocktail. If nothing else, it acted as a powerful aperitif and when we had dinner I scalded his Jewish propriety by exclaiming greedily as I helped myself to kosher: 'Casserole, how absolutely delicious.'

After dinner three people turned up 'to smoke a pipe of peace'. There was a girl with straight fair hair wearing a kurdah and pyjamas, introduced as 'The Light of Asia', an English Buddhist with long, long hair and an American jazz-lover with a crew-cut. Buddy rolled reefers and put on some Indian music and we settled down to a nice anti-social.

Hash does different things to different people. For me it

slowed down time and thought and even the movements people made about the room. When the Buddhist threw himself down in an armchair, the gesture almost hurt it took so long. People were like reptiles. I looked round at the young men and the girl, sitting or lying against the padded furniture and the contact seemed vaguely repulsive, like fish in an empty bath.

I think I was as high on the music as anything else, for Indian music too seemingly defies our ideas of time. According to Buddy, Pandit Shirkuma Sharva was able to produce a continuous sound on his flute by separate control of each lung, inhaling and exhaling simultaneously. I was past disbelief.

Luckily it wasn't that day we visited the burning ghats in Old Delhi. I think flaming corpses would have come out as something worse than fish in empty baths. As it was the scene was too sunny and defenceless to be morbid. In a large open compound by the river Jamuna, the funeral pyres smoked or blazed on their raised platforms. Some of the pyres had finished burning, leaving their little crooked reliefs of fallen bones in the ash. Others had not yet been lit, or else had gone out. Here and there the dry kindling wood had burnt through, exposing a blackened hand or foot. 'Face down on the fire,' wrote Allen Ginsberg, 'slowly lifting up their skulls like breaststroke swimmers.' On one of the raised platforms was a huge white holy cow, peacefully chewing the cud. In a corner was the long handcart used for collecting the dead bodies off the streets each morning when the live ones lying beside them have got to their feet again. In its shade two dogs were mating. Suddenly a party of near-naked young men came striding and laughing through the compound. One was a young Sikh, his hair in an idle pigtail. Their bodies were silky brown, their chests like classic breastplates. Long pieces of red cloth hung down between their legs. They didn't glance at the pyres. Nearby a very old man was squatting, shovelling bones into a sack which he would empty in the river. There seemed no great space or tragedy between his still just moving skeleton and the bare ones lying about.

A few days later I went to Agra, arriving late and sleeping in the station waiting room. No moon, so: see the Taj at dawn, I thought. Two Londoners were in the waiting room too. They said you don't ever have to pay on Indian railways. If someone asks you for your ticket you look out the window or say you've lost it. After Independence most Indians thought they had inherited the railways too and no one bought tickets.

'All the same, it takes the gilt off it, travelling third,' said one and I thought he meant 'guilt' and agreed in quite the wrong tone of voice. There is always a certain amount of guilt in the idleness of travel, even if it is supposed to be good for the mind. Somehow, travelling rough is the least one can do to atone, to take the guilt off, so to speak.

In the morning it was raining. I got into a tonga and was borne out of Agra to the Taj entrance. It was 5.30, the sun neither here nor there, but a fine black light in the sky. The gates to the Taj were still closed and a few people were sheltering from the rain under the tree where I was let down. When I had the usual row about the fare, they gathered round impassively. 'Honest Injun' is a contradiction in terms.

At 6 the great doors slowly panned wide and there it was framed in a giant arch, far away behind rain and flat-looking, white on black. The rain didn't slacken, so after a while I left the entrance house and walked up the famous waterway to the first steps, where I was told to take off my shoes. Inside the dome a swarm of Indians were testing the echo with yells. There was a strange fractured light filtering through the double screens of filigree marble that are the walls, spotting the murals of semi-precious stones. The precious ones that were once among them are now in the Imperial Crown. I think there was even a scheme once to transfer the whole Taj to Hampton Court.

As you go in, there are the false tombs of Shah Jahan and his wife Mumtaz Mahal, hers in the middle, smaller than his. Then down a flight of stairs in the incense-heavy sepulchre are the real ones, covered with mosaics. I thought of the unceremonious burning of the poor dead beside the river Jamuna in Delhi and then of this timeless memorial, also overlooking the Jamuna, to the love of a king for his queen: forgetfulness and perpetuity.

Outside again, my boots were full of glistening Monsoon. Vermilion parakeets shot like thunderbolts through the closed air.

Back in Delhi I took another crammed train to Benares. All this talk about trains! But there's no way of avoiding them in India. They are part of the landscape. Half the population travels on them every day. Indians are essentially migrants. Their lives are pilgrimages. If there was a rail strike God knows where the population of the trains would live.

On the floor of the compartment sat a blind boy, banging finger-cymbals and playing a drum with his toes. He began to sing in ghastly staccato agony. Then he got up and felt his way over to me, as if he had smelt my fear. He begged and I turned away, furious at the guilt. Outside the paddies were flannels of cress. Long beams, worked like see-saws, stretched over them, dipping, rising, emptying. Through the spikes of rice stepped peacocks like landowners. Mowglis driving goats – the goats held their heads high and nervous, they had little hairs springing from their horns – or astride monumental water buffaloes, pushing forward like gargoyles.

It was 6 p.m. The carriage was bathed in night-club light from the sunset. A sleepless night, then a nightmare arrival at the holy city in the small hours. There was no door to the compartment, so I made my way along the corridor. At the door was a hoard of possessionless Hindus, struggling and fighting to get in all at once: elbows and cheekbones and gagged open mouths. As they wedged into the door I was forced back bodily down the corridor. I had a typewriter in one hand and my case in the other, so I couldn't resist and they were soon being wrenched from my arm sockets as I tried to stand firm. I felt hot skin pressed all round me, muscling as if for survival. I was soon back where I started and it took a coolie ten minutes to get to me and lift my suitcase over the crowd and for me to pinch myself out the door. It was no place for an epileptic.

In the waiting room: peace, another half-night on a wicker chaise-longue, then with a vague idea of bathing in the Ganges to cool off, I made my way to the bathing ghats. Here men and women, fully clothed, were flopping about in the treacly water, being purified. The Ganges was high and fast and yellow and the temples along its banks were half-submerged, the water lapping at their stunted spires. A 'guide' soon attached himself to me, saying that he would be my 'guru'. 'All religions are tributaries of one stream,' he said, 'but that stream is the Ganges, the River of Life,' and he showed me where I could buy a little pot sealed full of its muddy holiness at a reduced price of 1s 6d.

'You interested in Nepalese Temple of Love?' he asked, changing from guru to ponce. 'It has carvings of all thirty-six positions.' I said nothing, but followed him through a tunnel where cattle were standing. I hadn't asked this man to show me round and I wasn't going to pay for it. It had happened too often: a sort of tourist tax, levied out of hand.

The Love Temple was tiny and ornate, with no room inside for anyone except the god. It was built in pagoda style and its long rafters were covered with erotic wood carvings. 'To put idea of generation in mind of man,' said my guide soberly, as if the craze had spread outwards from there. I spotted one figure with a child sitting on his head, casually taking a woman who was feeding her baby.

On the way to the burning ghats, we passed dozens of little cupboard shrines, set into walls, most having a lingam, symbol of destruction and life, set in a symbolized 'yoni' – vagina, and sprinkled with jasmine petals. I had glimpses of sun-filled courts, banned to outsiders, full of men and women offering garlands and sweetmeats to brightly-painted idols. One, the god of physical fitness, was a monkey, sometimes draped in red sacking.

'No photographs of the following items, by Government order,' said the guide. 'Women, cremations, lepers.' We had reached the ghats. Heat swung off the flaming platforms, driving back a crowd of spectators. A black Indian swung a hatchet at some kindling wood. I raised my camera, but he was swiftly added to the list.

Ranged along the tideline, here even higher, were the Hindu holy men under their fibre umbrellas, perhaps evacuated from submerged temples. Fifty yards out some boats were wheeling at a gold-sheathed spire. Near the holy men were sandalwood vendors, splendid behind the pyramids of red and yellow powder which the priests use for marking the forehead in blessing. Everything was hot and alive. Nowhere was there anything of the sadness or slowness connected to our funerals. The black Indian was breaking up a stubborn corpse with a pitchfork. Yet the friends and relations of the dead were gathered together in a little observation turret, seemingly unmoved.

The next morning I caught the train to Calcutta and a journey began through a landscape which defeats all similes. In England we have to exaggerate to say what we love about a place, otherwise we can't make ourselves clear. That's why our nature poetry is the most wonderful in the world: the poets had to electrify the hesitant shades and contours with their imagination before they could begin. They had to guess what lay behind the mists. Here, in India, the poem of the landscape is already written. The colours are squeezed straight from their tubes. There is nothing more to say.

A station: peanuts, plantins, puris (chepatis), paan. Cigarettes made of biri leaves, plates of curry made of fig leaves. The click-clicking of earthenware chai cups smashing as they are chucked from the train windows. Curd, Coco-Cola, coolies. Two thousand coolies round one American. One coolie with two cabin-trunks and a bed roll on his head, neck like barbed wire. And a man quietly flogging little copper ear-picks for twopence each. Indian stations are their community centres. Nomads, businessmen, beggars, beatniks, cripples, soldiers, gangsters, cooks, MPs, even passengers, make their homes here, oblivious of timetables. Most platforms I saw even sold copies of *Encounter* – though they may have been a special order for the 'Suicide of Britain' issue.

Thunder. Now the sky, reflected in the water-logged paddy fields, was veined marble and the greens a lifeless jade. Umbrellas began to go up in the distance. Suddenly the Bengal jungle, which had seemed out of reach, was close and the eye sank into it uselessly. It began to rain heavily, but without violence, and a strange mineral light, which seemed mixed from neither sun nor moon, spread across the clouds.

I tried to sleep.

'You are coming from . . . ?' A Sikh was blearing at me. Death might be immunity to genial Indians, but it's doubtful.

'Benares.'

'Of course you saw the Golden Temple.'

'No.'

'Oh, you shouldn't have missed seeing the Golden Temple. Oh dear me, no.'

Later, when I did get to sleep, my typewriter was stolen off the seat beside me. 'You see you shouldn't have gone to sleep,' said the policeman later. 'We must never go to sleep in trains. Once the back of my box was cut open on a train and all my possessions removed. Now I have a steel box. We live and learn. What did you say your name was?' I was witnessing the fabulous might of Indian bureaucracy as it shook its sleepy head, stepped into its trousers, spat out a gob of betel and selected the inevitable form for me to confess my guilt on.

Howrah Bridge, Calcutta, is one of the ganglions of the world. Along its rails are tinkers, magicians, lepers, monkey-pipers, snake-charmers, doctors, astrologers, dying septuagenarians and glassware salesmen. The eight-lane roadway is blocked with bullock carts, taxis, phaetons, herds of goats, stray cows, double-deckers packed like pigeon crates, and coolies, crazy with merchandise, dodging them like matadors.

The Salvation Army Hostel was old-world and Britannic. Just what I needed. Calendars of Cornish villages and the Queen Mother and 'frankly we prefer to see white faces around here'.

My room had wire over the windows to keep out the monkeys and a door on to a roof where an Australian was asleep on a sleeping bag. The bag had an Aussie flag stitched to it. I looked out over the city. In the sky were a hundred jigging kites, some twined in battle, others severed and tacking downwards. The trees were dotted with the fallen squares of coloured paper. And the buildings with monkeys. On window sills, locked out, they sat like gossips, hearing, seeing and speaking evil.

Next morning I half-heartedly looked up Satyajit Ray in the telephone book. If there was one man I wanted to meet in India it was him, but I knew you didn't just ring up international film directors and ask yourself to tea. I didn't even expect to find his name there, but there it was and almost before I had woken up properly I was speaking to him and arranging to go to tea with him the same afternoon. I had six hours to get briefed. I rushed out and bought all the film magazines I could find, then went to the British Council Library and started writing down long questionnaires out of *Sight and Sound*, all destined to be useless.

At 4 o'clock I put on my suit and got to his house half an hour early and had to hang about in the street outside, the only person wearing a tie in the neighbourhood.

His flat was small and luxurious. Sketches for scenes and costumes lay scattered on a table. Ray was a tall, powerfully sculptured man, wearing a collarless Indian shirt over loose white trousers. His deep voice was without accent. Tea came and I began to understand that anything I wanted to find out would have to be discovered through conversation and simply remembered. Ray was prepared to go through the social graces, but not to be quizzed. I put away my pad. In fact I had trouble getting the talk away from myself. Eventually I said I'd heard he was going to the Melbourne Film Festival and afterwards to make a film in Australia. He said yes, they'd been trying to get him to go for seven years and he'd finally given in. It'd been suggested he make a film of the late Albert Namatjira, the aborigine painter whose brief moment of fame petered out in alcoholism and imprisonment. But though the Australian Government had offered to make the film financially feasible, Ray said he had read Namatjira's life and felt that such an intensely personal and Australian subject could only be properly dealt with by someone familiar with Australia and its attitudes towards aborigines. He said he felt he should use the tools he'd been given – his language, Bengali – and the material – India – with which he was familiar. Even the prospect of working with Jeanne Moreau, whom he greatly admired, would not, at present, interest him. He had a horror of star 'personality'. More often than not his own actors were amateurs, discovered by advertising and auditioning, like Fellini's.

So that put paid to that. My next ploy was to produce a copy of the *London Magazine* with a notice of *Two Daughters* in it. The critic said Ray's was a literary talent, comparable with a writer like Chekhov's more than any modern film-maker's and that if his camera was taken away he'd probably go on creating in another medium. But Ray didn't agree. He'd been a commercial artist when he made his first film, but now he didn't feel he could manage anything other than film making. I asked him how he came to make his first film and he began to tell me about the birth of *Pather Panchali*, the film which made his name.

Returning from London in 1950, Ray met Jean Renoir, on location for *The River*, watched him on the set and received encouragement to go ahead with plans for a version of a two-volume novel he had illustrated for the firm of commercial artists he still worked for. Without any experience as director, actor or technician, he somehow bought the film rights and set to work on the screen play.

During the 1940s it had been his practice, before seeing the film versions of well-known works, to write a complete screenplay, later comparing it with the finished picture. In this way he had gained some idea of the cinema's potential and his own.

Once the script was finished he began the search for a backer. Since he had bought the rights of the famous *Pather Panchali*, discussions started promisingly; but sooner or later he was always asked, 'Where are the songs, the dances, who are the stars to be?' Ray would show them the manuscript in which he had written the entire screenplay, specifying camera angles and even including on every page a series of sketches to indicate the composition of key shots. They were impressed but wary.

Meanwhile, Ray was still working for the advertising agency, putting by every penny for production. He sold his art books and records and began tentatively to cast his film and look for locations. He chose a village, a wood, a meadow, the boy and the girl. After some difficulty he found the right person to play the old aunt, a toothless hag who had once been a beautiful and popular stage actress, but whose career had been cut short by meningitis. Now painfully stooped, she lived from day to day on opium tablets and said she would be glad to play in the film if it would mean the continuation of the tablets. He even found a backer and with £1,500 went into production.

The backer withdrew, however, after seeing the first scenes, but Ray again received encouragement, this time from John Huston, who said he would mention 'P.P.' to Monroe Wheeler of the Museum of Modern Art, New York. Ray then appealed to the West Bengal Government for funds, and a Government official, hearing of the interest from New York, put up £15,000. The State, therefore, became owner and producer of the film.

Progress was slow, but two years after he had finished the script, the film was completed and an invitation came to have it premièred at the Museum of Modern Art. After days and nights of intensive editing, Ray took his package of film cans to the air-freight office of Pan American and fell asleep leaning on the parcel while waiting his turn in the queue.

The première won *Pather Panchali* a showing at the Cannes Film Festival, but it was scheduled for a morning showing, when few people would be up and about. Ray's American distributor, Edward Harrison, arranged for it to follow a Kurosawa film in the afternoon, but this time the Japanese delegation had arranged a large party after their film and very few judges attended the Indian entry.

Next day the French critic André Bazin protested and the film, re-screened, was given the award of Best Human Document. It was the beginning of a long series of prizes for Ray.

Since then he had made seven feature films. I asked him what his plans were for the future, and he told me he had just finished a picture the day before called *The Big City*. He'd wanted to send it to the Edinburgh Festival, but couldn't get it subtitled in time. I asked if there was any chance of my seeing it and he said if I liked I could come to the first screening in three days' time. I was delighted and agreed to come to his flat just before, so we could go to the studio together. Then I left.

I think it was the next evening I spent looking for the Hungry

Generation. Someone had forwarded their Manifesto to me from London. 'Poetry is no more a civilizing manoeuvre, a replanting of the bamboozled gardens,' it declared, 'it is a holocaust, a violent and somnambulistic jazzing of the hymning five, a sowing of the tempestual hunger.' The movement was based in Howrah. But when, finally, I located the miserable shanty of an address, I was told that during the week the inmates were scattered all over India earning £9 a month in various Government posts. So I left a message saying I'd be back on Sunday. Actually I was staggered they existed at all.

Sunday came and the little room was without a fan, the pending monsoon stifling the air. There were five of us sitting round a very high bed, leaning on it. On the bed were the poems. I was given some to read and while I read someone fanned me. The poems were sensitive, beat-orientated, but though the Hungries knew Allen Ginsberg well – he had lived with them once – they said they were not Beat poets. The object of Hungryalism, they said, was '(1) To disclose the belief that world and existence are justified only as artistic phenomena. (2) To lash out against the values of the bi-legged career-making animals. (3) To abjure all meretricious blandishment for the sake of absolute sincerity.' And politically: 'To de-politicize the soul of each individual, to declare that existence is pre-political, that the conception of an Elite and that of the Politician differ absolutely since the death of Gandhi and that the actual position of a politician in a modern society lies somewhere between the dead body of a harlot and a donkey's tail.'

But the face behind the mask of jazzing anarchy was meek and anxious. It was touching how keen they were for the understanding of someone who spoke the language in which they had chosen to fight.

Outside the humidity pressed downwards like a tent roof holding water. Then there was a rent and the storm broke in a shining wall across the window. It was a great relief and our talk seemed to run more naturally after it. I wanted to go on sitting there by the bed, asking them things and translating poems, but they were embarrassed by the cramped room and kept asking me if I would like to see the botanical gardens and the Banyan tree which covered three acres. It turned out they'd never seen it themselves, so in the end we went. The bus took three-quarters of an hour and when we got there the garden was closed. A smell of wet jasmine and creeper came temptingly through the high iron gates. Two officials were turning people away. Three o'clock on a Sunday afternoon. No reasons given or known. We walked round like caged leopards, each disappointed for the other. Then I had to go and see Ray's film.

When I got to his flat the Hungries seemed like a dream: so urgent, yet out-of-this-world.

I went with Ray in a taxi, slightly out of Calcutta, to a studio laboratory. There was no officialdom, no over-excitement. Ray introduced me to the stars of the film, all very composed, then to a Yorkshireman who had worked with him on it, who said he would explain it to me as it went along.

The film began with a prolonged close-up of the flashing connection between the pick-up arm of a tram and the overhead wires. At each flash the titles changed. The film itself was about two people inside the tram who were destined never to descend, being bound by the customs of their society to the lines laid down.

A middle-class family are going through a financial crisis. The husband hears that the wife of a friend of his has taken a job and hints to his wife that she should do the same. This is against the most basic principles of Bengali life, but together they look through the 'Wanted' columns and a few days later she lands, with surprising ease, a job selling knitting machines.

She makes a success of the job, earns more in a week than her husband and one day brings home presents for everyone. This is one of the best scenes. There is a smouldering contrast between the skulking husband and the vivacious wife, as a young female relation tries on her first sari, managing to emerge from adolescence into womanhood simply by slipping out of sight to change.

But the husband is jealous of her success and writes a letter of resignation for her. The next day he is beaten up by an angry mob, clamouring for payments outside the bank where he works, and just manages to reach a telephone in time to prevent her presenting the letter. Now she is the sole bread-winner. The situation at home worsens. Ray cleverly uses the time of day to evoke a mood. It is dusk and things are out of order. You see them scratching a miserable meal. There are too many people in the small room. Each frame is perfectly composed and balanced; every wet rag adding to the hopelessness.

The husband makes a last bid for happiness and, unknown to his wife, gets a job in the firm she works for, entirely on her account. Meanwhile the wife has handed over the old letter of resignation as a protest to her boss, who has insulted her Anglo-Indian girl friend. They are both out of work, but as they leave the huge office block together, they are reunited and the camera unzooms to lose them in the crowded streets of Calcutta, the big city, which we become aware of for the first time.

The Big City – I think re-named since – was the kind of film you grow nostalgic for even while you watch it. The plot doesn't matter. It is the atmosphere and descriptions which count. Keats said a long poem should be a 'place to wander in' and that is what this was: a place to walk about in, looking over your shoulder as if you inhabited its world.

I suppose that film and my walks in Howrah were all I really saw of Calcutta. One other thing I remember clearly was the skeleton of a dinosaur prowling the vast Victorian museum on Chowringee like an ex-Imperial power, picked clean of its flesh, impotently haunting its latter-day domain.

Calcutta station was another Victorian museum, seething this time with life. I wondered would I ever get used to not moving on again. It had become instinctive. A shadow of familiarity and it was time to go. Once more I was heading south. One night in a second-class compartment for a change (middle-class Indian women all wear glasses; no lower-class woman is without a child) and I was at Puri, a vague coastal town where for once I wasn't touted. Deserted colonial bungalows rotted on sand dunes. I bought a sandalwood necklace from a beachcomber. Then hung about in the weird Vienna Hotel waiting for the bus along the coast to Konorak. This is where the famous Black Pagoda stands, a temple in the form of a mythical sun chariot, being drawn slowly towards eternity upon twelve sculptured wheels by seven prancing horses. Not black, but dark red, it is covered with wonderful erotic figures whose love-making is 'Karma' – eternal bliss – because it too is never ending.

Looking at them I realized I hadn't seen men and women kissing, holding hands, or even looking at each other in public, since Israel. Was it the hypocrite Islam which had dissipated the Hindu civilization these statues represented? Or was it the endemic disease of India itself? Here were the familiar features, but there were unfamiliar expressions of innocence and laughter playing across them, looks of such sublime consent as we are not used to seeing even at the movies. The young faces with their Epstein eyes were smooth of doubt. Their lips curled faintly in acknowledged invitation. Sometimes a giggle escaped, or a hand was raised to the eyes in mock embarrassment. One felt it was truly the sun which shone upon them, rather than a clouded moon.

Yet I was told that some people came from miles to visit Konorak and had to leave immediately they were so shocked. In the West we have our phrase 'sex and violence' and it is true that to a lesser or greater degree we have come to associate the two. At any rate sex and danger. But how did it happen? Did the chicken Freud lay the egg, or was it there all along?

In the West we cubicle Life, Religion and Sex. In India they are, or were, one. No couples are seen in the shrines of the Christian Occident. Even Joseph and Mary are denied their love affair. The first couple are driven out of Eden. They are signs of banishment and fear – the same fear perhaps which prompted an early Christian missionary to write of the figures at Konorak: 'The Bible must supplant the narratives of their false divinities. Their temples, covered now with sculptures and paintings which crimson the face of modesty, even to glance at, must be demolished. The vile lingam must be levelled to the ground. . . .'

But the Black Pagoda still stands among the sand dunes, though time has begun its slow censorship.

Puri-Madras was a long, sleepless jolt, beginning one night at 1 o'clock and ending two mornings later in the small hours. Through the lurid rain forests: rags and umbrellas, ochre and torquoise saris. No blouses. Imprisoned, rag-clothed Indians covering every inch of floor and luggage rack, resigned to it.

A station. Plantains are aborigine bananas. There are aborigine tribes in this part of India. A young man got on and handed round slips of paper: 'Humble Request,' they said. 'He that hold the letter is Yadava by caste. ['Caste' is the same word as 'colour' in Hindi.] His mother had three daughters and two sons. His three sisters are studying in Roman Catholic Boarding. His brother is studying First Form. He is reading SSLC in MG High School in Kuntur. His father worked as Engine Fireman in Railway. He is now unfit to work owing to sight defect. This boy has no help by his parents. He is a very poor boy. So I request you all to help him what you like. His name is China Venkateswarlu. Signed, Yamarthi Viswanadham, Headmaster.' No one gave him anything.

Opposite me a middle-aged couple were systematically handing one another betel nuts and paan leaves. Between them on the seat was a little silver tree.

Outside, date palms with vultures growing in them.

Evening, and the world turned the luminous pink of theatre intervals. Fireflies in a tree like fairy lights.

Above my head was a beautiful, flat, empty bunk, owned by someone who hadn't slept in it all day. My spine felt like cigarette ash looking for an ashtray.

The first morning in the Madras YMCA I woke up late and found my camera and passport gone. I was in a dormitory with two Indians and an American, and the night before there'd been that vivacious German I'd met in Lahore there too, but in the morning he was gone – the American's camera too. I rang up the High Commission about my passport and they said, incredibly, not to worry, 'after all you must make your journey, mustn't you'. But then I remembered I'd left it with the YMCA reception. So it was just the cameras. The American and I went to the police station and they were marvellous. To impress us, the officer started yelling English military commands at his subordinates standing at attention out in the sun. Then he put agents disguised 'in mufti' at all bus and railway stations, rang up Bangalore, Bombay, Hyderabad and Calcutta station masters and alerted Madras dealers. Unfortunately I was feeling sick and didn't care.

The next day I was in St Isabel's Nursing Home, thinking I'd got (1) typhoid, (2) cholera, (3) yellow fever, (4) hepatitis, (5) smallpox. They never did say, or know, what I'd got, but put me on Ledermycin at 1s a capsule for two weeks.

Outside my window palm branches brushed like the skeletons of great fishes. On them raccoons scampered, suddenly jumping round to face in the opposite direction with terrible nerves. I dreamt I'd arrived back home and everyone was busy and couldn't spare me much time. My mother was washing her hair. I had come back too soon. Everyone was disappointed. I told my dream to Sister Cecilia and she said life was just a journey anyway. Something we pass through on our way elsewhere. So that was cheerful. One day she wouldn't admit to having made my orange juice, perhaps because that would have shown pride. She made the place bearable.

I left St Isabel's after two weeks, no wiser about my illness, and booked a passage to Penang, Malaya. Four days to fill in. Once or twice I went to Elliot Beach, vast and Antonionic, one of the longest in the world. Little raffia lean-to's, sweet-sellers, shell-sellers, talkers in groups, kite flyers, poor people, promenaders, children and old men alone. I changed in a lavatory and had a strange, surrealist swim. There were hundreds of people on the beach, but only me in the water, looking at them, and the hats of temples sticking up above the dunes behind them like the tails of enormous chickens.

Back in town I sat in the Kwality Café with a grape juice. Outside a cot was hanging up to dry on a street lamp. Under it three new Japanese motorbikes were parked. I read in *Blitz* – 'India's Greatest Weekly. Let The Voice Of India Thunder Over All' – that the first kiss in Indian films had taken place between Sonia Sahni and I. S. Johar in the film *Goa*. Hoorah!

Normal complement

When the time came I went on board S.S. *Rajula*, bound for Penang.

What looked like a white man in a Buddhist's saffron robe was strolling round the deck ahead of me.

'Are you from India?' I asked.

'No. I'm Brazilian, but I've lived in India five years. You are English?'

'Yes. Your English is excellent.'

'Not really. Did you like India?'

'I'm beginning to. It's not a place you can really like being in. But now I want to go back.'

'My visa expired ages ago and the authorities caught up with me. I'm on my way back to Rio for a while.'

'But you are a priest?'

'I'm a disciple of Vedanta. A wandering man.'

'And you've been wandering round India for five years?'

'Four years,' he said, and a moonish, slightly embarrassed smile spread over his face as if he had admitted being top of his class at the end of term. He hardly looked twenty. There was a dainty plumpness about him which suggested the Great Indoors.

Nothing could have been further removed from this self-styled Oriental than the cohort of paratroopers we found eating the 'Western-style' dinner with us that evening. They were from Birmingham, off on some exercise in Malaysia. They were big, tough chaps with knees like broken headlamps and enormous bull-nosed boots which trampled round the unfortunate decks as on the bones of the enemy. The nice thing about them was how fascinated they were by my monk. After they got to know him they would seek him out and quiz him about his strange life with all the frustrated goodwill of missionaries. As Swami couldn't understand their woosh accents, I always had to be there to translate. Was he allowed to marry? No. Not to marry, or smoke, or drink, or have any possessions but his begging bowl made of a hollow gourd. Why? Because in order to be completely happy on earth, one had to renounce those things which compromised independent thought. Loyalty to one person, one place, prejudiced one against the rest of the world till one was fighting against loneliness. That was the cause of all the world's weariness. The paratroopers would retreat to muster their values. Once Swami told me how it had all begun.

'Two things my mother would tell me,' he said. 'First, that since I was born a man, I should try to act like one and not make them liars who christened me. Second, she would get me to stand at the open window in the early morning and repeat into the rising sun: "I am strong, I am pure, I am strong, I am pure" and all my life I have been looking for that strength and purity.

'When I was seventeen, my father died in hospital. He was in an oxygen tent at the end and once while I was there he became drunk with it, shrieking for more and more till the orderly in charge began to cry because he didn't know what to do. I saw that my father was simply getting too much and told the man to turn it down. Later he was calm, but very weak. He said he knew he was going to die, so where was the use of fighting? I told him there was no use and we even discussed how he should fold his hands. I think that was the turning point of my life. There was to be a death – so there must be a funeral. I would have to comfort my mother and try to curb my emotions. I began to realize that depression was just a wilful misunderstanding of things. I guessed there was something more to life than that. So I went to Paris in search of it. I was to be a painter. I had great ambitions, but I hated the life there. Even the artists were cheap commercialists and they persecuted me. Perhaps I should be grateful to them, for they made me realize that my talent was receptive, not creative. It was about then I decided to go to India. I walked all the way from Paris and I've been walking ever since – from the Himalayas to Kerala and back again. I've made the journey three times in four years.'

'But how did you live?'

'I am a Sanyasin monk of Veda and we are permitted to beg for food. We may ask five houses a day and if we receive nothing we must go hungry.'

There was one character on board who took lunatic exception to Swami. This was a poor mad Malay Indian who yelled insults at him whenever he passed him on deck. Swami giggled at him girlishly, but in fact he was rather a sad figure. We would see him sitting in the bar, making strange, silent gestures to absent companions – probably the Japanese, whom he said he'd joined when they conquered Malaya – turning down drinks he hadn't been offered by them, or helping himself to people's cigarettes. Then he would mutter something about his imaginary wife and child who had been seasick the entire glassy voyage and run off to change his clothes again. One minute he'd be parading in British Army tropical kit with a malacca cane. The next he'd appear in just a sarong, which he'd open and look into like a treasure sack, or occasionally lower as he walked away from one. Once he handed Swami a bible and whispered a text into his ear. Swami looked up the text and read 'Your life is in danger'. But he wasn't in the least afraid, he said, not because the Indian was mad, but because, according to his philosophy, the phrase was a contradiction in terms.

I think the only passenger who wasn't somehow involved in all this moonshine was the only first-class one, a Madrasi called Mr Lourdes. Mr Lourdes was 74, the same age as Nehru, but well preserved and immaculate in club tie, white suit, and co-respondent shoes. He was making his thirty-sixth crossing on the *Rajula* and could apparently remember travelling on her five years before she was launched in 1918. In those days, he said, he would often find a little Indian page boy posted at the door of the bar to turn away Asians if Europeans were drinking there. That was a long time ago, but when, on this trip, he had been invited for the first time to dine at the captain's table, he had had to refuse. He bore no grudge, but it was too late to change now

I sat in his first-class saloon, listening to his unmarked elegant phrases. *Tales of the Vienna Woods* came bleary-eyed over the antediluvian speaker.

'The sad thing is they could still be here,' he said. 'But they never would behave naturally. Like all the other races who've come to this accursed sub-continent, the country spoilt them. The country's to blame in some ways. Everyone's miserable there. It's a losing battle. Of course, there were a few school-masters and individuals who resisted it, as your E. M. Forster says, but they were not "Pukka Sahibs" and their own kind ostracized them. The English weren't unpopular. Look at me, I've copied their way of life ever since I can remember. But they would ride their high horse.' He shook his white head at the memory and I remembered seeing the statue of a Governor in Madras, stuck about two storeys up on a great plinth, scanning the horizon like a conquering general from his steed. Just then the first-class dinner gong sounded and the old Madrasi got up to go.

'But they are gone now,' he said, 'and there is no one left in the first-class for the captain to dine with.'

Later, in the Tourist Restaurant, the paratroopers asked me if

I wanted to see round the engine room with them. They had made friends with a Birmingham engineer called 'Mush', and he was going to take them round after dinner. Primed with Emu wine, we descended to the lower deck and I became aware for the first time of the two thousand deck passengers, seething in the darkness like the pilgrims on board the *Patna*. According to Mr Lourdes, the *Rajula* had once held a deck passenger licence for 8,000, the largest in the world. But in those days anyone could travel who wanted to and people weren't told how much they could put up with. After independence the licence had been revoked and now everyone had a piece of deck five feet square and a place in the twenty-four hour queue for the lavatory. So far only one of them had died this trip. No Europeans were allowed to travel Deck, but for £16 there were always some who managed it.

We picked our way among restless cotton-wrapped forms. Then Mush opened a steel door and we felt burnt-out air rushing up at us from a rhythmic crashing far below, a noise which in another world had been a tapping beside our bunks. We entered the engine room on a high catwalk, covered with black grease. Below us the engines like buildings tossed in their interminable sleep. Then down a thin steel ladder into their presence. Within touching distance a piston like an oak tree shot up at one angle and down at another. Everything I touched was quivering and felt like graphite. Grease on the floor. English under-engineers hanging about under ventilators. Bewildering cautions on pieces of machinery made in Birmingham. Mush was mouthing something, but all human sound was obliterated. We went into the boiler room and two of us had the immediate impression of imminent explosion. It seemed impossible that such a thing could be held up by a ship. We walked along the 75yd. propeller shafts and slowly the danger and noise receded. The shafts were turning soundlessly. In the rudder room at the back of the ship a charming piece of mechanism waited to construe the movements of the helmsman into hydraulic pressures which every now and then would spring to life to operate the twin rudder pistons. Then back the way we had come and a two-minute walk in the quiet starlight to the bridge. The quarter-master was standing in the dark, steering by keeping a red light on the mast fixed between two stars. We had to whisper, because of the captain. The doctor came on to the bridge for a breath of air. He had just delivered a baby on the lower deck. There had been a death, now there had been a birth, returning the ship's complement to normal.

III – SOUTH-EAST ASIA

D. J. Enright

The railway to Singapore cuts through rubber forests. The sight is monotonous and debilitating, for there is nothing to use your eyesight on. Unlike India's voluptuous fields and lunatic stations, Malaya has a floorless jungle without light among it and bordered, lifeless platforms. It is the second richest country in Asia.

Twenty-two hours in the train and I telephoned a friend and poet, Dennis Enright, from a bar near Singapore station. He is head of the English department of Malaya University.

'Where are you? We're expecting you,' he said. It was like coming home. How marvellous to be *expected* again. For months I had been neither expected, nor unexpected, but an arrival, an occupier. As he himself had said in a poem on Chinese hotels:

'Not "Guest" –
The Chinese, those corrected souls, all know
A guest is never billed, whereas the
Essence of my aspect is, I pay –
But "Occupier", good words cost no more.'

Now the excitement of a new country seemed almost commonplace by comparison. I found a cheap hotel, rang up again and he came round to pick me up.

The pleasure of seeing him was especially great for me

because he is not the kind of expatriate who seems even stranger than his surroundings by exaggerating his differences from them. He seemed hardly to notice them. He was unemphatically at home, bridging the distances for me with every glance round of his soft blue eyes.

I suppose, looking back, there *was* something Oriental about him, but then there is something Oriental about the English anyway. But not in the Orient. One trip there and they are Occidentals for ever.

His house was a lovely Maughamesque villa on a hill in the campus. Inside, the high ceilings and verandahs were better than any air-conditioning.

I think he saw that I was tired so that that first meal was quiet and undemanding, establishing facts only. But he did say that he could never travel round like me, seeing a little here, a little there. He preferred to live in a place. He had lived and taught in Alexandria, Bangkok, Kobe.

We listened to Britten's *War Requiem*, which had just arrived, and some Japanese folk songs. Then after dinner he took me back to my hotel, promising an expedition to Sago Lane, Chinatown.

At 7 the next evening he and his wife picked me up. Oh to meet at a given time once more! I think the essence of what I missed while travelling was the chance of seeing someone I knew in the street, or the telephone ringing and a date made. One could make dates, but they weren't the same thing. If they had futures, they had no pasts.

In the two cars were a couple of other dons and their wives and a girl called Patsy, who bubbled and squeaked. Dennis was acknowledged MC and managed to generate a party atmosphere without actually saying much. With his benign expression and fluffy, clean hair, cut round at the back, he was rather like Harpo Marx.

We hid the cars on the fringe of Chinatown and walked towards Sago Lane, feeling the life of it gathering as we approached. Men in gym shoes and damp underclothes trotted by with barrows. English gave way to fizzing Chinese neon – an ideal medium for the detached, jagged characters, each one like a small kinetic sculpture in the night.

Only the street names were in English now. Upper Hokien Street, Upper Nankin Street, Chin Chew Street, nailed to the mildewy, paneless buildings, which had drawn closer over our heads, forming pillared arcades. On some of the pillars were bunches of glowing joss-sticks in wooden boxes. Under the arches hung revolving lanterns casting jots of colour up the walls.

In one raucous street were the Death Houses, corridors of shelves like opium dens where the ancient were brought to peter out while their relatives got drunk next door. There was the impatient snapping of mah-jong boards and a rhythmic hammering of coffin-makers. Here and there among the restaurants and bars were incense stores, red-lit, perfumed caves with paper dragons and prayers in gold on red crêpe. We saw an old crone being carried through the clutter and drinking to her last place in it all and I imagined her lying in there, smelling her own funeral, hearing the nails entering her coffin lid. Better than being lonely, I suppose: at least she would go out with a bang; a whimper would never have been heard above the din.

We turned a corner and the curtain went up on the set-piece. Sago Lane was a new kind of daytime. The cool and darkness of the night had given way, like the flat English lettering, to the heat of bodies and the flare of pressure lamps. A jam of street stalls challenged every step with piles of imaginary fruits, cheap dresses, tinware and mooncakes – for it was Moon Festival and everyone must buy, buy, buy. We bought some of the tacky little bombs and picked our way among silks and puddles of neon to the restaurant stalls. A sidewalk gramophone blasted sino-American jazz to the chop-chop-chop of knives cutting orange-rimmed pieces of pork into fragments for 'mee'. We sat down on stools in the gutter and ordered about eight bowls with plenty of bottled beer. Everyone tucked in with chopsticks except myself, who began knitting it until I was told there wasn't a fork in the neighbourhood, when it seemed to come more easily.

When we had finished we moved to another stall for something else with more beer. Then to a bar where there was a drunk Chinese judge, whom Dennis said only recognized him when he was drunk enough to apologize for not recognizing him when sober. The judge wanted to take us all to his air-conditioned island, but was too beer-conditioned to move. I think that was the end of the evening as a logical progress of events. After that it became a bit starry, but I know we didn't find the cars till about two.

The next day it was so hot I stayed indoors and tried to cultivate my hangover into rich descriptive blossoms of the night before. But as it turned out I didn't manage it till two years later. From where I was sitting I could see a class of little white-starched schoolgirls, sitting in rows under a tin roof, looking at some out-of-sight blackboard. '1—2—3—4—5 —6—7—8—9—10 . . . 1 plus 1 is 2. 2 plus 2 is 4. 4 plus 4 is 8 . . . ' came their new English voices, far more interesting than the tangled images of Chinatown buzzing in my head. I must have sat there for hours. 'Twinkle, twinkle, little star, how I wonder what you are . . . ' Arithmetic was over. Palm trees like ballerinas brushed the tin roof with their fins. Sun dropped from the centre of the sky, casting undistorted black shadows. I longed to hear rain on the tin roof and to see the little classroom become a birdcage.

In the afternoon I went swimming at Mount Emily with one of the lecturers, who had a Rolls Royce. Afterwards we met Dennis in The Coffee Shop and everyone was very sweet to me, letting me taste Chinese wines, one with something like a parsnip inside which increased potency. Then we went next door to *Maxim's* for the 'weekly masochism' with Li Pey, Doris and Irene, who were all having hysterics for some reason. Dennis said half the population of Singapore was under twenty, so the young had to fight for survival. Apparently Irene was trying to decide whether to marry an Australian and to go and live in Australia. She had the idea that he would turn against her once he got her among his own people and the thought of losing a man she didn't love in a strange country was more than she could bear.

Before we went home, Dennis invited me to go to dinner with a friend of his at the Chinese University in two days time. He said he wanted to go because the place was in a state of siege and no one was allowed out or in without special permission. A communist element had rebelled against the government when Malaysia was created the week before. Courses had been suspended, all work forgotten, and every night there were fervent rallies on hilltops with speeches and vows and dancing.

Till then I had a couple of days to fill in.

At my hotel, which was the cheapest in town, I met the usual sex-starved English adventurers, longing for Australia, having just learnt that it would have been cheaper to go from Southampton. One boy, called Norman, had begged his entire way from Calais, only to find that there was no way of crossing the few remaining miles to Darwin. He'd have to go to Sydney and couldn't afford it. He'd almost decided to walk home again when someone offered him a job selling cod liver oil pills. The game was to call at people's doors with a Chinese interpreter, saying you were the firm's representative from Australia, here to launch these new 'un-heated' tablets in Asia. Apparently sales had fallen off because the pills made people sweat and gave them indigestion. 'We Aussies also have a hot climate and we have understood the fault in these pills and checked it,' he would say. 'The present pills are newly formulated and un-heated. I am not here to market them officially (a fine understatement), only to launch them. We do, however, have a few advance crates . . . '

It seemed that the white face was still good news in the world of medicine. When the Chinese came to sell their own patents they had a harder time of it. Wandering about with Norman, I saw a large crowd round two quacks touting their cure for that much-feared Chinese ailment 'internal injuries'. One spoke rapidly in Pekinese, while the other interjected the Cantonese equivalent in a kind of music-hall cross-talk. They did some dancing and tumbling, then one swallowed some large pebbles and a snake to prove the validity of their medicines, which looked like packets of little pink Christmas tree bobbles. The snake was small and wet, but very alive. Norman said it was this kind of burlesque which lent credence to his own act. He was making £3 a day and planned to be in Sydney in six months. He told me that when he got there he was going to make use of his experience in Singapore to import pharmaceuticals on his own behalf. But *not* cod liver oil pills. He drew me into a chemist's.

'The Chinese make the best contraceptives in the world,' he said. 'Non-existent. Made from the spittle of a nightingale as one of our friends back there would say. And if you like that kind of thing, there's feathers, fur, nodules, extensions . . .' He made a sign to the shopkeeper who took two boxes from under the counter. In one was a nine-inch rubber penis with a long tube and a rubber bulb coming from it. When the bulb was pressed, the knob swelled up threateningly. In the other box was a heart-shaped inflatable cushion with two vertical pink lips, parted in a cynical smile. They were both expertly made, yet it was amusing proof of man's strange aspirations that the two organs might have been those of different species so wildly did they differ in proportion. The stallion phallus was no more meant for the diminutive vagina than eagles are for robins. But this does not mean that each is not the other's secret dream.

Something more homely was the Magic Love Ring. This was a circular piece of rind, apparently from the tail or limb of some animal, for there was a fringe of hairs springing from it. 'Soften Love Ring in hot water or tea,' ran the instructions, 'and place round the neck of the member. Exquisite and indescribable pleasure will then be experienced and this will result in conjugal bliss.'

In search of something less than conjugal bliss, we went that evening to The Happy World, not a brothel, but an amusement park with a dance hall. At the door we each bought six dance coupons for five shillings. 'Good for one dance only', said the ticket. 'N.B. Dance partners must submit this coupon within one month of date of issue otherwise it will not be valid.' Round the floor sat the 'partners': bright, thin little figures, not speaking to one another and springing jerkily to life only when the necessary coupons were handed over. Above the bandstand a revolving indicator announced in lights the next dance: waltz, quickstep, foxtrot, tango, waltz, quickstep, foxtrot, tango, and the puppets dangled in the arms of their redeemers waiting for the lights to change so they could return to lifelessness and peace. As we watched, a bleary-eyed European tacked across the entire floor and stood bowing in front of one, impotent to make the situation work without a ticket.

We circled through the tables and chairs behind the partners, trying to see their faces, but the little features had long ago disappeared in the gloom. I danced with one beautiful one, but she only reached my elbow. I remember beautiful little soft, pointed fingers in my hand and a straight white parting. Then she ran off to a Malayan boy who was waiting at the door before I'd used up all my tickets. I still have one of them before me as I write.

The next night it was the rebellious university. At the gates the car was surrounded by ugly, red-arm-banded Chinese, who wanted to know who we were, where we were going and exactly why. There was latent violence in their questions and we all felt we might at any moment become cause for further victory celebrations. But they let us through. Inside all was quiet and we were soon entering the polite atmosphere of a dinner party. Through the windows we could see the bonfires of the blood-hungry Communists in the distance, but they were no longer real. Instead we had a very real clash of personalities between Dennis and a fat Dutch American called Van Cloef. It all started by the American reading out a letter in a paper written by Dr Leavis, who had been Dennis's tutor at Cambridge.

'Now what is one to make of this,' he said. 'Just listen to this sentence a minute and see what you think of it. "And for a moment I was moved towards something which might be called assent." My, that deserves a Bronx cheer. It really hits you between the eyes, doesn't it?'

'Leavis is always hitting people in the eye,' said Dennis. 'Anyway, what's wrong with it? Do you object to the airs and graces?' The American said he objected to the self-importance and they were off. I don't know if Dennis thought that Van Cloef knew he was Leavis' pupil and thought he was needling him by proxy, or whether he was just defending Leavis' right to tease his own language a bit, exercise his *droit de seigneur*. Anyway, for a while every nuance of Anglo-American incompatibility was hanging in the air, more violent than the Capitalist-Communist one we had survived earlier. The evening was becalmed and the rest of it was a sailing home under pressure. Dennis's sad eyes regarded the American as a man watches a crowd from a bus, while the American sat up very straight, trying to remember his opinions. Once he turned to me and said: 'Mr Williams, are you just passing through Singapore, or . . . ?' I started to say how things were for the hundredth time, when I saw Dennis light up his pipe and wink at me through the smoke. Soon we left. Really, I loved that man.

Lieut. Bingo Williams

At home it was always 'in time', 'or else', 'in case', 'for fear', 'too late'. My earliest memory is of people's impatience outside the lavatory door and of a blue-ringed hot-plate, more or less permanently in front of me. Later it was a blue-ringed eye, accusing me of being 'too late' again. It must have been this urgency I never shared which made me begin to write poems: they were the only thing I could get done 'in time'.

In Malacca, time was away and I was beginning to falter into a piece of prose about India. It took infinitely more effort: not to find ideas, that came later, but to link them up. I discovered that you can't go on saying 'next morning', 'that evening' indefinitely – witness my present attempt at a bridge passage. You have to invent a bit – something new to me. The freedom was agoraphobic.

One of the things Dennis Enright had said about some poems I showed him in Singapore was that they were too careful. His French wife – and later mine – made the same mistake when she began to shop in English: a simple word like 'Strand' became incomprehensible if over-pronounced. Less, rather than more effort was needed. But at first it meant more.

Dennis also said Malacca was a place to work in, 'The Sleepy Hollow' as it was called, so there I was, ensconced in the New China Hotel, giving form for the first time to my vague ramblings, and loving every minute of it. It gave me a kind of smugness I had always thought the property of adults.

Not that it was peaceful. Outside my window Helen Shapiro's deep voice shook like a rat the loudspeaker in front of a record shop. She was riding the last crest of her wave before the Beatles broke on the world. Outside my door a Chinese radio crackled. Below a restaurant clattered. But I wouldn't have preferred silence. Silence I find tense and soporific.

Drunk with sentences, I would light a cigarette and step out for a coffee like a resident. For a brief moment I had caught the mechanical hare and for once had no desire to race on. I knew how Grosely felt in Maugham's *Mirage*: 'The mirage shone before his eyes. The illusion held him. He was happy. I wondered what would be his end. Well, that was not yet. For the first time in his life perhaps he held the present in his hand.'

But Grosely had Maugham to talk to and his wife to make love to. If it's not one thing it's another. Writing seemed to quell the urge to travel on, but to bring with it an overpowering desire to make love and to hear the high chatter of a girl's conversation.

Perhaps it was the place's fault. The warm evenings with a light breeze in my face as I swerved along the port in a trishaw were almost unbearably suggestive. One night I did go to the Dance Hall, but that was something else. More of that later. Nothing thrilling, mind you.

One night as I was walking back from the food stalls on the port I came across a rowdy Buddhist procession. Box shrines, gaudy as sideshows, were being carried head-high through the hum-drum streets. They were flanked by girls bearing inscriptions on red paper and boys with pipes, cymbals and drums. Between the shrines came the religious men, skeletal beings in saffron with glazed, staring eyes and a man on either hand to steer them through the crowded street. Long bamboo rods had been pierced clear through their cheeks and decorated

144

with ribbons. The rods bounced up and down as the men went with their curious skipping step. There was no blood because they were in a trance. They had the vacant air of tightrope walkers.

The next day I decided to have a look at the Buddhist temple in daylight. It was called The Abode of Merciful Clouds and was far removed from the sinister gaiety of the procession. Inside, an old woman was sitting at a treadle machine mending a saffron robe. Around her were all manner of household goods: a cooker, a fridge, bookcases, a dressing table and a dining room table with bowls of fruit and nuts and cases of beer under it. Near the front of the temple was a little stall for straw hats and souvenirs. The little woman got up and came scuttling round a vast cast-iron boiler to see if I wanted something. So I bought a little clay replica of the Buddha I now saw crouched among the bric-à-brac. As I left I thought I saw him wringing the air with his fists.

The first Chinaman to come to Malacca was Admiral Cheng Ho, the Three-Jewelled Eunuch. He brought gifts and promises of protection from the Ming Emperor, but he doesn't seem to have kept his word, because in 1511 Malacca fell to the Portuguese under Alfonso d'Albuquerque. Today half Malacca is Chinese, but all that remains of the Portuguese is the solitary Porta di Santiago and the exhumed grave of St Francis Xavier. St Francis was long ago transferred to the Portuguese territory of Goa but his grave still lies open, a hideous mess in the ruined Church of Our Lady. The Porta is all that's left of the massive fortifications razed by the British during the Napoleonic Wars. But by the time that happened the Dutch had conquered the Portuguese settlement in 1641, and the Dutch merchants had put up the sturdy houses on Heeren Street. These and the Cathedral of Christchurch were built with salmon pink bricks brought from Zeeland and are still the best buildings in the town. In 1824 the Dutch exchanged Malacca for the British settlement of Bencoolen in Sumatra, willingly or not isn't known, but they had had their walls knocked down by us a few years before and Bencoolen hardly seems a fair swap. The British promptly made the cathedral Anglican and began adding their own gravestones to the Latin, Portuguese and Dutch ones in the crypt. Outside the cathedral, a plaque says 'The Diamond Jubilee of the Reign of Her Most Gracious Majesty, Queen Victoria, Empress of India, was celebrated in this settlement on the 21st of June 1897 and to permanently commemorate the completion of the 60th year of Her Majesty's most glorious Reign, a fund was subscribed by her subjects of all nationalities residing in this settlement, out of which an annual scholarship has been endowed and this tablet erected as a visible and permanent record and memorial of the loyalty and affection for her beloved Majesty felt by her subjects dwelling in this corner of her far-reaching Dominions.'

The scholarship still exists and the two 'Queen's Scholars' who win it each year are generally considered the most intelligent in the Federation. But it's hard to imagine any loyal Chinese mason chipping out a similar vote of confidence for the Queen today.

The Commonwealth troops in Malacca were not unpopular for themselves but because they were always fighting each other: New Zealanders and English against Australians, and everyone against each other, rather like the Commonwealth in general. In fact the Capitol Dance Hall might as well have been the Commonwealth Relations Office. Whites aided natives with vouchers called dance coupons. But natives were only obliged to stay faithful to whites while the music lasted. Then they could declare their independence, or rather break off diplomatic relations again.

One night I was down at this supermarket buying a few frozen smiles, when I met a coloured Australian from the Thursday Islands. His name was Lieut. Bingo Williams. He said he had Welsh blood, we might be related, etc. Then he said he knew a better place than the Capitol and we got in a taxi and drove out of Malacca to a place with the coy name of Suzie's Massage Parlour. Inside it was very bleak and dim and empty. We sat on a sofa and a big fat girl came and asked if we wanted a drink. Bingo didn't want anything, so I had a coke. The girl brought it and came and sat on the sofa with us. She lit a cigarette, crossed her legs, opened her mouth and seemed suddenly to remember that she had nothing to say and no English to say it in, so she said 'You want massage?' She was speaking to me.

'No thanks, my friend's first.'

'No, you first,' she insisted. 'You do massage with me first.'

'I'm not massaging you, love.'

'Why don't you? Don't you want to now?' said Bingo.

They were both looking at me.

'No, thanks very much.' I got up and walked outside. Lieut. Williams was a pimp. I was on a dark and deserted trunk road, the brothel an incongruous dark hangar behind me. Bingo followed me out.

'You bring me all the way out here . . . ' he said.

'No. *You* bring them all out here. How much do you get? They must need you.' He cursed me from a distance for a minute. Then he said:

'Look, I'm sorry. I've got to get back to barracks. Can you lend me a quid?'

'No.'

'Ten shillings then?' He began to whine. 'Five shillings? . . . Just don't you come to the Capitol tomorrow night.'

We set out in opposite directions, and as I walked down the long road into Malacca the whole thing seemed rather typical. This was my trip in miniature: a kind of surprised arrival at the top of a garden path at the end of another ride. I was the patron saint of ponces but I had no courage in the clip-joints.

I went back to the New China Hotel and sat watching the lights going on and off in the cubicles of another brothel opposite. Just a narrow street away it seemed like the answer to everything, a cradle of erotic possibilities. But closer up it gave the lie. I'd already tried myself on it more than once. When I first arrived in Malacca someone gave me a card with its name on. 'Cathay Hotel,' it said, 'Most leading Hotel in Malacca', but it should have been 'the most mis-leading'. The rooms were roofless cubicles, sharing windows with the one next door. A yellow Chinese woman came forward. 'You want girl? Short time? Malay girl? Chinese? Very beautiful girl?'

Pounding bed-springs reinforced her words.

Yes, yes, I want, but not now. Yesterday or tomorrow, not now. And I retreated down the stairs, out of the looking-glass world into the human street again.

At home I had known a pedestal and violets kind of adoration for as long as I could remember feeling anything. Three unintentionally platonic love-affairs, unfinished and forever unfinished. Then a few other nights elsewhere of babyish sexual graspings. But the two things were as separate as oil and water, separated by this same narrow street and united only in the imagination. I longed to be demonstrative but people were always speaking of other things.

I had just read *The Dead* by James Joyce and I felt I knew so well that bewilderment as you open a door, expecting to find your own passion in a mirror there, her eyes, but see instead only the thoughts, the unsentimental normal whims of another person, who might be alive, but might be dead, she is so far off. I remember thinking that it must be this dissatisfaction with one's own passions, this impossible wish to please and be loved at the same time, which was both self-destructive and creative, for it made one search out another means of seeing oneself take effect on the world.

So I sat in my hotel writing. I didn't cross the road again, or go to the Capitol. Instead I went down the road to a barber shop where two or three pretty girls in pinafores gave me a haircut which took about six months to grow out.

Lily

Across the border in Thailand, the women's voices got louder and their houses poorer. The laughing, golden women on the train were an immediate assertion of the country's traditional sovereignty, for it has never been colonized and the people have never had occasion to feel inferior, superior or even equal, to Europeans. In fact they are rather like Europeans: almost Mediterranean.

The temptation to generalize on arrival is great, almost instinctive. Anything to stop the racing strangeness of a place. One may even be right, but after that it becomes harder to be sure. First impressions get blurred back into the vaguer truth of things.

I was at the Station Hotel, Haadyai, in the south of Thailand and no one spoke a word of English. I was longing to sleep, but there were mosquitoes all over the place, just waiting for the new blood to turn in. They had two legs at the back they didn't use, which arched back and up. 'Flit', I said to the manager, but he wasn't even insulted. I might as well have said 'Lyle's Golden Syrup'.

That night I went out. I was with an English corporal and we went into a sort of café which was a brothel. It was terrible. Tons of hopeful chairs everywhere and strip lighting and a row of girls by the wall. They sat there like wallflowers, waiting to be asked to dance. But there was no one to ask them. All that waiting. That must be the worst part. Waiting and waiting about for your youth to fall. We sat down and joined all the eyes vacantly fastened on a meaningless television, sneaking glances round for a sympathetic face, but finding none. Then we got out.

The night-club was rather smart. Spots revolved on the floor and up the walls and there was a small band. Near the bar were about ten girls. We ordered drinks and two of them brought them over and sat down with us. We offered them drinks, but they didn't want any – or cigarettes. So we danced. Mine was called Lily. She looked rather like Sophia Loren, about 20 and taller than most Thai girls. She was also very inquisitive – not about why I was there, or how I'd got there, but about my family, how many brothers, sisters, rooms I had, what my father was. Anything about myself she merely found amusing. She wanted to know how old I was and when I told her she threw back her head and laughed and laughed and said I was her brother and I could come and stay with her if I liked. I gulped. I couldn't believe it. I thought she must be joking. But she soon said her flat-mate was with some Americans at another night-club and we could go there if I liked. They had a better band or something. But if I wanted to go I would have to buy her out for the evening. I think I would have given all the money I had to do so, but it was only 25s.

'The Rainbow' was open air and Lily's friend Pia was there with some other girls and half a dozen American Military Advisers. We stayed there till it closed, then Pia and the other girls went off in jeeps with the Americans. Lily said Pia wouldn't be coming back that night so I could stay with her if I wanted. She just seemed to think it was the simplest thing to do in the circumstances. But I was nervous and pretended to be worried about money. Money didn't matter, she said. I'd bought her out of the club, hadn't I? So we began to walk through the dark streets to her house. Even then I couldn't believe it. I had the idea she was keeping me occupied while my room was being sacked, or else she was leading me into an ambush. The streets of Haadyai look very like those of a Wild West town and I knew they had gunfights there. We seemed to be walking so slowly and to be going round in circles. Who were we waiting for? I must have been mad. Life just isn't like that, I would have said a few days later. But for some reason I can never take for granted the singularity of people. I must have learnt too young at school that people hunt in groups and think collectively. I am always being surprised to find them individuals, sometimes lonely.

And I suppose Lily was lonely. As soon as I saw her room with its old radio and pin-ups, I knew she was human.

Before I left the corporal in the night club he had said: 'You watch these Thai girls. All they're after is your money. You can buy anyone's friendship in this place.' But either he'd been unlucky or Lily was an exception. If anything it was my friendship she bought with hers. As for money, it lay about the flat like telephone messages. The first morning she asked for some to buy food with and I gave her all the Thai money I had, about 30s. She took it and promptly leant out the window and threw it down to a boy to go and get some chicken and rice and coke. Later she told him to take me to my hotel to pick up my suitcase and when I came back she unpacked my things and hung them in her wardrobe. I was to stay, she said and I was beginning to believe it. There was something so whole-hearted about her decisions. She didn't seem to suspect, as we do, the easy way out, the obvious solution. She merely took them in her stride. It was the kind of trust which begs deception and I supposed that was why she was a tart – to protect herself. She seemed to lack the subtle gift of antagonism and part-playing which are the weapons of the sex war in the West. There was something defenceless and rather sad about her using 'happiness' for 'pleasure' and 'sleep' for 'make love'. If she had been in the

sex war she would have been defeated and lovingly sub-
sidized for the rest of her life.

Her room too was sort of undefended. In daylight, the
luxury disappeared, leaving the dressing table, the mosquito
net over the bed, the radio, the pin-ups, as islands in the bare
boards which reached half-way up the walls to where wire
netting separated her room from the next. At night we could
hear the breathing of a family next door. And during the day
her friends wandered in to speak a few words of English to me,
try on one of her dresses, or dance a bit to the radio. How our
privacy would have frightened them.

All day the lilting, minor-keyed Thai songs warbled from
the radio, the wistful, childlike voices ending always on the
same note of helplessness. Lily knew all the singers and all
the songs. The sound was like her and part of the room for
me.

One morning, after I had been there about three days, Lily
suddenly gave me a medallion. She stood on a chair and took
it down from a little shrine she had on top of her wardrobe.
The shrine was of Buddha under a glass dome with dried
flowers, fragments of gold leaf and medallions cast in temples,
laid round it as offerings. The medallion she gave me was of
To-wat, Buddha's disciple in this part of the world. It was
shield-shaped and Lily said it would protect me in battle.
She mimed machine-gun fire and clearly believed it. Then she
yelled out of the window to her trishaw boy and he came running up straight into her room with a smile like a melon on
his face. He had on a new hat and Lily immediately had to
get it off because he'd just had his head shaved. He was going
to be a monk, she said. We all laughed, but it turned out to be
true. Then she gave him the medallion and some money and he
ran off. Ten minutes later he was back with the medallion
sealed in a little perspex container and hung on a chain. Lily
took it and hung it round my neck. I was knocked out, but
that was the kind of thing she did. With an uncertain look

on her face she would do something utterly memorable and touching like that.

I supposed this was what Maugham meant when he talked about Eastern girls knowing how to make men happy. Europeans, he said, were sometimes psychologically unable to leave the East on account of them and I believe if I'd been thirty years older I'd have stayed and been willingly milked to death of my past. As it was I knew all the time that I was getting the best of it, because all my means of returning the compliment were at home. In fact that's what being foreign meant to me: a kind of impotence. The best I could do was accept and thank. I could never really prove anything. Even our few common words were not enough to amuse with stories of my trip. So the happiness was only the passive one of enjoyment. I could only let the place happen to me, like a holiday. That is why I didn't fall in love with Lily.

We used to tell the time by the sun. Every few hours a woman came out on to her balcony opposite to move a bird-cage out of the shade. All day I sat about the sunny flat in a shirt and sarong, reading, or watching Lily stitching something. There was a pregnant cat living with her and when it lay in the sun you could see the little forms snuggling under its skin. Haadyai was preparing for a holiday and every now and then a jazz band went past in a lorry and Lily and Pia would run to the window to watch it. At 9.30 every day they had to go to English classes, so after lunch I had to help them with their homework: 'Pat is good *because* she works hard.' 'Pat works hard, *therefore* she shall be rewarded.' Perhaps that was why Lily always insisted on referring to herself in the third person: 'Lily doesn't like working at the club, *therefore* she shall not be rewarded,' she said.

Once when I was helping them I made some habitually un-American remark about an American spelling, which didn't go down at all. 'We like Americans here,' they said, speaking a lot for Thai humanity rather than their hospitality for they didn't seem to think strangers any different from themselves and certainly not strange.

Sometimes Pia didn't feel like going to school – she had caught her American – but Lily always took off her make-up, put her hair up, got into a black and white dress and bicycled uncertainly off, usually into a light storm.

I had lived there ten days. Twice I tried to go, but Lily made me stay and that was all I wanted to hear. I don't think she loved me, but she did hug me very hard occasionally, for no particular reason, rather as she hugged the cat, and I was very fond of her. I think she just wanted me around and above all to do as I wanted. Everything she did had to have my blessing: 'Hugo want us to go dancing?' 'Hugo want Lily to wash her hair?' She wanted me to stay with her, whether as a status symbol or a pet I don't know, but the ironical thing was she wanted more than anything that I stay because *I* wanted to – though probably not forever. I don't think she cared about forever. It was always by giving into each other that we pretended to come to our own decisions.

I soon discovered what it was all about. She had to go back to the club 'just as a waitress' and she couldn't expect me to stay just because she said I must after that. It had to be my own idea, and of course that is what it became. I realized I would stay anyway and as soon as Lily realized it she decided not to go to the club and we went out to the pictures instead. It was an Italian film with little high-pitched Thai voices bubbling higgledy-piggledy from the lips of a giant Romulus and Remus. Lily adored it and wanted to see it round again, but I refused. So we bought some beer and talked about our favourite subject, our families.

Perhaps we shouldn't have. Next morning the trishaw boy came running upstairs very worried, saying that Lily's brother-in-law was waiting for her downstairs. Lily was frantic. She said he'd come all the way from Bangkok to take her back to her family and she wasn't going. She hated it there and she hated her brother-in-law. But she put on her black and white dress and went down to talk to him. She was away about an hour and when she came back she was livid, not with him, but with me, for jumping about on the floor like that. I had only walked up and down, but he had looked up at the ceiling and she'd had to make up some story. What would he have said if he'd known? I apologized, but she seemed more worried than angry and couldn't remember her English. I suppose that was the end of it there and then. Her home came between us like a wall. I felt utterly superfluous, like a walk-on actor or a ponce. What was I doing there? I had a sudden horror at my pigmy ways. I should have taken her to the seaside, or Bangkok, or married her. But I realized I still felt selfish, and that I was not only unable but unwilling to go further. Lily must have known I wasn't worth waiting for, because that night she went back to work. She came home early with two bottles of beer, but she was talking forcedly, already distant. I remember wishing her brother-in-law hadn't turned up and that perhaps I loved her. But it was too late.

Next day I left Haadyai. The trishaw boy was sent off to buy me a ticket for Bangkok. At the station Lily waved me goodbye with tears in her eyes and her eyes wandering over the other people on the train and platform. I think she was crying at her own restlessness. As the train drew away, I felt my face setting in new lines as the expression of sympathy and regret was wrenched from it into the distance.

Ten minutes later, how long ago it seemed, how many stations back: the station hotel, the corporal!

In some ways I wished it had been different, that I hadn't waited for the dream to break before calmly packing and moving on. I disliked the complacency I felt. It took the poetry out of the landscape. Outside the window the flashing paddy fields looked flat and meaningless.

A fool like Pagett

Based with friends in Bangkok, I journeyed luggageless to Ankor, Cambodia.

Officially the border was closed, but when I got there all I had to do was move aside a bundle of barbed wire placed half-heartedly in the middle of a bridge and walk into the next country. People in capitals imagine their countries with hard, map-like edges round them, but the actual edges get rounded off by the people whose lives they run through.

The first sound I heard in Cambodia was 'Bonjour Monsieur' and looking round saw a little man with a beret on, waving to me from a van. I got in beside him and started exhuming my French. For some reason I hadn't expected to hear the language spoken there. It's so much more indigenous to France and French existence than English is to our own. English isn't ours any more. Nowadays we have 'funny British accents'. America, Australia, India, Africa, Jazz, Hollywood, Advertisements, Pop, have colonized it. But French has a certain integrity still. It is still French.

My van driver spoke it perfectly. He might have been born in Paris, but he was a fisherman in the great Cambodian lake. We drank cafés filtres and he put me on a bus for Siem Reap, the town near Ankor Wat.

From the bus the countryside seemed made of water: fields growing in water, rushes like watered silk, mountains like islands. As you looked down the rows of rice shoots set at right angles to the road, everything was water and reflection, but if you looked back at it, diagonally, it became a green field, the green of pistachio.

Beside the causeway of the road was a passage cleared through the paddies for sampans of lotus nuts, lily stalks, rice and fish, which are sown and harvested here like a crop. There were motorized sampans too, with propellers on long shafts which could be lifted and dipped according to vegetation. The boats could run through mud and over small islands and sometimes one saw a head gliding behind a bank of reeds like a bicyclist's, apparently on terra firma. The place was a lake in disguise.

Suddenly we stopped. A Landrover coming in the opposite direction had nicked our off-side wing. Allegations were flying. People were getting down into the road, making themselves at home. Several men started walking off through the paddies, whistling at girls. I sat, refusing to believe it. The old pile was a living wreck. One scratch could only improve it, yet here we were settling down for the weekend. I looked round for fellowship and my gaze met that of twenty passengers, staring at me vacantly as if I was somehow connected with the halt. In fact I think I was the only person who was. No one gave a damn. Crouched by a misty ditch, their sarongs stretched tight over their knees, they chewed contentedly on betel nuts, or hacked at their dry, staccato language with betel-stained tongues protruding from their mouths like those of parrots.

'Parlez-vous Français?' I tried. I must have been joking. Not even the driver spoke French. I mimed an enquiry and he nodded at me with the familiar coy smile spreading over his face as he looked round for reassurance.

I strolled up and down the road. Half an hour passed. It was terribly hot, so I got back into the bus and started writing: 'A red ant is crawling through the hair of the man beside me. He rakes phlegm into his throat and spits on to the floor of the bus. I think he is going to take snuff. He fills up a little bent tube with the stuff, puts one end up his nose and blows down the other. He goes on doing this till he has to spit again. A little boy with the Brahmin thread round his neck is staring at me through the window.'

The police had been sent for and an hour later they arrived: four Americanesque gangster cops with dark glasses, cigarettes and private jokes. They stared dreamily at the damage, then got out a measuring tape and started measuring everything in sight: width of road, width of bus, width of Rover, height of Rover, height of bus, height of driver, length of bus, length of Rover, length of tape (red tape). Then, presumably in accordance with French justice, the character and past of the defendant had to be weighed up in a notebook and taken into consideration . . .

Three hours after the accident – now I am calling it an *accident* – we moved again.

Siem Reap was only twenty minutes down the road. A typical French small town, with a gentle river, swirling market, trees and cafés. It was too late to see the ruins that night, so I found a hotel, then a restaurant. *Au Rendez-vous Des Coloniaux* was a shack beside the ciné but there was nothing colonial about the familiar, battered menu, written out in blurred violet ink, offering oeufs en gelée, châteaubriand, tournedos maison, compotes de fruits, even crème de marrons. The food was delicious, hauntingly European, and afterwards the supreme luxury of a stale Gitane completed the illusion.

In the morning I got a lift with a Frenchman down the broad, mile-long avenue to Ankor. He was working for the government maintaining the ruins, but he had a distinctly proprietary air about the place. He said it was entirely due to the French reconstruction and planning of Ankor in the old days that it was now the country's biggest export and that they were right to put a picture of the Wat on their national flag. He said the Wat – main temple – was best seen in the afternoon and the Bayon in the morning. So I went to the Bayon, for me the greatest moment of Ankor.

The building is like some fabulous growth of fungi. You can't see that it has been built at all. It looks too ancient. All signs of mankind have been outlived. It is a mansion on the sea-bed, its edges eroded, colour indefinable, shape ambiguous as the ghostly towers formed by a dripping black candle. At first it is hardly there. Then it grows upwards with the trees and undergrowth, dwarfing them.

The Frenchman who re-discovered Ankor while chasing butterflies – it's hard to believe the Wat hadn't been spotted before as it towers above the jungle – said he experienced a strange chill as, looking upwards, he discerned the giant masks on the towers of the Bayon gazing enigmatically down at him from the surrounding foliage.

Alas, there was little fear to be had by the time I arrived at the Bayon, unless it was that of crossing an American's camera angle. The poor sweating septuagenarians tottered everywhere, recording, recording, lest what must have been some of their final hours should be wasted in frivolous looking. Mounting the near-perpendicular stairway, balancing, their cameras fixed to their foreheads like cycloptic eyes, they seemed prepared to risk anything for the final winning shot that would reveal all. Till one old linen-clad lady, posing on a Buddha's knee, let her bottom slip off it and all but fell over a wall into a dungeon. What a moment, my dear, I almost died.

Why am I so scathing suddenly? I was a day-tripper myself, and with a camera, what's more.

At the entrance to the Bayon were boys selling bamboo Jew's harps and polished wood crossbows. I got one of them to shoot and he laughingly aimed at a monkey, 'sure thing dead', then at a tree, putting the bolt between his teeth in readiness, while he pulled back the twine with hands and feet. Setting the bolt in a groove, he touched a trigger and the twine smacked against the bolt, sending it straight as a bullet two inches into a tree eighty yards off. I wanted to buy a Jew's harp, but only had enough for a coke and wanted a drink more. After luxury in Bangkok I had under-budgeted the trip as a reaction and was regretting it. I would now have only one day in Ankor.

Outside the Bayon were terraces where elephant fights were once held and towers between which tightropes were stretched for trials by ordeal. I wonder how they found out about that. From there, immaculate paths edged away into the jungle towards various smaller temples. The whole complex covered ten square miles.

I chose a path and was soon alone, twitching slightly at the screeching, rattling, warbling, buzzing jungle which seemed to be playing cat and mouse with its tutors. The sound was electric, coming from all sides like in an echo chamber. Parrots gargled, monkeys looped above the path, their eyes not caring where their limbs were going if there was something more interesting to watch on the ground. Smells were of swarthy tropic blooms and the armpits of banyans. Leaves like dinghies.

The Hindu-Buddhist temple of Preah Khan, which I soon came to, was a vast low complex of buildings, half exhumed from the jungle, half clamped still to the earth by its great white roots. Inside it was dark. Tunnels led to crossroads where Buddhas instead of phalli budded from Hindu yonis. I walked through it and came upon a party of very jungli Cambodian teenagers making a campfire. Four boys and two girls, one of whom gave me a burnt runner bean.

Finding another, less beaten track, I went on, actually afraid by now. There is something about the jungle which is dark even in daylight. Perhaps because it is evergreen, constantly thickening, creeping up on you like children playing grandmother's footsteps. There is no truce for autumn or winter in the jungle. Every now and then a leaf detaches itself in old age from a branch and falls heavily to the ground, hitting it with a dry click, and that's autumn. Otherwise it's summer and war.

But it can lose. Suddenly I came to a cleared space where a film set of a fort had been erected. English technicians were rushing about with long knives and light meters. I asked one of them what the film was and he told me to go away, it was *Lord Jim*.

My first thought was work, but back in Siem Reap at Columbia Pictures' office a PR man told me they only wanted Oriental extras. I heard from someone that the crew had been there four months. Everything had gone wrong and now the carpenters and electricians who got drunk every night and fell down the stairs of their hotels were being turned out because no one could get a room.

Next day I had to go. I don't regret Ankor, but I regret skimping on it. All the time I was there my eyes were in a panic to print their photographs on my mind. But they came too quick and too bright, leaving me a blurred collage, like someone else's story at a slideshow. I hadn't got time to focus. I'm afraid the trip was valued more than usual by the prospect of being able to say I had been there.

On the way back the bus held out, but the road gave way. One of the many bridges had slumped in the night. So we all had to get out and watch as the driver edged forward, testing it. But the bridge just gave a little like a tired camel and he had to retreat. While we waited for a bus to come from the other side I was plagued by a pock-marked man who said he had been tortured by the Japanese and tried to get me to eat some kind of spice.

That night at the border I had about 10d. So I went to the police station and slept in the prison. It was on stilts over a bog and under it was suspended a cage with a man in it.

'And I thought of those fools like Pagett, who write of their "Eastern Trips".' – Kipling.

IV – JAPAN

A murmur of boundaries

If you travel first class on Japanese Airlines – 'Wings of the New Japan' – you are given a short blue kimono by a stewardess. If you travel economy class you are given a little fan. With my fan I stepped down into colder weather than I'd been in for a year.

In the customs shed our suitcases were dealt to us by a revolving distributor. Mine was opened and on top of all the clothes were two daggers. 'Are these your weapons?' asked the customs official.

'Yes,' I said, feeling like a gun runner, 'souvenirs.'

'They look dangerous. We have a law against this kind of thing.'

Under the official's clean fingernails my knives had become exhibit A and B in the murder trial of an aged Japanese schoolmistress. A detective appeared with a tape measure and proceeded to measure the blade of each. One of them caused some trouble as it had a curved blade and the detective was uncertain whether to measure it round the blade or straight from hilt to point. The difference made the difference apparently. But the verdict was guilty. I could not 'import' it. The other, a more poisonous stiletto, I could keep providing I didn't carry it in my pocket after dark.

'Supposing I had some antique English swords,' I asked, 'would they be considered too long? I know Japan exports ornamental Samurai swords all over the world.'

'I'm afraid we must confiscate this weapon. You may re-
deem it when you leave our country.' Kill yourself by all
means, but don't get blood on *our* lawns.

'I shall be leaving by ship from Kobe. May I reclaim it
there?'

No, that would be impossible. Why did I not do as all
the European athletes had done the year before? They had
deposited their weapons (javelins?) with the authorities without argument and reclaimed them on departure. Why did I not
leave Japan by air? It would be so much simpler.

Simpler still to fly right out that minute. I asked for string
and paper, made a parcel of the knife and made my way with
the detective to the nearest P.O., where I mailed it home.

Then I started to look around. I seemed to have energy
for anything. I was like a bull looking round for friends or
enemies, tired but terrified of falling asleep. Japan was the end
of Asia for me and it seemed like a last chance. I could have
walked round Tokyo all night.

But I went to a Japanese inn.

Sliding paper doors slid back and two little Easter eggs
bowed to me from the waist.

'Shoes, shoes, shoes,' they said. Take off your profane boots
and don our dainty slippers. In my room I was not allowed to
wear even the slippers.

Everyone knows about Japanese rooms. They have this very
low centre of gravity, and nowhere to hide anything—least of
all oneself. One feels like Alice grown big in Wonderland and
I had the impression that my suitcases, particularly a green
plastic one, standing squarely Occidental on the raffia floor,
were in very poor taste.

There was no furniture in the room but a low mahogany
table. Above the table hung a lamp of balsa wood and rice
paper. By pulling a cord hanging from it you could adjust its
brightness. There were two brightnesses and a nightlight. In a
corner of the room was a little recess pillared with the trunks of

two artificial trees. In the recess was a painted scroll and a telephone.

A girl in a kimono came in with some green tea. She put the tea on the table and went and knelt in the doorway, nodding and smiling.

There was no bed in the room so I asked where I was going to sleep.

'You take bath? You take bath?' All my life people are telling me to wash. She pointed to two kimonos lying folded in the corner of the room, one light black and white one and one heavy black and brown padded one. I put them on and went to the bathroom. I wondered would the bunny come in too and wash me, as I had heard happens in some Japanese inns. But I was left alone.

This room also seemed to take place largely below the ankles. The floor was pebbled and there was a miniature milking stool standing beside a huge sunken bath, which was covered with wooden boards. Beside the bath was a little pine tree, shrouded in steam. Above it was a notice in English:

'Don't you soap in the tub.
Don't you pull the plug.'

In Japan they don't believe in sitting around in dirty water. You wash sitting on the stool under a waist-high cold shower and afterwards get into the bath with your friends or wife for a soak and a talk.

When I got back to my room there was a bed made out on the floor, its head within easy reach of the lamp and the table. On the table was a little pattern of food on a bamboo tray. Shark fin soup, rice, raw tuna, dried sea-weed.

The first morning was so cold that the sun and cold seemed to intensify each other. Outside in the street there were people with white masks over their faces – to keep out the cold or keep in their colds, I never discovered which. I chose one without a mask to ask the way. I wanted to get to the Imperial Palace where the American Express was, with perhaps some letters for me. But he didn't understand and seemed to laugh at me, glancing round. I was to get used to that.

I bought a map and got on a tram going in the right direction. In the tram everyone stared at me, quite politely, like an advertisement. Wrapped up in fur, some of them looked like Eskimoes. Just as we approached a stop a young girl student came and sat next to me, in order to be near the door I thought. She was holding some English language books. I turned my head half way in her direction and she said 'Do you mind if I speak to you, I study English.'

'No. Yes. Where are you going? I'm going to Yurakucho.'

'So am I. I can take you to a coffee shop. You are American?'

'No, English.'

'Would you like me to show you Tokyo?'

'Yes, that's exactly what I would like.'

'We get down here.' We walked for about five minutes in silence, separated by a foot's difference in height now we were out of the impersonal bus.

'What's your name?' I said.

'Mitsué. And yours?'

'Hugo.'

'This is the shop.' We went into a coffee bar called 'Chopin'. At first it looked like a chapel, with stained glass windows and a staircase going up and up and choral music being played very loud on a gramophone. On each darkened landing were young people listening silently. We sat down and good American coffee came with a free mid-morning roll.

Mitsué was small and bespectacled, like a little pekinese with round appealing eyes. She was shy and I wondered what had made it possible for her to speak to me. When I asked her she said that everyone did it to improve their English and show visitors their city. But it didn't answer my question.

'But you didn't find it hard to speak to me?'

'Yes I did.'

'Well, I admire you. I can never speak when I want to. But it's different in London because there's no way of telling who's a foreigner.'

'I think I am very lucky to be speaking with you. You speak with the Queen's English. I hope I will see you again.'

'When are you going to show me Tokyo?'

'Saturday I will introduce my friends and we will take you all over Tokyo.'

'Shall we meet here?'

'O.K. What time?'

'Half past ten.' We talked for a few minutes, then suddenly, like the White Rabbit, she was gone.

A schoolmaster in Bangkok had given me five pounds to buy Handel's *Messiah* for a Japanese schoolmistress he'd met in Canada. Her name was Miss Suzuki and I was looking forward to turning up out of the blue with a present for her.

But she was hard to find. I took a train to the right suburb, but postal addresses only came to greater Tokyo with the Americans and hers turned out to be no more than a name and a district. I found a policeman and together we went round a maze of cinder tracks, asking for her in person.

Eventually we found her mother, who told me through the policeman that her daughter was teaching at Tokyo University. She gave me the telephone number of a common-room and I immediately rang up. Miss S. was in class. I took the train back to the middle of the town and tried again. 'A foreign gentleman to speak to you, Miss Suzuki.'

'Hello, Miss Suzuki speaking.'

'Hello, Miss Suzuki. My name is Hugo Williams. I have a present for you from Mr Chen in Bangkok. I would like to meet you and give it to you.'

'That is most kind of you, Mr Williams. May I meet you tomorrow?'

'I only know the Chopin Coffee Shop at Yurakucho.'

'Would twelve o'clock be convenient for you?'

'Perfect. I look forward to seeing you then.'

Just before twelve the next day I approached the Chopin. Miss Suzuki's fresh, obedient little voice had excited my imagination and I decided to have her record playing for her in the coffee bar when she arrived. A tiny, suited, middle-aged lady with a large handbag was standing outside.

'Mr Williams?' she said. 'I am Suzuki.'

'Oh, how do you do. Have you been here long? If we go inside we could have coffee and hear your record. Mr Chen sends his kind regards.'

'I'd rather not if you don't mind. A friend of mine is expecting us at his house. If you have time that is. He has prepared lunch.'

We took a train and sat dusting each other with small talk. Canada. Mr Chen. Music. Tokyo. English. Food. The cold. I wondered how far the day would take me. A chain of events seemed already prepared to knit me with the Japanese people forever. I seemed to have an unlimited claim to their attention.

From a suburban station we walked through low muddy streets. The houses were fragile, uneven, like card houses. A man with bare feet in stilted Japanese clogs was picking his way over the puddles. I wished I had an overcoat.

'This is his house.' Mr Hadachi was in the doorway with his wife and daughter. They greeted me with bows and English and apologies. Keiko, the daughter, a beautiful girl of fifteen, was introduced and vanished. The house was warm and bright with the smell of cooking coming from a Western kitchen.

'Just a tiny old house I'm afraid,' said Mr Hadachi. There was a staircase but we went into a small, chaired room off the kitchen.

'Do you take saké?' he asked me.

'Japanese rice wine,' explained Suzuki.

'Yes, thank you,' I said.

'Don't you mean "yes please"?' said Mr Hadachi.

'Yes I do. Your English is really marvellous.'

'This is dried crayfish, I think. We eat this with saké.' He poured the saké from a bottle heating over a flame into a little pitcher and from there into tiny porcelain bowls, covered with a pattern of finest cracks like cobwebbing. The crayfish was tough and sweet and salt against the soft, dry drink. Being warm, the alcohol was soon in our blood and we were talking eagerly. There was, as always, nothing and everything to say. The Japanese in them forbade anything but veiled compliments to pass between us, but the Western education they had both received added a query and stringency to their talk which made them original and absorbing.

One can almost never meet Asians half way for our knowledge of their viewpoint is always smaller than theirs of ours. The circles are expanding but they usually still clear each other. Here for once I was met with something like gratitude inside my own ground. What was said I have no idea.

Soon it was time to eat. We were to have sukiyaki, the dish of welcome which means 'chosen'. Until this year there were two places you could get this in London. One was chic and dear in Chelsea, the other sparse and excellent in Irving Street. Chelsea is still going, but the Asiatique has just been replaced by a dread Golden Egg, where the usual South Sea idols hope to divert your attention from the food with their red glass eyes, and breasts.

Sukiyaki is slices of beef fried in soy and sugar along with cabbage, leeks, bean curd, carrots and onions. There is a hot-plate on the table and the cook stands up and decorates the bubbling saucepan with food like a painter with his palette. It was one of the best things I've ever tasted, but then my favourite omelette is cooked with apricot jam.

After lunch we left the 'Western-style' dining room and climbed the stairs to the Japanese living room – the best of both worlds. Here it was shoes off on the tatamy, kimonos for everyone, and L-shaped arm-rests to lean against on the floor. The room would have been a small sitting room but in the spare Japanese style it was spacious. In Japanese rooms no floor space is wasted on permanent furniture. The springy blocks of tatamy on the floor are furniture in themselves and the paper walls which filter and abstract outside light are all the decoration. Rooms in Japan are less distinctly indoors than ours and they are settings rather than aids to life. In the inn I had been critically objective. Here, as a guest, I was part of my surroundings.

We listened to Handel, Christ's voice vibrating the house. Then I was asked to read aloud from Kipling. Hadachi had a tape-recorder and said he could use my voice for teaching. This flattered me so much that I went on far too long. I changed to Eliot and recorded *Prufrock*, then Keats' *La Belle Dame Sans Merci*. This was in a 1928 Oxford Poems and the first line went 'O what can ail thee wretched wight,' instead of 'knight-at-arms'. I think I could have gone on for a day without them stopping me.

But we were going to the Boro-ichi, the rag market. Before leaving, Hadachi's wife gave me a tea-pot and some sweets made of chestnut. She and her daughter had been absent till then.

The rag market was much like Petticoat Lane, except that wares were spread on the pavement. I bought a second-hand overcoat for £1, a new kimono for £3, a pair of round dark glasses and some candy floss.

Before I left, Miss Suzuki said she would get some of her students to take me round Tokyo. The chain was lengthening.

Saturday was Mitsué. At ten I entered the dedicated atmosphere of the Chopin once more: students in duffle coats already hunched to the passionate music. Mitsué came in and said her friends were outside. A girl called Mitchka and two boys, Shirokawa and Hidioshi. Mitsué noticed straight away I had on a new coat. I said it cost 1,000 yen – £1 – in the rag market and they all laughed at the joke.

All day we travelled round Tokyo but I remember only their attentive faces, and questioning. They gave me the impression that though I could see Tokyo any time, they had only now to see me. They were irresistible because they seemed curious in spite of themselves. Questions were always apologies, seeming only to pay tribute to a culture they obviously preferred to their own.

There would be a slight pause for decency's sake, while an archway or shrine was pointed out, then another shy, illuminating misunderstanding to be cleared up. I even found myself defending Japanese art. I fancy I was being tested. Alec Douglas Home's son had just failed to get into Oxford and Shirokawa claimed that such a thing could never happen in Japan. Britain must be a true democracy, he said. It was an elaborate experiment.

I remember waiting hours on islands in the middle of roads for street cars and no time at all for equally crowded tube trains. At each station there were professional pushers who just forced passengers between the doors of trains like icing sugar through a cake decorator. I noticed that wherever we went people knocked and pushed us aside without a word.

'People are very rude in Japan,' said the sensitive Mitsué. But she did not explain to me, as someone did later, that were they to bring their manners to bear, that would involve recognizing one as a person and an almost endless series of elaborate courtesies and formalities would ensue, such as few of them have time for. The alternative is, at best, called impersonality. D. J. Enright in *The World of Dew* is more lucid: 'To push back is in order – it should be done as impersonally as possible; if you trample some old woman who is tugging a bundle bigger than herself, that too is accepted, even by the victim. But to protest by word or gesture about being needlessly shoved about – that is a gross offence against the non-existent manners of travelling, it is unheard-of, it is altogether "unexpected". One is arrogating to oneself public opinion, which, alas, practically fails to exist in Japan.' Elsewhere he notes however that 'The guiding principle of Japanese manners is not mere attention to form, for they will display a positive ingenuity in their determination to make a guest comfortable. Those foreigners who find Japanese politeness an empty and unfeeling form might be asked what exactly they expect in the way of manners. A kick in the backside to show the fullness of the host's heart? The Englishman and the American in particular make a fetish of what is called "casualness" – the Japanese would call it open rudeness, and my sympathies are rather with them. We Anglo-Saxons are too ready to see something "sinister" in polite and thoughtful behaviour. Unfortunately Japanese good manners seem to be peculiar to personal relations and die a sudden death in the ruder atmosphere of public life.'

If the trains were rough, they were fascinating. More immediately so because they were within one's experience, unlike the orange-painted shrines or temples which were going to take more understanding. At one station we stopped at there was a man giving PT instruction on the platform. He was standing on a box outside our window and half the people in the carriage got out for a quick kneesbend and a stretch. In the more central stations there were quite a lot of kimonos to be seen. I know of no dress which so effectively breaks down the human figure in favour of its own peculiar charm. The little white bundles tottering through the tunnels with their strange, forward-leaning half-run looked like pretty Easter eggs tied with a bow. They seemed no part of the hostile complex about them, yet they manoeuvred without fuss.

'They are bar-girls or hostesses,' said Hidioshi, and I noticed that they were always alone or in pairs. He explained that some Japanese women wore kimonos for holidays, but you could always tell the hostesses because they wore them back from the nape of the neck – considered the sexiest part of the body in Japan – and with the *boti*, or sash, tied in front, denoting easy virtue.

'But they aren't always prostitutes,' he said defensively. Later he said: 'You see those slips of paper under that telephone? Those are the telephone numbers of call-girls.' The ground was snowy with them.

On the way out of the station we passed a poetess selling her work on some steps. I bought a poem called *Chain*, but they told me it was no good.

'Do you like modern jazz?' asked Shirokawa. It was a confession of faith.

'Yes.'

'Tokyo is full of jazz cafés. You must definitely see some.'

The tiny Mama's jazz café was quite unlike the dignified Chopin. Music and customers overflowed into a rumbustious alleyway. Inside I thought I smelt something more than tobacco. The usual scarves and duffle coats were there in lonely dedication. But perhaps the white cool faces and spiky jazz haircuts were a shade less innocent than elsewhere. No one spoke. Round the walls were pinned record sleeves with their titles spelt out beneath them in bold black lettering. Gerry Mulligan, Paul Desmond, Cannonball Adderley, proclaimed Japan's preference for the 'white' fluency of West Coast jazz to the hard, emotional playing of New York. With the fine American coffee came a slip asking for requests. We wrote 'Charlie Parker' hopefully, but the girl said it would take an hour to come up. I felt at home here as I had not done for a long time and soon we began to talk and argue. After a while a little note was put in front of me by the waitress. 'Hush. Hush. Why listen to jazz music?' I had under-estimated the seriousness with which certain Japanese could swallow America whole. The humour which goes with it is a custom no amount of goodwill can learn. We left Mama's and pressed on through the cold evening to Riri's, where Mitsué said we could make as much noise as we liked. Riri's was a singing café – a kind of music-hall. You hired a book of words and sat at a long, crowded table like at school. There was a stage where a young man was leading the singing and, like the exercisers on the platform, everyone was joining in the hearty tunes. They came from Scotland, Israel, Russia. But the atmosphere was not American this time, or even 'folk'. The marching rhythms, the fellowship, was more like Germany. There is a fleeting resemblance between the two nations of industrious, lately warlike technicians, but here again I felt that Japan was using something inherently foreign to her as a gadget with which to escape tradition and enter an Eldorado Western World which did not become her. I preferred Japanese America to Japanese Germany. As yet I had hardly glimpsed Japan itself at all.

A home for everyone

After a few days at the Japanese Inn the cross-purposes were getting knotted, so I moved to the YMCA. This is one of the few pre-war buildings left in Tokyo. It is a club, a school, a hotel and *the* tourist exchange. Here I started to meet large numbers of foreigners and a wistful Japanese intellectual called Hidenowa. One of the foreigners was Henri-Claude, who looked like Gerry Mulligan. Another was a German named Herman. Herman spoke perfect Deep South, had flown jets, trained horses and been arrested for the kidnapping of Frank Sinatra Jnr., of which he was innocent he said. One night Hidenowa, Henri and I suggested finding some tarts. Henri had a card which said: 'Do you know Turkish Bath? It is the pleasant place where with sufficient sweet-smelling soap you are washed from head to foot and refreshingly massaged your burning body concealing clear shame in glamour figures. Turk girls are waiting for you. Fee Y1200 for 1 hour.' We doubted if any Soho landlord could have come up with such suggestive ambiguity had fate made it necessary for him to conjure with Chinese characters! But Herman said pompously that he'd 'never pay a woman'. So we went without him, failed to find the Turkish Bath and wound up at the Silk Rose Jazz Club, where for 10s you got a girl to sit with, a bottle of beer and a lot of Japanese Dixieland. It sounded cheap and it was, even though the girls spoke hardly any English. They were very pretty and they sat very close, trying hard to express themselves with the words of pop songs. 'You go for sweetheart in America?' 'You baby-face.' 'You like Tokyo?' 'Tokyo swingin'.'

'You same same Gerry Mulligan,' I heard Henri's telling him. But I didn't catch on so quickly when mine chose to compliment me by pointing to my face and repeating 'Audley Hepburn, Audley Hepburn.' When she had got this across she leant back and suggested the reward for her trouble. 'You buy me drink?' I said yes and an eyebath of Coca-Cola came which the waiter and the girl seemed to agree was 'whisky', costing 7s 6d. I paid, knowing that elsewhere you could pay £7 for the same thing. With the drink came a fresh interest in me from the girl. She produced one of the club's cards and wrote her name on it, 'Mimi,' and said I was always to ask for her when I came. I could even ring up and reserve her. When I asked for her own number she was less enthusiastic and told me I was 'crazy'. This was for 'business' not 'funny business'. She told me she had a Japanese sweetheart and 'I'll always be true'. This is the light-hearted public life of Japan which can run parallel to an unknown private one, probably financing it. It should have been depressing, underlining one's foreignness, but such is the Japanese female's talent – almost her *raison d'être* – for uplifting the male spirit, that one goes away feeling gay, witty, attractive, even loved.

After that night at the Silk Rose, Henri and I spent whole days exploring the endless districts of bars and cafés and clubs in Tokyo. Endless because one hundred bars are said to close each night, while another hundred and one open. One quarter known as 'French Alley' especially pleased Henri because of the names of the bars there. 'La Vie en Rose.' 'Avec.' 'Moulin Rouge' and 'Sous les Toits de Tokyo'. One I liked was the 'White Lion'. This was a weird place. It was like a small chapel with pews, laurels in copper, lace doilies, aspidistras, a huge cast-iron boiler and an altar, with candles, which was really a huge loud-speaker. On going in we were handed a programme of the music that was being played that day: Bach Organ Recitals. Coffee was the usual shilling.

Henri heard of another café which had something called a 'kissing balcony'. It is apparently difficult for some Japanese couples to find a place to kiss in and the semi-official nature of this place makes it easier for them. But as Henri said 'You gotta find the girl and you gotta find the place' and we found neither. Every night I would go back to the Y, my pockets full of matchboxes, each representing a bar or café. 'Chopin', 'Opal', 'Mama', 'Dig', 'Pony', Ki-Yo', 'La Mer', 'La Cave'. A home for everyone. I would climb into bed and the lights of Tokyo, under arches, down alleys, in water, in the sky, would stay on in my head long into the night.

I never tired of our pub-crawls, because in a way they endorsed my way of life at that time. A kind of search through self-indulgence for something to write about. I felt that by wandering endlessly, aimlessly, in public places, I would get in the way of things best. Or that was what I told myself. Henri on the other hand had a more defined purpose and a longer stay to finance. He was an industrial psychologist, there to study Japanese business management. But where to begin? So far all he had done was drink a lot of coffee and make an agreement with a certain 'madame' to give her girls some French lessons in preparation for the coming Olympic games.

While his more serious introductions were maturing, he decided to put an advertisement in the *Asahi Evening News*. Together we wrote it out:

'Young French psychologist, speaks English, seeks exchange with student of Japanese business methods,'

and took it along to the newspaper's offices.

In the morning we scanned the personal column. At the bottom we found: 'Young French psychologist seeks exchange with Japanese student. Box 207.' Our first reaction was government censorship: industrial espionage. The truth we would never know, for the explanation was a printer's error. All we could do was sit and wait for the results.

A day later they began. I didn't see them all as Henri did, but I did go one day to the Fugetsu café with him, where he'd been assembling them in batches, for audition, so to speak. As soon as we walked in two people detached themselves from different tables and drifted towards us. A third arrived soon after. There was still one missing, so I went up to a man who seemed to be bracing himself to meet us and asked him if he was 'Hadachi-san'. He replied no, but that he had a friend called Hadachi, a cousin. His own name was Pinto-san. He said he was waiting for the leading anarchist of Tokyo. I asked him to join our troupe and it seemed that that made quite a nice cross-section of Japanese youth as well as of the kind of people who answer advertisements in papers. We had a giggling, stiff-collared country bumpkin from Hokkaido, a rather smooth, apparently queer PR man, a cultured graduate from Tokyo University – the real Mr Hadachi – with a Cambridge accent which must have come to Japan with some mad old gentleman before the first war, and Pinto-san, whose card announced him to be on the 'Editorial Stuff' of *The Ladies Own Weekly*.

I spent most of the time talking to the PRO who had just come back from Europe. He had some photographs with him of his trip and he showed me pictures of Switzerland, Paris and London. Amongst the ones of London was one of the American Embassy.

'And this is the Gillette factory,' he said as he showed it to me.

'Who told you that was the Gillette factory?' I asked.

'The taximan.'

'He was pulling your leg. That's the American Embassy.'

'Pulling my leg?'

'Joking.'

'He didn't like the Americans?'

'He didn't like the building.'

'There is plenty of anti-American feeling in Japan also.'

Three days later I went skiing with Pinto-san and his sister. We travelled all night in a coach, skied all day and came back in the coach the same night. It was murder. It cost altogether less than £3.

The birth of Father Christmas

As Christmas got nearer a fever of commercialism broke out in Tokyo. On every pavement rows of little plastic Father Christmasses were being sold for 17s 6d each. On the corners were Father Christmas sandwich men, thin as reeds under their short tunics, stamping their feet to keep warm. They advertised strip-tease and Christmas Fare at the *Moulin Rouge*.

Christmas in Tokyo was a strange affair for it seemed to affect everyone, but for no apparent reason. The details of the tradition were there, but they were not rationally connected by the tradition itself or by any understanding of it. Most people thought that it had something to do with the birth of Father Christmas. All were involved. Shops were sold out. People were on holiday. Presents and parties were given. I was invited to one at the English Speaking Society of one of the universities. It was held in a classroom. Red bulbs had been substituted for white ones and many streamers and bells put up. As soon as each guest arrived he was handed a sheet printed with the three Christmas songs most popular in Tokyo: Rudolph the Red-nosed Reindeer, Jingle Bells and White Christmas. Being members of an English-speaking society, they still felt obliged to speak nothing but English and, when there was an un-Christmassy lull in the conversation, someone always suggested a song. We sang those three songs twelve times. By the end of the evening they had all taken on other meanings nothing whatever to do with Christmas, but always I suspect latent.

After dinner I had to make a speech about Christmas in England. I described the day as it normally is at home, emphasising food and presents and drink and those things it seemed to have in common with the present occasion. It was thanked with 'We always thought the British were narrow-minded, but now we know better.' And answered by an old American adviser who said that in the States Christmas was celebrated as a deeply significant and holy religious festival, that though there were some rowdy business parties, most families felt this to be a time . . . and then the king-pin holding up a great plastic bell to which all the streamers and hopes for merriness at Xmas were attached, gave way and down it all swung into the coffee. It is easy enough to be patronizing from this distance, but it really was a depressing party.

On Christmas Day I wanted to be host. Mitsué and her friends had shown me Tokyo for almost two weeks and I wanted to repay the compliment. It was one of the things I felt homesick for: the pride of ownership.

I was going to take them all to an English service and lunch, but they arrived at the YMCA before I was up and came into my room with presents. Mitsué had knitted me a pale blue scarf and stitched a sequined Christmas card. I had got framed photographs of us all for them.

Downstairs I asked the receptionist where the Anglican church was. Church? His eyes clouded with suspicion and I think he scanned a police notice showing the faces of twenty or so wanted foreigners, which I knew was pinned inside the counter. Not finding mine, he reached for the telephone directory and looked up 'Church,' then 'Anglican' without success. I telephoned the British Embassy and the Scot I woke up said there was no one there but him. If I waited he would ask the Japanese porter. The porter came on with a gay 'Happy Christmas' and said there was an English-speaking church called St Albyn's at the foot of the Tokyo Tower. There we went.

For me, the day was made by one member of the congregation who had on a kilt. As soon as Mitsué saw this she leant across and whispered 'I am so happy today.'

After church we went up the Tokyo Tower and saw the new prestige motorway cruising over poverty-stricken rooftops from the airport to the Olympic stadium, ready for the games. Below us a baseball game was going on in a field without grass. Above and quite near a little red weather balloon floated against the winter-blue sky.

We had a rather bad lunch in a Western restaurant, then they all had to go back to their families.

I spent the afternoon crawling jazz parlours.

In the evening I was to meet Henri to go to dinner with an American journalist, Dan Sutherland. While we were waiting for him to pick us up we started guessing at the purpose of a large number which kept lighting up in bulbs outside the station. 76, 77, 76, 74, 71, 73 it went. People passing by? Number of cars? Number of trains? Buses? I asked about six people what it meant, but none could tell me. Eventually Dan turned up and said it was a noise level recorder. We shouted at it, but it remained inscrutable.

We were to take the tube to Dan's house, but instead of going down in the lift, we went up. The lift seemed to serve a department store as well as the station, but the store was closed. Dan said something about having a few minutes to spare while his wife cooked the dinner, handed some tickets to someone and we suddenly found ourselves in a theatre, watching *Kabuki*, the traditional Japanese drama. It was as if a lift from Waterloo tube station had taken us straight into the Old Vic.

A play was already in progress and Dan explained that you just bought a ticket for the scenes you wanted to see. A whole performance might go on twelve hours and people brought their families and picnics and wine. The atmosphere was very relaxed and every now and then members of the audience would shout out something, like an *olé* in a bullfight. Dan said this was usually the name of an actor. Acting was a family business in Japan and the actors names were as traditional as the plays. It was part of the tradition that the audience spur them on by anticipating their entrances and key lines with their family names, or even the number of their generation. It was the kind of audience participation Western theorists have striven in vain for, though I doubt if our actors would remain as impervious. Dan told us he was in New York when the Kabuki went there. He was the only one in the audience who knew the actors' names and the first time he yelled one the actor was so surprised to hear his name he completely dried up.

Happily spread out in their seats, the audience here were obviously on holiday. Yet the playing itself was of a curious, almost operatic formality. Speech was stylized out of all recognition, not into song, but into something more like animal sounds, like the language in Kurosawa's Samurai films.

The stage was very wide and low and we were watching two men guarding a vat of saké for a wine merchant. Each was remonstrating with the other not to touch the drink, while quietly helping himself to it. The play ended with a drunken dance and the return of the merchant with their punishment. It was pure pantomime.

Next came a very different piece about three people committing suicide in a boat on a lake. In this we saw the main attraction of Kabuki: the female impersonator. Long ago, women were forbidden to act by law because of the wrongly-directioned interest they provoked in male spectators. The custom persisted and women's parts are still played by men. These men also live normal lives as women and are said 'to understand more of feminine ways than women themselves'. If such a man had no son, my guidebook said, and it seemed more than likely, he would adopt a son and pass on to him his art.

185

When I had read that I thought nothing more could be said for the tact and humanity of the Japanese way of life.

When that play was over we left and as we went through the foyer someone came up to me and said 'Hello Mr Williams, did you enjoy the Kabuki?' 'Yes, very much indeed,' I said, thinking I recognized one of the players. I was just on the point of saying how good he'd been when I remembered I'd met him in Bangkok.

'It's good to see you again,' I said. 'How long have you been in Japan?'

'All my life,' he said. 'I work at the YMCA where you are staying.'

I put this in not to say how alike all Japanese look, but how different. It was not a mistake one could make easily and I cursed myself. The Japanese face is at least as varied as the English, and in a crowded tube or wet street it can even look English, though there is an Eskimo type which cannot.

Dan's house was Japanese, large and delicate. The paper-screen rooms were built inside the main walls so that the large windows running round the whole house lit up the internal walls. It was very quiet and newly-wed and Dan was very quiet and respectful of his surroundings, which he seemed hardly to believe in. One felt the image he had of his home was breakable in his mind – as indeed it was. There was a moment's awkwardness while our three nationalities produced a complete vacuum. Then Thankful, his wife, appeared and we started jabbering about France where her family had originated from. Candles were lit and Thankful came and went with nice things to eat. Instead of turkey we had sashi, tender raw tuna fish and instead of Christmas pudding a tacky rice cake called ozoni. We drank warm saké and soon the edges were rounded off. The truth was we were all very excited. I, at any rate, felt these three people to be valuable and the occasion somehow permanent, like a memorial dinner of a meeting long ago. Yet we talked about the future and poetry, agreeing with everything, running down our countries, but loving them. It was the kind of self-conscious pride that is only possible far from home when you think you have managed to re-form there, independently, something of what you are homesick for.

Time flew. But by midnight their marriage had begun to fidget and we thought we'd better go.

New Year's Day 1964. I decided to telephone my family in England, which would be still in the old year. I thought half an hour before their year ended would be a good time to speak to them, but that was half an hour before the International Telegraph office opened in Tokyo on the morning of January 1, so I had to book the call in advance and take it at the YMCA.

I went to bed early, got up at seven, had a quick breakfast and by eight was standing by. There was no booth at the Y, only a public telephone attached to the wall in the foyer, but it was still quiet and I wasn't worried. I knew what I was going to say. I had written it down. 8.30 came and I went over and stood by the telephone, pencil and paper at hand. Suddenly it rang and I snatched it up. An American voice said 'Is that the YMCA? Can I speak to Captain Grant, please?' I fetched the receptionist and he told the American that Captain Grant hadn't arrived yet and could he call Reception the next time. I sat down and tried to relax. It was a quarter to nine, a quarter to midnight. At five to nine the telephone rang again. I'd made it! I ran to the telephone. But no, there'd been a delay. Lines through Asia were very crowded. They were running an hour behind. Would I like them to re-route the call via Anchorage and New York? It might take half an hour. I said yes.

Three hours later I was still waiting. It was mid-day and the hall was crowded with GI's, calling one another 'brother'. Captain Grant had long ago received his call. I was cold with nerves. In England it would be 3 a.m. Everyone asleep. I decided to cancel the call. I got up and it came through. 'Mr Williams, your call to Chelwood Gate, England.' Three minutes wait and a familiar, clipped voice was coming from under the sea to me. I spoke and it sank. Another came on. I tried to explain how I'd wanted to call from the New Year. Nothing.

'Are you all right?' came a frightened, sleepy voice.

'Yes. Yes. Happy New Year.'

'Happy New Year.'

'Congratulations on your grandson.'

'Don't tell me you've marr . . .' My father was suddenly awake, but the line had died. No response. The GI's were all round me, joking, waiting to use the phone. I kept reading a plaque above my head which said 'A Merry YMCA Christmas and A Happy YMCA New Year. Tomorrow's Leaders Are Made Today. Practise Hospitality.' Eternity.

'No, no. I mean Thomas,' I said.

'Oh, yes, thank you. When do you reach Australia?'

'Your three minutes is up, Tokyo. Would you say goodbye, please.'

'February fourth. Goodbye. See you in the summer.'

'Goodbye. Goodbye. Goodbye.'

My good Japanese friend

Mitsué and Mitchka were going to spend their New Year holiday showing Herman and me round Kyoto. They had got permission from their parents to stay with cousins there.

In the train I wished Herman wasn't coming. He seemed to think we were off on some illicit weekend and kept peeling oranges for Mitchka and trying to put the pieces in her mouth. He was all bounce and argument and dirty jokes. I didn't laugh and he turned to me and said what I needed was a spell in the US Marines. They'd soon smarten me up. Life wasn't all buttercups and daisies, you know. At that I rose like a stupid little trout. I said I supposed he thought life was all dirty jokes and mucking-in and obeying orders. It was exactly what he wanted. He asked me if I were a conscientious objector and whether I thought the world owed me a living. He said I was the sort of person good men died for. We were back at school. I remembered those long early terms of learning how to pare away the laughable twigs of one's own character and spy out those of one's neighbour. Terms of sucking up and bullying to stay alive. It was a game I had forgotten how to play, and it left me shaking. For Herman it came naturally, like a doodle, almost as if he were not responsible for how far he went. He even managed a certain charm with it. He was bored, so he tackled. Five minutes later he was offering me an orange. He had maddening vitality.

As we got down from the crowded train at Kyoto, we heard a tearful child of two or three yell from its mother's back as it was yanked along the overcrowded corridor: 'Anyone who cries will be carried off by the devil.'

Kyoto is in a very cold pocket of the mountains. It was night and Mitsué's cousin Sadamu was at the station in an anorak. He took us to a hostel which had closed down for the holiday and we waited half an hour in snow while he persuaded the manager to let us stay. Inside was a vast area of tatamy, partitioned here and there into sleeping spaces. One was allotted to Herman and me. It was icy, but we had the whole hostel to ourselves for 6s a night, including the kitchen. The two M's went out shopping and came back with steaks for us all, which they cooked. They were good, but cold and I had to stop Herman trying to heat his up over the little pot of charcoal, that ghost of a fire the Japanese warm themselves over. The two M's waited till we had finished before they ate.

In the morning they came round to collect us and we began to see Kyoto.

It was bitterly cold. Herman had on a sleeveless sweater and a light jacket and said it wasn't at all cold. The rest of us suffered silently for one another and the gods. Without Sadamu I doubt if we would have even found half the temples. He turned out to be a young priest and took us into his care.

From the bus Kyoto looked quite ugly. The wooden shacks and shops seemed to have collected beside the streets and against the modern blocks like the débris of a river. Nothing was straight and the sky was quartered with the heavy wirings of trams and telephones.

We got down from the bus and Sadamu began to show us the treasures which lay behind the careless façade. It was like leaving the pushing crowds in the Tokyo Underground for a rendezvous with one or two delicately solicitous Japanese, vaguely apologizing for their countrymen as if they did not really exist. Streets and crowds seemed unimportant so long as they sheltered this special charm. They may even have been responsible for it. With the temples it was the contrast which created order, just as the apologies produced an intimacy.

It was still the New Year holiday and a lot of people were walking through the temple gardens, taking pictures of their families under the Arches of Peace. All the girls were in white or pink kimonos, shuffling along on little pigeon-toes, their hair high-lacquered, their faces cloudy as peaches. I wondered had they put on kimonos for the temples or for the holiday.

In a Japanese house the lady should always sit with her back to the view, or if there is no view, to the scroll in the alcove, so as to be seen in the most attractive setting. Outdoors they seemed to follow the custom. Wherever we went they could be seen deploying almost unconsciously against every possible background. In gardens, by lakes, on bridges, they stood as if before mirrors, in mutual admiration with their surroundings. They even seemed immune to the cold, like brilliant, brittle porcelain. Beside them, Mitsué in her duffle coat looked very human.

In the evening we returned to the hostel. Sadamu said it was so crowded in his house they might as well stay with us. We made stone hot water bottles and put beds down all over the floor to keep warm in. Like that we spent the whole evening, eating and talking. There is no such thing as a bedroom in a Japanese house and beds don't have the same significance they do here. But the girls all wore combinations and well-knotted kimonos just the same.

After eating sukiyaki in bed, we listened to Sadamu playing a flute and then we all fell asleep in a great heap.

In the morning we visited the Koldiji temple to see the Miroku Bosatsu, Messiah of the Future. The statue was a slight, seated figure, carved from maple, slightly decaying, but strangely vital, perhaps because of it. One hand was lifted in meditation, its body graceful as a cobra's flowering hood, mouth benign as in sleep. Yet it did not sleep. It was merely at an end. Here was an image of the complete destruction and disordering of every human sense into the human dream of immortality. Here was the after-life, the future, the re-birth. 'Wait,' was all it said and one was terrified, for one could not wait. One's senses were secure and insistent on the fact. One could only watch in horror as the world turned over and began to putrefy and the Miroku Bosatsu offered you one more chance to be re-conceived into immortality.

Not long ago a student hit the headlines in Japan by leaping upon the dais and kissing the statue, breaking one of the fingers of its upraised hand as he did so.

Yet the statue is neither man nor woman.

The third day was much like the first: walking through snow from temple to temple, bickering slightly, occasionally getting hot soup or tea if Sadamu knew the priest.

Like Japanese faces, the temples soon ceased to look alike and I was hungry to find each new one, hidden behind its wall or hill: private property one could yet explore. Each temple was like a grove in the crowded city. Set in its garden or compound, it combined the peace of cloisters with the peace of countryside. In fact the architecture followed the course of the landscape. Roofs were precipitous as mountains, upturned like pine branches. The temples seemed to have dictated their settings, not vice versa.

Yet it is not only art which imitates nature in Japan. 'Very few effects are accidental in this country,' said an American we walked with. 'You see those pine branches? The needles only point upwards because each twig is pruned. If they clip the leaves back each year the whole tree will become stunted and crooked like the trees in Japanese painting.'

It is not until one sees the Japanese landscape that one realizes how realistic their art is. I always thought it must be a basic difference in style or eyesight, but there are the toy mountains like stage scenery on the plain, the little brush-strokes on the tufted hillside, the clouds like streamers, the eccentric cherry boughs, the hunch-back pines, the sun like a porthole in Mount Fuji. It is not the art which is stylized, but the landscape which is somehow created. Like everything else in Japan, the landscape is a product of the imagination.

That night was our last at the hostel. Next day I went alone to Nara, first capital of Japan. Mitsué came with me on the train as far as the first station. I never saw her again.

More than a year later I had this letter from her in England:

'Dear Hugo,

How have you been? It's long time since I saw you last. Just yesterday I heard from Henri that you had been sick in hospital. I hope now you are fine and you enjoy lovely weather there in England. I think your country has beautiful scenery the same as our country has. Everybody seems so happy and fresh. In spring we always expect something new and wonderful. Anyway everything on earth loves this season I think.

Well, I think I'm going to tell you myself. I graduated from high school in March. I'm now working one of the biggest trading company in Japan. My part of the job is to export cans. I like it very much. It's very interesting. You may have seen canned Mandarin oranges called 'Tokyo Menka'. Yes we sell to London. By the way what do you do these days?

You had such a wonderful experience when you were young, yes of course, now you are young. The experience helps you. Experience is a good teacher.

You remember? Hugo whom I know was very short temper. When I met a person who is like you sometimes, I remind you and you said to me "Please don't mind if I get mad, this is English nature." So I try not to mind any time.

I know they must have nature like you. But I know you are a nice boy who likes modern jazz.

I'm looking forward to finding the book "Hugo's Travels Alone" at book store. Did you write or when do you finish to write?

Don't be surprised if I wrote. Wouldn't you write a letter to me sometimes when you are at a loss for killing time?

Please take care of yourself.

Your good Japanese friend,

Mitsué.'

Nara

When I arrived in Nara I decided to do nothing. I was in a
very good mood and thought I could get away with anything.
I wanted to be passive. I would just wait and see what happened.
I found a café and sat down with my suitcase showing and a
map spread out. When the coffee came I asked if there was a
youth hostel in Nara. The waiter didn't know but someone
overheard me and said there was one, but it might be closed.
How about the YMCA? It was just round the corner. He
would take me. When we got there it turned out to be just a
school – no rooms. A European lady who was there said I
should try the university. She said she was just going to a
meeting of the English Speaking Society and I could go along
if I wanted. She couldn't put me up, but she had an idea who
could.

At the ESS I was welcomed like an invited guest. There
were about twenty people of all ages sitting round a Japanese
room, drinking tea. Everyone wanted to know something
different about me, but they all wanted to know first what I
thought of Japan. What had I expected? Was I surprised by
what I saw? The Japanese have a pathological fear of being
misunderstood or under-estimated, and since they have turned
their backs on their 'ancient traditions' and embraced the
Western way of life, they have looked more and more to
the West for recognition of the feat. In a way they are like

foreigners in their own country, imagining slights where none exist.

At one point I was handed a magazine open at a certain page. On it were four pictures. The first was of a girl sitting elegantly in a Japanese room, holding a writing brush and making a letter on a scroll. The second, admittedly, was an absurd picture of a girl having what looked like a swim-suit tattooed on her naked back. The third was a kindergarten illustration of a rickshaw and the last was an old photograph of two women, one in a kimono, the other in sadly out-moded Western clothes. Was this the Japan I had found, they asked. No. Yet these were pictures from European school books. Why? How could they get away with such misrepresentation?

It was a good topic, but I chose only to defend the rickshaw picture. This the article objected to because rickshaws were long ago abolished in Japan as a kind of slavery. The runner even had bare feet, they said. It was touching how much it meant to them. But didn't they realize, I said, that this was just something for the imagination of children to rove on? They could learn soon enough that it was history. What good would it be to tell them Japan was just like America? Anyway, people in England at least had always had dreams about the Orient which ran parallel to their knowledge. 'Confusing it,' said one of the crusaders, 'I think some people in your country like to live in the past and forget the present, which is not so glorious.'

'We are as interested in seeing what is different about a country as how it resembles our own,' I said.

'I think you are right,' said someone else. 'This is a very bad magazine.' He had sensed hostility and his nature had forbidden it. We went on talking about Japan and my route from England. Then it was time to go and several people offered to have me to stay for a night. I was to move around. We put my suitcase on someone's bike and pushed it through the dark streets towards his house. On the way I tried to photograph some workmen mending the road by the light of flares.

The first person I stayed with was Mr Takeshimiyazu. He had a very nice room with bunks, hi-fi, tv, a heater, a map of the world, a photograph of the Miroku Bosatsu and a print of something it resembled: the Mona Lisa.

In the morning began four days of bicycling leisurely round the most beautiful city in Japan. Nara is a very old village-city, falling through the trees of a hillside park where deer wander. All round are paddy fields, divided by avenues and bridges, and among the paddy fields are the antique, empty temples, two thousand years old. In Kyoto they were perhaps too crowded by the town, too much like museums, clearings in the neon. Some were frankly commercialized. One Sadamu took us to there had a Zen garden of raked sand and rocks – the rocks were arranged in the Chinese character for 'heart' – but on the wall hung a notice:

'Scrubbing, raking, brushing, sweeping. Your labour of love is willingly accepted if you wish to make an exercise in Zen. (250 yen – 5s – for 10 minutes).'

Yen Buddhism is a thriving light industry in Kyoto. But in Nara the gardens are full of pine needles and the pine trees bow down over the roofs. In one temple where the giant Buddha sat, I did however buy a poem. For a shilling it was wood-block printed in my notebook and Mr Takeshi wrote a translation of it underneath (every day he shortened his name by one syllable, till in the end it was just 'Tak'):

> If you go to see the Buddha from nearby
> You must suffer the loneliness of his spirit.

In a garden at Kamakura there was another giant Buddha, about thirty feet high. If it had stood up it would have been a hundred feet high and in case it ever decided to there were a pair of huge stone sandals behind it, each with a prayer written inside. In front of the statue was a tactfully worded notice: 'Please do not climb on the statue as it is considered sacred.'

In the evening we went back to Tak's room and a girl came round to cook some noodles for us. She was Tak's girl-friend. He said he thought her face was like a Noh mask. She didn't eat with us, and when we had finished she put some saké on to heat and left. We drank the saké with peanuts and shreds of dried cuttlefish and read the paper. It was January 11, 1964. The two lead stories were 'Johnson Confers with Chiari as Riot Flares in Panama' and a report on the 'Imperial New Year Poetry Party' in Tokyo. 'A record total of 46,886 entries were received for the annual New Year Poetry Party, which was held in the Imperial Palace yesterday morning,' said the article. 'This year's subject was "Rami" (paper). Among the compositions recited yesterday morning were those by Their Majesties, The Emperor and The Empress, and members of The Imperial Family.'

There followed the Imperial poems in phonetic Japanese and in English:

'A sorrowful light
Is projected on Braille dots
And a shadow is cast
As they are raised
On Braille paper,'

ran the Crown Prince's, easily the best.

'The Imperial Household Agency', the report continued, 'announced yesterday morning that the subject for next year's poetry party would be "Tori" (birds).'

The four days and nights which followed were much the same as the first, except that after two days with Tak, I was with different people, according to their spare time. One liked Brahms, another liked the Firehouse Five, a third liked Western girls. But they were all polite, infinitely touching and peaceful as true pacifists. I became convinced, probably wrongly – I would like to believe wrongly – that they knew nothing of the petty antagonisms which are part of everyday life in this country, at home, at work, round any table. Yet the restraint can stagnate. There is a sort of refusal to challenge any relationship with the comment of a single point of view. The Japanese seem unwilling but obedient slaves to convention. I once saw a man standing on a curb in Tokyo, bowing to a taxi, which had just spurted away from the pavement, showering him in mud. (I swear I saw another bow seven times before sitting down to have breakfast with two friends in a café.) Their conversation is the same: civilized, but one-sided. It may not even be a refusal to challenge, it may actually be an inability. Once, when Henri and I got fed up with being stared at in the Tokyo tube, we bought Japanese newspapers and sat reading them upside down. Several people noticed and actually moved up to the other end of the compartment they were so disturbed. One young man became transfixed as I pointed out an amusing paragraph to Henri. He got out of the train to escape the apparition, thought better of it, got back in just as the doors closed and sat down again with his back to us.

Rage in the Japanese male is cut back and cut back, almost from birth, like the leaves of their pine trees, producing the unique but sometimes impotent Japanese sensibility. Girls, being less important, are not considered worth the same training and are usually gayer and more natural. Mitsué for instance would have come over to us and told us we were mad.

The last person I stayed with in Nara was an Englishman from Rhodesia. He'd been to Trinity, Dublin, then begun travelling and had already been going for three years. Canada, Germany, Hawaii, working wherever he went. He was a kind of Englishman rare in England now: confident, patriotic, aristocratic, buccaneering. At 26 he already had a bamboo cigarette holder.

In Nara he was teaching business men to speak English and saving £100 a month – he said. He spoke Japanese, had a Japanese girl-friend, a Japanese mistress, and a black-belt at Japanese swordsmanship, which is called *Kendal*.

At 3.30 in the morning we got up for me to watch him practise this sport.

It was still dark and raining as we walked for ten minutes, eating mandarins, towards the club.

In the anteroom of the club were a great many men either naked or hung with leather and lacquer armour. Michael buckled on his armour – specially constructed for his great height – grasped his bamboo sword and led me into the hall. All round the long walls men in black armour were kneeling with their heads bowed. At the end of the hall was a small shrine at eye level. A child was beating a large drum which stood in one corner, the strokes gathering and slackening speed. Michael told me to take off my coat and get down on a piece of tatamy beside the chief Samurai. The older men were very still, summoning their spiritual strength and their spiritual defences about them.

Suddenly the drum indicated a prayer. Everyone stood up and bowed towards the shrine, then began to yell the words written underneath it in staccato monosyllables. The prayer sounded like a war-cry. After the prayer were exercises, every movement accompanied by that peculiarly Japanese ejaculation 'Hiye'. Michael darted over to me to explain that the cries were all part of the science, which was one of attack and intimidation rather than defence, and that there were four targets: head, hips, forearms and adam's apple. Then he was back in the line-up of fearsome black knights. Helmets were donned, vizors lowered, and the game was on.

I had expected something more like a fencing match, single bouts between equal combatants. But suddenly, regardless of height or age, they were all battering their opposite numbers about the head and shoulders with a smacking of bamboos and a chorus of battle cries which would have terrified an Apache. Swords whirled in great circles through the air and looking down the room one could see twenty or so rising and falling as in the multiple exposure of a golf drive.

The handle of the sword is held with two hands, as far apart as possible. Arms are held straight and above the head and a stroke is made downwards, with a quick, jerking, jab-and-withdraw action. As the stroke is made, the left foot prances up and forward, coming down with a smack on the floor to emphasize the blow and the cry of 'Hiye'.

I later asked Michael why the sword was always held above the head, leaving the body unprotected. It seemed a suicidal stance to take up. If you got a spear between the ribs the best you could hope for would be to take the enemy with you as your sword came down. But he got very excited and said that no European could defeat a Japanese swordsman. *Kendal* was a method proved in battle by the Samurais over hundreds of years.

Each bout lasted two minutes, then the child, who was also in armour, beat the drum and everyone bowed to one another and meekly exchanged opponents as in a square dance. The fierce bashing continued for an hour and was followed by more exercises, which I at first mistook for a prayer. I obediently took my place in the ranks as before and prepared to kneel, but someone told me kindly to sit down and as I did so I caught sight of my unhelmeted foreign face, grey in a huge practising mirror.

After the session, everyone became naked again. It was bitterly cold, but much to the amazement of some of the younger swordsmen, Michael picked his way through the crowded changing room and into the cold shower.

Soon breakfast was brought into the changing room. There was rice, bean-curd soup and vegetable stew of cabbage and potato.

Later in the morning Michael had to go to Osaka to sell a

little of his own culture to some radio salesman there. I never saw him again.

I am sitting in a little café in a covered shopping arcade in the centre of Nara. The café is called The Dolls' House, but the dolls are made of wood. It is nine in the morning.

I have left Michael and Takeshimiyazu and the others and tonight I travel to Kobe. I wanted one last day alone in Nara, just to hang about and write.

But how do you do it? You can either stay still and write about other people, or you can move about and enjoy yourself. I doubt whether you can write about yourself moving about and enjoying yourself. Consciousness is too unreasonable. It is like a great surface which things jab upon and across at random, some things falling only from the imagination. There is no form to it because there is no end to the imagination. Imagination is stupidity and ignorance, intelligence and knowledge, indefinably mixed forever. But what can you do about it? You've always been taught to fight down stupidity and ignorance, to cover them up with what you are sure of. So the picture you paint will always be false, painted by reason and conscience, instead of consciousness. That's what makes it so hard.

So I will sit very still like a Zen Buddhist and copy out what I see before me. It is more worthwhile to copy out a page of another book than describe a mountain you saw a week ago: Katherine Mansfield, *Je Ne Parle Pas Français*: 'I do not know why I have such a fancy for this little café. It's dirty and sad, sad. It's not as if it has anything to distinguish it from a hundred others – it hasn't; or as if the same strange types came here every day, whom one could watch from one's corner and recognize and more or less (with a strong accent on the less) get the hang of.

'But pray don't imagine that those brackets are a confession of my humility before the mystery of the human soul. Not at all: I don't believe in the human soul, I never have. I believe that people are like portmanteaux – packed with certain things, started going, thrown about, tossed away, dumped down, lost and found, half emptied suddenly, or squeezed fatter than ever until finally the Ultimate Porter swings them on to the Ultimate Train and away they rattle . . .

'Not but what these portmanteaux can be very fascinating. Oh but very! I see myself standing in front of them, don't you know, like a customs official:

"Have you anything to declare? Any wines, spirits, cigars, perfumes, silks?"

'And the moment of hesitation as to whether I am going to be fooled just before I chalk that squiggle, and then the other moment of hesitation just after, as to whether I have been, are perhaps the most thrilling instants in life. Yes, they are, to me.'

That must have been what set me thinking. I sympathise, though I see myself, not as a customs official, but as a smuggler, trying to bluff my way through ports with a lot of goods I don't really understand and certainly don't know the value of. All I know is that I want to get through and not have to open up.

But in the end I have to open up. Alone in my hotel, or now that it is all over and I have rattled home on the ultimate train, I need to remember, to feel again. But how? There is so much more to it than one knows or can ever explain. So much more each day until I decide to stop. The past doesn't slip backwards into the past, it advances day by day, expanding and multiplying like a family.

So what do you do? Scraps? Jokes? Scraps of information? Or a sort of padded-out lie which makes sense? The letters I write are mostly like that. Parodies of what it *should* be like to travel. Letters are so false anyway. They are written by those who receive them. Or else as wedges in a door you think might close. Caricatures of yourself, big enough to fill the empty space or animate the photograph you imagine blurring over. It's too good an opportunity to miss of drawing the picture of yourself you'd always dreamed of. Walter Mitty should have left home and taken to letter-writing. That way he need never have woken up from his dreams.

I am homesick I suppose. So I try to make myself at home by appropriating a coffee bar, sitting quietly in a corner and writing objectively. But why do I feel so exhilarated at the same time? It must be because there is nothing nearby to remind me of the past, or how I normally behave and feel. I can change at will and nobody will notice the difference. I have the illusion of a fresh start at hand every minute. I am responsible only for the future. It must be the dream of murderers: to be unrecognizable, even to themselves; to be able to begin again from each minute. I sit in this café as if I owned the place, or as if at any minute I might own it. Anything I do now is new. If I go somewhere, meet someone, see something, they are mine because they were not introduced to me. They came out of me. I am a roving planet in an anchored system. At last I have taken over my free will from the other influences. Homesickness is a birth pang of freedom.

'The same old flights, the same old homecomings,
Dozens of each per day,
But at last the pigeon gets clear of the pigeon-house . . .
What is home but a feeling of homesickness
For the flight's lost moment of fluttering terror?'

(Rilke)

The noodle vendor's flute

I arrived in Kobe ready to go on board my freighter for Sydney, but it was still in Yokohama and not expected for two days. I had two days' grace but hardly any yen. I began to try to find an address I'd been given in Tokyo, but the person had moved and by the end of a morning of futile enquiries I thought I would go mad next time I heard the sound of a Japanese sucking in his breath through his teeth and tilting his head to one side in the habitual compromise of a negative. If only they could say 'no', but 'no' is impolite in Japan and 'yes' is often used instead. For instance where a Westerner answers 'no' to 'Can nobody speak English around here?' a Japanese answers 'yes' – confirming your statement that nobody does. Occasionally you don't even have to put a negative in the question to get the old affirmative negative.

'Why is the museum closed today?' 'Where have all the porters gone?' would both get reassuring nods and yesses.

Anyway I couldn't find anywhere to sleep free, so squeezed into the YMCA again.

Next door to the Y was an illuminated sign:

INTERNATIONAL TURKISH BATH
SPECIAL TURKISH BATH
GRAND TURKISH BATH
MAMMOTH SALOON

205

I went into the Mammoth Saloon where businessmen were waiting for their favourite masseuses. There was a television showing some boxing. Girls in quite decent bras and panties were hurrying about bringing lagers and messages as if they were fully dressed. I watched one go briskly up to an old bald European and lead him away down a corridor. I had the price of a lager but not of a Turkish bath, even an International one. Anyway, I'd been told that this place *really was* a Turkish Bath.

I left and went into a bar called *The $64,000 Question*. I was beginning to understand how so many bars and baths and cafés and clubs could keep going. In his family life the Japanese is severely restricted, socially and sexually, but he feels a gravitational pull towards a broader view from the pace of Western living. The style of a Japanese home and the way of life it illustrates has nothing to do with 'a good time' in our sense of the word. So the Japanese seeks a substitute by forming a kind of public life, separate from his home. In this life he is his other self, his American half. It is for this other Japanese man that the thousands upon thousands of bars and clubs and beer halls have been created.

Here the Japanese is alone, in another world, unrecognizable to his friends. Anyone who talks and behaves as if this public life were his true life is considered 'teddy boy', 'mal elevée', 'not from a good family' and it is true that a girl who seems to be wearing Western clothes a bit too enthusiastically, or a boy with hair tinted slightly auburn, will seldom know much English. On a higher level, those who study Japanese Philosophy at university usually speak better English than those who are doing English Literature – the easier course.

There is very little snobbery in Japan, but what there is has to do with the dignity and integrity with which each person makes the compromise between East and West.

The next day I was to see a version of this snobbery at work. I was sitting in a café called *Bambi* with a very intelligent young man from Kobe University. We were talking about girls and he said he supposed he would have to smoke when he got a girl-friend – a word for which there is no equal in Japanese, or any other Asian language. I asked him what sort of girls he liked and he said Italian, or did I mean for marrying? Later I said I thought a girl sitting near us in the café was rather pretty and he lifted his hand and signalled her to come over. He didn't know her, but he was a man and she was not. The girl came over and the boy explained that I was an English student who would like to meet a Japanese girl. She sat down and spoke her few words of English to me, her soft eyes with their double eyelids clicking up from her lap whenever she spoke. Once, quite by accident, she jogged my friend's arm and he said 'Don't touch me. No relations. Only friend,' and the girl blushed crimson, sure that she had overstepped her role. It was an interesting case of moral snobbery, too Japanese ever for me to understand.

That night I was lying in my bunk on board my freighter, listening to the two fragile, falling notes of a noodle-vendor's flute. I remembered lying in bed in Tokyo and hearing the same haunting sound going through the night. Some ragged middle-aged man squeezing a rubber horn between gloved fingers as he ladled cooling macaroni out of his saddlebags, or pedalled his bike under the neon arches and the left-on lights of office blocks. Once in Tokyo a woman in a kimono came up to me and asked me to read a postcard for her. It was a picture of Hong Kong. It said: 'Dear Mimi. Thanks for everything in Tokyo but you might like to know that since we saw you Dave and I have both got the clap. You might pass on the good news to your friend. Your loving Bob.' I explained the situation to Mimi as best as I could and she smiled gratefully at me, gave me a little bow and shuffled on.

What was it about her smile I was finding so hard to give up?

V – AUSTRALIA

Down at the Mobilgas

The journey began at Armidale where my mother was born, a town 200 miles north of Sydney. We were there for the picnic races, a meeting held mid-week in Australia to exclude the working class and designed to auction off the young ladies to the local gentry. Binoculars scan horseflesh and human alike.

Andy and I were staying with some cousins of mine and the day after the races we set out northwards. We had changed into jeans and straw hats and posted our dark suits to Sydney.

Jungle mists and mellow fruitfulness. The road far below us, then far above, and every feature of the land signposted, being essential. Purgatory Creek. Mulligan's Folly. In Bell-Bird Gully the bell-birds chime like distant sleigh bells. In Grafton 'Zot spat here' is chalked on the ironwork of the bridge.

Within two minutes of walking out of Armidale we were in the back of a station-wagon, hoping it to be a good omen. Already today we have travelled 300 miles.

Ironbarks, koolabahs, wrists of dead gum trees, like memorials on a battlefield. On through sugar cane and banana country. Blue bags over the bananas to keep off flying foxes. Then downland and a view across the Wallam, or mangrove swamp, to the sea.

We sleep on the beach and in the morning set out past the resorts of 'the Gold Coast', which is hard. Hips slung brown and dimpled in their bikinis assert a contrary influence on our tramping. One sees a short cut to heaven.

We watch the gods standing on their waves. This is the walking-ground of the whole surf culture. The worship of the fine gold hairs on the fore-arm of a continent. Near us an Ajax-blond surfie is lifting down his ten-foot surfboard from the roof of his American car. Long beef-strong thighs. How many hours can he cram in?

We walk on. Holiday-makers flash by in their Holdens, Australia's own car. Polished elbows poke from every window. Surf-news on the car radio. Six-foot body-shoots at Dee Why. Tomorrow it's Curl Curl.

Soon we are picked up by a young man from Victoria. He has driven up to Queensland to find his brother, who owes him £5. He sets us down in Coolangatta and an hour later picks us up again. His brother has moved north, to Brisbane, where we're driven into town by three yobs in an old Chevrolet.

They have tattoos covering their arms. Kind of inland pirates. They shout at everyone, open bottles with their teeth, brag. One says he once waited four days beside the road outside some godforsaken township and was kept alive by schoolboys giving him their lunches. 'You know all this shit you hear about northern hospitality? Well, it's all fuckin' shithouse. Ask you in for a beer, my tits. Ask you in for a brawl more like. Nothing better to do.'

Now we're on a tram in Brisbane. I was hoping to see the conductors in topis, but now they wear plastic caps. Our Dutch conductor says he preferred the old cork topis which allowed the air in and 'didn't plow off fen yer stuck yer head out t'findow'.

We visit a friend of mine called Hilary. She is a very attractive girl with a long plainish face and beautiful eyes and legs. She is wearing shorts. She has a friend called Jane and they live in a small flat just outside Brisbane. They are both English. They tell us they have just come back from South Molle, a resort island on the Barrier Reef. They were waitresses there and we almost persuade them to drive us straight up there again. But they take us to Mount Cootha instead and we have a view of hideous Brisbane and a look into a modern chapel upstairs in the convent of the Sacred Heart. Andy talks with one of the nuns and like a fool mentions that we'll be leaving Brisbane either this evening or in the morning, thereby forfeiting any chance we might have had of leaving in the morning, because I see the girls glance at one another knowingly. I was right. They cook us a meal, then run us out of town in their mini and set us down under a moth-bombarded lamp outside Nambour, near a railway. We get over a fence into a small memorial park and kip down under a green bay tree. During the night three trains crash overhead and signals change with a sound like the guillotine. When I wake up I find a little wooden cross at my feet and at my head a monument to the unknown warrior. Handy Andy has found a tap.

After some luncheon-meat and bore water we hitch into Gympie, town of a hundred pubs, all closed. We ask an old fogey where there's a café. 'Don't you have a billy?' he says, 'black fella can make water boil in a cyclone.' Andy tells the man that we don't have a cyclone and we walk on till we find a grocers open, where a bored girl makes us milk shakes. In a shop window next door there is a genealogical tree showing that the Queen is directly descended from Judah.

On through interminable scrub. Dead-living gum trees like dogs, fish, men, antelope. To Childers, a wide colonial township of the Old West, with swing doors, pillared arcades and wagons up to take in the month's supplies.

A circus labours past. A drunk stops in the middle of the road and says he is going to Gin Gin. A gin is an aborigine girl. Gin Gin means plenty of aborigine girls. The drunk has a shining red face and his teeth keep slipping forward. He is a nice old man and he keeps apologizing for being tipsy. 'I was drinking with me brother-in-law, but he went home.' We shoot along the road in fits and starts. Luckily there is no traffic for a hundred miles in both directions.

'Where you fellas from then? You Americans?'

'England.'

'Oh, England, good Old Mother England. O to be in England, now that April's there. So you're seeing a bit of the world are you? What made you come here?'

'We wanted to see the country.'

'I wanted to see the world when I was young, but I was only 19 when the war broke out and me dad wouldn't let me go. All me mates went, but I never went. Had to stay home and look after the property. Sugar. Very important, sugar, you know. In my opinion it's the only worthwhile industry, sugar.'

'Why?'

'Well it's stabilized see? I mean everyone eats sugar, don't they? People aren't going to turn round and say they've suddenly had enough sugar, are they?'

'I don't know, anything can happen nowadays. Things happen overnight sometimes.'

'Not yet anyway, I hope.'

Down at the Mobilgas, outside Gin Gin, with the autos going past so steady and self-righteous. They throw up the dust and the dust settles back over us again when they have gone. We throw stones at beer bottles, chipping off jewels for the coming Stone Age to unearth. It's going to be one of those days. It is one of those days. It's going to be one of those nights. It was one of them last night.

There is a dead flying fox hanging like a paper kite from a telephone cable. A dried-up snake lies in the gutter. Swamp gums, blackwoods, parakeets, kookaburras. The laugh of the kookaburras seems to spread through the bush like a dirty joke. The parakeets streak overhead like green-flighted arrows, aimed at the doughy sky.

After nightfall we pick up a semi-trailer going to Rockhampton. The cabin is like a boiler room because the engine has to be inside to keep the overall length under 45 feet. The great arms of the Yugoslavian grip the wheel and we hurtle over the gutted road. Every now and then we stop and get out for a draught of cool air and a mouthful of cold water from the water-bag suspended on the front mudguard. A rectangular water-bag is as emblematic of the Australian outback as the surfboard is of the coast.

We stop and sleep for a few hours on the roof, then on into rocky Rockhampton and a clean-up in a Caltex station.

I buy a two-month-old *Encounter* with a translation of Baudelaire's *Voyage* by C. D. Lewis. 'One morning we set out, our heads on fire, our yearning hearts sulky with sour unease.'

On the way out of town across the usual bridge, we are picked up by a nursing sister on her way to play a little bowls. She has on a peaked cap inscribed 'The Rockhampton Ladies Bowling Club'. Suddenly she drives over a huge iguana standing motionless in the middle of the road.

'Once went over a little six-foot brown snake,' says the intrepid sister, 'and she flipped right up and came in through the nearside window and on to the back seat, seething about there, so I opened the door and got out and left it there. You have to skid on them to really finish them off. . . . I'll put you boys down here, and don't you go hanging about in this sun without any water.'

Two more rides to The Caves, a two-dog dump where the only car has no wheels or engine. In the pub there is a death notice: 'I Regret To Announce the Death on Sept. 25th of *On Credit* At The Caves, Queensland. Please Beer With Me.' A handsome old grazer comes in, sits his baby boy on the counter and orders a schooner of Mac's. All day we hang about. Somewhere nearby is the tropic of Capricorn, but no one seems to know whether it's up the road or down.

The Caves is a railway station and once a day something called 'The Horror' stops here. By evening we are so demoralized we decide to jump it. We enter the carriage from the off side, turn out the lights and lie down on the seats. Someone opens the door.

'You've got tickets, I assume.'

'No.'

'Where are you going?'

'Depends how much it costs.'

'Mackay'll be about a pound.' He goes away to get some tickets. When he comes back the fare's £2 5s. It's obviously been a long time since anyone bought a ticket. We pay up and get a night's sleep on the seats.

Mackay seems African. There's a sleazy, yellow-haired old river and she has foul, humid breath which she wafts up to us as we stand on the bridge.

Someone offers Andy a job digging a cess pool, but he turns it down. Then we get a short ride to the Panorama Motel on the outskirts of the town. Underneath the new paint of the motel we make out its maiden name: Bona Vista. A memento from the days when Italy was still a figure of speech up here.

All morning we wait in the dripping sun. Looks like rain, Looks like rain. Over and over we speak the words for everyone's hopes. But rain, we come to understand, is in the eye of the beholder. There are places in Australia where it never really rains, but no matter where you go, the phrase is valid. If it looks like rain to you, then it looks like rain. It's a beginning anyway. There's nothing more to be done about it.

In the afternoon a Landrover bears us to Shute Harbour where we embark for South Molle. It is a Butlins with a little South Sea sand sprinkled thinly over the pretty rough ground beneath. There are prefabricated chalets with aborigine names and a wartime atmosphere of cut-price fulfilment. We scrub our jeans in the washroom, which stinks. Things like turnips for tea and after tea we walk to the top of the hill and have a rather beautiful view across the Whitsunday Passage where Cook sailed on his voyage of discovery. There are spotlights of sun coming through the brown clouds and luminous pools of it in the sea.

The island is £3 10s a day, so we only have one day, then back to Shute Harbour eating coconuts, where we wait near some toads under a gnatty lamp. The lamp attracts the gnats, the gnats attract the toads and the toads bounce occasionally into the road and get squashed by cars. You have to wait under a lamp so drivers can make snap judgments about your appearance, the honesty of your eyes, etc.

We get a lift to Townsville with a man whose father is dying there, but in Bowen he meets a woman, so the lift is discontinued. We sleep beside the motorway with potential lifts keeping us awake all night. My sleeping bag is hot and damp and my face and arms sticky with insecticide. In the morning I stand up and look about me. I feel very tall because the land is so flat and my sleeping bag looks so low down and far away. It is covered with rich red earth and dew. We make tea in the billy can. Andy's turn to carry the billy, which clanks when you walk.

This morning Andy is testy. He crept out of his sleeping bag the wrong end and said our trip was losing its sense of purpose (his sense of purpose). I'm too volatile or something. I have no urgency and drivers sense these things. Actually Andy is in love and he can't make up his mind whether he's running away from her or back to her, so he just runs faster and gets testier and bears the road upon his back like a cross.

He also left his second hat in the last car.

We hump our packs and lean off down the road, heads thrust forward like bloodhounds on the trail. Take away our packs and we'd fall on our faces.

Soon a handsome old ranger in a Falcon takes us on to Ayr.

'One of you get in the back and mind my rods.' He has on a wide-brimmed, oily hat and the same Oshkosh work-shirt everyone seems to wear in Queensland: grey with a faint pink line through it. He tells us his family has had a property near here since 1864 and adds 'when my family emigrated from England,' in case we should think they were sent.

In Ayr we buy new hats and haircuts and have huge plates of liver and bacon served by a pretty Italian girl.

Next it's Charters Towers, an old Catholic town with high verandahs, green gabling and wooden crosses on all the roofs. I say I want to look around the town, but Andy says we must push on to Mount Isa at all costs. I don't feel like stamping off martyred, as that would be asking too much of the place, but it seems mad to campaign on in blinkers.

As it was we waited hours in the suburbs and nothing happened all day.

Except one thing. While we were there a girl went past once or twice, then disappeared into a house opposite. A few minutes later her father came down to the fence with a paw-paw in his hand for us. He had just picked it and it was warm and sweet still from the earth. We ate it sitting beside the road, while the girl watched us from an upstairs window.

Slowly it got dark and we spent another night hugger mugger on red volcanic rock thinly disguised as pale green grass. Buzz of cicadas and parakeets like green lightning streak into booming skies. Hoot of beef-trains in the distance and nearer at hand the roar of night transports coming up the hill. It's difficult to sleep in dreams of lying in the middle of the road. Mosquitoes like Spitfires. The bowl of stars tips slowly up. They are set in a broad band down the middle of the sky.

Now we're 40 miles up the road under a rhododendron in Homestead. Most of the names you see on a map of Australia represent a single sheep station or roadhouse. This one didn't even have a name. Ten tin huts, a store, a bar, a petrol pump. This is how I remember Homestead, the great industrial metropolis that was once a hole in the road.

Maybe one car sends up the dust each hour. If it's my turn I bolt out of the shade, thumbs wagging, eyes pleading, but as

soon as they see me, a dazed, pre-occupied look comes over
their faces and they swerve to avoid the alarming apparition in
khaki, that out-of-work guerilla who seems to be getting at
them in some way. Perhaps Andy is right and I just don't
transmit urgency. The truth is I rather like just lying about in
the dust, reading and smoking and going over to the pub when
it opens. Anyway I don't notice any immediate acceleration in
our progress when Andy's in charge. It's my belief that certain
people have a deep-seated compulsion to pick up vagabonds
and others a deep-seated aversion to them. In the end you
learn to tell which is which before they know it themselves.

At last a shearer stops for us. He is driving 350 miles for a
date in Prairie. He has an over-hanging upper lip which makes
his cigarettes point downwards. He looks like George C. Scott.
He says he has no time for young girls. He's not the kind of
fool who drives 350 miles for a peck on the cheek. What is he
doing out here, this swordsman? He certainly doesn't do it for
love of shearing. He tells us that what he'll do tomorrow will be
the equivalent of carrying a sheep four miles and walking
twelve. But the rate is £8 10s per 100 sheep shorn and a 'gun'
can shear 200 a day and if his back holds out he can gross
£2,000 per annum, working only eight months of the year. He
says he is planning a trip to Europe for the winter. He and his
brother are nicknamed Saturday and Sunday because they are
ex-union. They are fast shearers and hard livers. They are the
mercenaries, the carpet-baggers, the lone rangers, the wildcats.

Sensible Creek – a trickle of water, Breakfast Creek – nothing.
Silver-leaved iron-barks. Gum trees in the sandy creek-beds.

Prairie, and our long shadows spread down the main drag.
Cars are coming in from nearby stations for their beer. Black
men wander about here and there trying to be of service, half
unaccepted, friendly, shy. Once they were beautiful in the
manner of their country. But their country is being changed by
a people more beautiful than they, so that they have become its
jackals, its gnawed bones. They were charred when the country

was created a desert. But the country is deserting them. It is leaving them, as it leaves its gum trees, long-standing after they have died, in a mockery of their former lives. They gravitate towards the pub, uncertain what the law is nowadays about them drinking. . . .

The Beatles' gay affirmatives fill the saloon.

The shearer comes out of the washroom with his hair wetted. He goes over and cleans up his car for the seduction. Then he fetches a heavy-set, plainish girl out of the public bar and they go off to Hughenden for the night.

A Scot comes out and talks to us. I go in to have a drink with him and he tells me he'd give anything to be back in Dundee. He is lonely, he tries to push a 10s note into my hand. He tells me he once had £300 in Townsville. He gives me some names of taxi-drivers in Alice Springs. I can see that he needs his dour northern land.

Outside people keep offering work to Andy, who is a barrister. But he is beginning to be rather ashamed of it and won't shave.

I snoop about for lifts and find a trucky mending his lights. 'Ah ha ha, I got the message, I got the message,' he is muttering to himself.

'Your back lights still aren't working.' I tell him.

'We're not going backwards, not tonight, sonny.'

'Can you give me a lift to Hughenden?'

'Sure.'

'What about my mate?'

'Up to forty, no more.' We fetch our packs. 'Come on, we just left.'

Straight on till morning

Next morning we shave sitting in a field in Hughenden. Later a beef dealer takes us over the bad road to Richmond. Andy pretends he's a hardened old digger and talks about breeds of cattle and wool prices. But no sizing-up goes on anywhere here. Anything one says is merely superimposed on what one really is. Or what they would have one: sensible, adult, predictable, permanent and appreciative, in short, human as they. With them there is no struggle for new words. Words flow quick and sure as their stylized, gentle greetings. 'G'day, how are yer?' 'Looks like rain.' 'Be seeing you then.' The Australian is straightforward and open-hearted, but he is also materialistic and immutably earth-bound. Sometimes I feel them looking at me as the grain must look at the chaff, still eddying giddily, about an hour after the winnowing.

Englishman: 'It's possible.'

Australian: 'But unlikely, boy.'

In Richmond we swim in the green water of the public bath, while hawks wheel above us, thinking we are drowned sheep.

After lunch we move straight on to Julia Creek with two shearers. 'There's a crate of beer in the back if you feel like it.' We open the bottles on the side of the truck. The beer is cold and fizzy. The bottles whistle in the wind as we bring them to our lips. We lie back on some old sacks. It's a hard life you might say. . . .

In Nelia the car comes to a slow stop. Something wrong with the cooling system. 'She's a good car. She won't go past a pub.' There are blacks on the verandah underneath potted ferns and caged cockatoos. Whites inside in the cool, dark bar, talking cricket with a Kiwi in a New Zealand cricket cap. If a New Zealander isn't talking Rugby, he's talking cricket. And if he isn't talking cricket he's too drunk to talk at all.

Flaming Tree Creek, Afternoon Creek. 'To which particular names adhere by chance. From custom lightly, not from character.' Thom Gunn.

So far I have seen no emu, koala, brown snake, jack rabbit, or kangaroo. I turn around but they duck back down their burrows.

Julia Creek, which is a town, not a landmark, has a thin coat of locusts over it. The cloud expired here last week and millions of flies are now settling on their crisp, stinking carcasses. There are heaps of them beneath every lamp post, on every window sill, on roofs, and in the gutters. They chose a good place to die. The town is a necropolis. There is a sour look about it. The buildings seem vaguely rancid, the trees petrified, the dogs mangy, and the inhabitants all seem to have the death-wish upon them.

It is 6 p.m. We hang out our thumbs. Flies come at us like reporters round an accident. There is a boy called Gary with two suitcases and an umbrella. He has to reach the Mount Isa Mines by tomorrow for a job. No cars to be had, so we sleep on the cracked, locust-scattered earth outside the town.

In the morning the flies start up again. During the night 'Wally' seems to have joined us. He gets up from behind a bush and walks over, swatting flies. Gary is still here too, though he sat by the road half the night in case something went through. Gary, Wally, Andy and me. The ten little nigger boys in reverse. I say we should split up, or hitch in relays, but Julia Creek angst seems to have affected them and they sit around playing cards on one of Gary's suitcases.

I walk up the main street to buy some cigarettes. There is a man sweeping up locusts outside the Town and Country Club, or rather redistributing them. He gives me some cold water for our bottle. He is from Leipzig. He says Julia Creek is the worst place he has ever been in. It is an old, forgotten settlement and the town and countrymen hate newcomers. They are taciturn, frustrated and in-bred. I ask the station master in his big house when the train goes through west.

'Who told *you* to come over here,' he says.

The train to Mount Isa goes at 5 o'clock, so we decide to jump her if we're still here by then. Meanwhile we haunt this ghost town. Gary sells his electric razor in a pub to pay for his train fare. He has too much luggage to jump with us. Wally finds a few old beer bottles and collects enough on them to pay his entrance to the swimming pool. He has WALLY home-tattooed on his right shoulder, PAM on his left, and TRUE LOVE across his groin.

The train is two hours late so we have the dark on our side. Eight o'clock comes and we lurk quaking behind some sleepers. Men with lanterns walk past scaring daylight out of us. We see Gary standing with his umbrella like a saint in a halo of light on the platform. We move behind a signal box. A lantern swings by and we scramble under the box and into some stinging nettles. This is all wrong. You have to bluff your way, look official, ask the way, wear your hat, smoke. But Andy is the full Scarlet Pimpernel and is going to terrify himself if it's the last thing he does.

Suddenly the train is in and we start to board her like pirates with grappling hooks. A lantern approaches and back we dart into the shadows. Wally has left his Gladstone bag lying beside the rails. Will it be seen? The man walks along tapping the wheels with a hammer. He looks briefly at the bag and passes on. We climb into a truck and flatten ourselves against some iron pipes. I feel my sunglasses break in a pocket somewhere. Footsteps pass back and forth beside our noses.

We don't breathe for ten minutes. Then the diesel starts ticking over like a car engine and we begin to move. I turn over and look up at the sky and see the Southern Cross swinging carelessly, like a necklace, low in the sky.

An hour later we're in a siding in Cloncurry. Yellow light pours in on our fugitive shapes. Our packs stick up above the skyline, offering their hunched shoulders to the executioner. This is the end. We'll be shunted into a shed, unloaded and locked up. Another train passes slowly and the driver looks in on us without interest.

Much later we move on again. I sleep a little on the tubes, but it is very cold. Over the side is tussocky bull-land in the moonlight: part of the old Cloncurry station, once the largest property in the world.

In the morning the country is softer: rolling foothills, wild flowers, white cockatoos and chequer boards of magpies, falling from the gum trees with their cries of children.

The railway bends slowly through the landscape and we have to keep down on corners, because of the guard who is sitting on a step at the back. Soon we will have to jump. But when? Which side? 'Jump when she slows down on the next corner.' Andy is on the linkage. Wally and I over the side. Which way do you face? I try to remember the buses in London. I jump and fall flat on my back and see Gary's face laughing down at me from a window. The guard watches us as we walk away across a swamp. Three minutes later we are in the back of a truck and going into Isa. Wally gets down at the Mine Employment Agency. That's the end of his journey: not even work, but the grind looking for it. When *we* arrive we eat, sleep, write up our journals, wash out our jeans, but for him the end of the journey is just the beginning. It makes one realize the different motives people have for doing the same things and that they are not really the same things at all.

The following day Wally stopped Andy in the street and

asked to borrow ten bob. He had already been to the vicar and got five bob off him for clipping his hedge.

We wash in the usual garage and then telephone a journalist friend of Andy's. He has a cubicle in a nissen hut which he shares with a miner called Dennis. He says Andy and I can sleep on his floor.

In the evening Andy and his friends go off drinking together and Dennis kindly asks me if I want to go to a dance. He has on black jeans, winkle pickers, white T-shirt and half a ton of Brylcreem. He asks me whether I'm going to change. I say no and he tells me not to worry, the girls round here like bodgies, the bodgier the better. He turns up the radio, gyrates. He is an interesting hunk of teenage manhood; almost illiterate, disarmingly frank, coarse, happy and humorously articulate. He is a worker and he knows what comes after work, so when he comes in he immediately puts on the radio and starts looking through a *Blighty*. Children's Hour is still on, but anything's better than silence. At all costs silence must be kept at bay. All round his bed tits are hanging out to dry. A friend comes in with a copy of *Man* he borrowed, comments on the latest outdoor girl on Dennis' wall and goes off with a bundle of *Parades*.

Later on the three of us go into a café and Dennis introduces me to Kaye, Scram, Bev, Janice and Vera. Kaye has her name embroidered on her blouse. I can't open my mouth. We sit round the juke box, mesmerized by a gliding star pattern on it. I buy some Philip Morris, but nobody smokes. I speak to Janice for some time about her name, which I catch as Denise. Dennis is drinking milk. I begin to feel I am cramping his style, which is considerable. He says he has to see a friend and why don't I go on to the dance. I go. On my ticket is printed *Ladies Auxiliary* 2/-. I dance with Janice and Bev and Kaye. Then I go home and lie down on the concrete beside Dennis's bed. Much later he brings home a girl-friend and stubs my toes as he opens the door.

Next day we look around the town. I imagine it to resemble an old Californian gold-mining settlement. Money is on everyone's lips and in every language. We hear Spanish, Dutch, Greek, Arabic. £40 a week? £50 a week? More if you're willing to risk your life in a new mine. And nothing to spend it on but beer. Nobody drinks anything but beer outside the cities. The only question is how much you drink. There are drunks everywhere. Men of all colours, waiting around for work, leaning against the buildings, their great shoulders going to waste. There are two men available to every one needed and one girl to every five men (excepting Dennis).

We hitch ten miles down the road to an aerodrome and then have to wait a long time on a speedway with the cars going past like deerbot flies. A private plane lands on the airstrip and I go over and ask the pilot if he's going to Alice Springs, but unluckily he's just come from there. An hour later a car going about seventy brakes and grinds to a halt a few yards from us. It is going four hundred miles in our direction. We settle back against the comfortable seats and feel slow involuntary smiles spreading over our faces at the thought of the miles ahead, already conquered in our minds. After a long wait one feels a certain smugness at getting a lift as long as this one. It is the smugness of being right after all.

Our driver is something very rare, an Australian interested in seeing his country. He has bought a camera and is driving to the four corners of his world. Darwin, Perth, Adelaide, Sydney. Just for a holiday. He stops to photograph some lilies in a creek, and some beautiful long-haired cattle. He makes me realize how far I have been to look at everyday things and perhaps how ridiculous it is to go batting off across continents, trying to understand them by racing on each day to a new town, sleeping beside roads, forcing myself against the roughness of the countryside, a roughness which can be found almost anywhere.

I too am taking photographs, but when I return and see them printed I notice how familiar those far-off landscapes seem and I can almost recognize my own home in each of them. Perhaps it is a trick Australia plays on all its would-be tourists. There is a quality of anticlimax about the place which only emerges in retrospect. Perhaps if we'd had a car we would have seen this as we went along, but when you're hitching you are one with the dust and the road and the chance of a lift before nightfall, and one also with the anticlimax.

At the Darwin turn-off we are set down and immediately get on to the Alice road and put the mosquito net over us to keep away the flies. Whenever a car comes along one of us has to disentangle himself like some escaping animal in Zoo Quest. It's going to be a long wait. As night falls the flies drop off and the mosquitos start up. They make us feel paranoic and we hurl insults at the passing motorists. 'Don't stop', we growl. 'Don't stop if it's going to strengthen that fearful self-esteem, that pride of ownership you guard so carefully from us. Shake your head at us, say "I'm sorry, boys" to yourself. Run your hand over the clean, empty plastic seat covers. Smile at us and we will smile back, for we can see the varnish already beginning to flake.' No, give me the yob who tries to run you down, laughs, yells, and screams off. He at any rate flings it in your face.

It's terribly ungrateful, but that's the way one goes on, even after a lift of 400 miles. One gets spoilt. One gets to think it's every car's duty to stop.

All the same, we get to Tennant's Creek that evening and are now in a billiard parlour-cum-barber shop in the main street. This used to be a gold-mining town, but the gold ran out and now there's only tin left. I ask someone if there's been much traffic through and he says:

'There were two girls here about a month back and they waited a whole week for a lift. Every day I'd wake up and look out the window and there they'd be on the other side of the road. In the end they had to turn round and go back. You won't get a lift out of here easily mate, not this week.' You trust him as much as the other man who tells you you're bound to get a ride within half an hour. We know that there's a chance and also that there's no chance. It's a free country and there's free-will and madness to be reckoned with.

We give it a try, but after half an hour we give up and find a place to sleep. I have just about got used to sleeping out and I sleep almost soundly, my right hip in a scooped-out hole.

In the morning we move to the Ti-Tree roadhouse with some Yugoslavs in red shirts. The Australian pub, verandahed about, is a ship on a lonely sea and the sailors in this one seem to be from all over the world. Everyone is talking very keenly about horses. There is a fat old aborigine woman called Pamela drinking brown ale and she is asked in behind the bar to see the latest baby.

When we are all drunk enough to go ninety we get into their car and go. The road is straight and made of bitumen by the Americans during the war. Here and there are windmills marking the bores of the old stock route from the north. They stride across the landscape with fifty-mile steps. The country grows wilder, lifts shoulder bones of rock and ant-hills like red snowmen standing ten feet high, stalactites of thousands of little dead insects. The road pierces through the flat-topped mountains and there is the Alice like a garden before us.

It is Good Friday and everything is shut up, so we look for the creek and roll out our sleeping bags in the dried-up bed. Out of the white sand grow the huge ghost-gums, wild with luminous paint and we look up into their filigree stems against the reddening night. A drunken abo is singing to himself down the stream, magpies fly over with their sticky gargle and an organic batter of wings. The sand is comfortable for sleeping, but when you change position the lumps turn against you. No mosquitoes, but everywhere ants, which crawl slowly over my eyelids all night.

It is Saturday morning and we are having breakfast in an

Italian delicatessen. There is a Chinese woman talking Chinese to her daughter nearby. This is not at all the last outpost of civilization, but a rather well-appointed neat little holiday resort, with big hotels and curiosity shops.

We walk up the main street and buy postcards. 'The Australian Aborigines make excellent stockmen', allows a big-hearted caption writer on one of them, but it's hard to believe that the stagey cowboys in ten gallon hats and high-heeled boots have ever been on horseback. To photograph, or not to photograph? Squat, thin-legged, the women big-bellied with miscellaneous sperm, or hunger, perched on the pavement outside the greengrocer's, seem short enough of pride that one hesitates to threaten the failing store.

In the shops are aborigine curiosities for the tourists; wooden snakes and lizards and patterns on bark. These are mostly made on the missions and sold by the missionaries in Alice Springs at worldly enough prices. The female mission-ary who sells me a boat hacked out of a piece of wood for 25s has a large bite mark on her neck which she seems unaware of. Unfortunately I only discover later that exactly the same products are on sale in the bush for the price in pence.

The best job held in Alice Springs by an aborigine is sanitary cleaner and we are in a store when he comes in with his wage packet to do his shopping. First of all he gets the notes changed into two shilling bits so he can see how much he's got. Then he begins making his purchases by pushing across one or two florins in exchange for each article.

While we are in Alice a young American takes us in his Landrover to one of the aborigine missions. You have to have a four-wheel drive to reach it. The slippery, dry sand of the creek beds bogs down an ordinary car. I am in the back of the Rover and the red dust shoots straight in the back till I am swallowing it in mouthfuls. It gets under my glasses and in my eyelashes and months later I find traces of it in the pages of a book like nostalgic scraps of confetti.

The American's girl-friend is driving. She goes over the non-existent track with one hand lying in her lap. She takes it too fast and the car leaps about. She looks very attractive driving. Girls often do when they attempt rather masculine things like smoking or climbing, or arguing. They look as though they are only pretending to do them. On the way back she felt sick and I was sitting in the front and she put her head on my shoulder. I had to wedge my shoulder-blade behind the tin seat to hold it steady for her as we went over the bumps.

The mission itself is more like an open prison. There is an atmosphere of hopeless waiting, but also of resignation. The women turn their backs on us and the girls smile slyly, twisting their round bellies inside ill-fitting mother-hubbards. Work is invented for about half the men and the rest hang idle and forgotten in the forgotten shadows of the old outhouses. Dogs trail after them wherever they go and flies settle and re-settle upon them wherever they rest. They are hunters and work is a convention they have never understood. They are nature's children and as with one's own, it is hard to think clearly what is best for them.

A member of the wedding

Easter in Alice Springs is a fallow time for hitch-hikers. But here we sit and hopefully wait for someone to come along who is brave enough to take on the Simpson desert in a car. But few are fool enough, for they can easily put their cars upon the train. We sit on, reluctant to forfeit the 24 hours already invested.

We are between the railway and the road, both of which leave Alice through a canyon in the flat-topped mountains. A nun with a blue scarf has just gone into a bungalow on the mountainside. She takes in flowers and bread. We are to see her go in six more times during the next two days.

There is something mysteriously rewarding, almost invigorating, about wasting days out of your life like this. It is a lesson in patience and relaxation, like Yoga, but you have to know when to give up and we don't. After two days we are exhausted and out of patience. We book seats on the train which goes twice a week to Port Augusta, twelve hundred miles south. For the last time we sleep in the ghost river Todd. 'Usually dry' but for once it rains large drops on to my face. There can't be much water up there in that empty ewer. I think of London insomnia and the long rain.

The following day we are heading south in the train. Camels with their Indian masters stare at us at the water halts. Emus lumber to their feet like startled debutantes and skitter away from the train, lifting their hooves like trotting ponies. All around us the red desert spins like a ring of Saturn.

Exactly eight minutes at Finkie for five ounces of South Australian beer, 'straight out the river', says a Queenslander. There are aborigines standing like lynched men in the black square of shadow beneath the water tower. Another eight minutes at Oodanatta, a phonetic caricature of the aborigine language: Oodanatta chatter, the dry clacking of their carved rhythm sticks. Eight minutes seems hardly flattering for a settlement two hundred miles from its neighbour, but that is its fate.

We eat the bad, obligatory, pre-paid food, sleep soundly in the large Victorian cabin and after 36 hours in the train, hop out at Port Augusta, and take up our position on the far side of a level-crossing. There is a fifty pound fine for motorists who fail to stop, so we are soon on our way to Adelaide.

We see little hopper trucks running over the Donald Campbell salt flats, scraping up the salt like ice rink tractors. It's getting colder, too cold to sleep out tonight, but when we arrive in Adelaide it is dark and Andy immediately gets over a fence into a park and makes himself at home under a tree. I walk to the station, but there is no waiting room, only a gangster cop casting his big shadow everywhere. I ask to sleep in one of the stationary carriages and he tells me I'm not in America now, you know. Englishmen in Australia are often mistaken for Americans because of their expecting us to speak like BBC announcers. In the end I sleep in a bandstand somewhere and wake up to the sound of people walking to work past my head. They look in on me through the bars as I stretch and yawn.

I find Andy where I left him, in a municipal flowerbed. He gets up and we walk through the rush hour to the park and lie down again in the sun and watch some schoolgirls practising baseball. One has on dark glasses and keeps adjusting her hips and dropping catches.

We leave town on foot and then in a Cummings Turbo Diesel, a magnificent dinosaur of a truck with twenty forward gears and four reverse gears and a sort of super-charged driver to crash them in and yell jokes at us above the noise. 'How can you tell an Alitalia aeroplane? It's got hair under it's wings.'

We go through Horsham and Gerung Gerung. Good Australian place-names. In Horsham there's a sign outside a newsagent saying 'Sports Goods—Novels—Easter Eggs.' The Australia beloved of its expatriates. All along the way are fire slogans: 'Charcoal paints a black picture.' And what is a Heart Assessment Centre?

Melbourne reminds me of East Croydon. There are those same curving streets with sodium lamps and a Woolworth's somewhere.

Andy was born in Melbourne, and says that that was enough for him. He gets on to a tram going to the northern suburbs. He wants to reach Sydney by tomorrow. In the end the call of the heart is stronger than the call of the road, and nowhere more than in Melbourne. I get out the map and look for a green patch in which to spend the night. My bed has no trestle, my trestle no bed, and it's going to be a cold evening my friend. It's about 11.30 and the streets are empty corridors. I see a Chinese boy in a duffle coat and ask him if he knows anywhere I can sleep. Perhaps I knew he'd offer me his bed. We go back to his room and he cooks me some noodles, locking the door behind him whenever he goes out to the kitchen. I am here illegally apparently. After eating he refuses to let me sleep on the floor and I fall back fully clothed on to the first bed for a month, while he climbs into my sleeping bag.

Next morning we have more noodles and I set off to find an address a friend has given me. I take a taxi, but the occupant has been gone two years and left no forwarding address.

233

I go to the museum and see Ned Kelly's square armour.

The streets are empty again and the litter is being caught up in little whirlwinds and deposited in corners. Outside the Labour Exchange is a huge Victorian weighing machine with a vast dial and a little panel telling correct weights according to heights. Long ago some friends took my measurements into a shop in New York, to get me some American Levis, and were told that the child whose measurements these were could not possibly exist. The weighing machine says the same. I should be either a foot shorter or two stone heavier.

I soon decide to follow Andy back to Sydney. No doubt there are people in Melbourne besides Chinese and weighing machines, but they are not in evidence. I get on to the north road and am picked up by someone who thinks I am an airman he always picks up.

We pass through Glenrowan where Ned Kelly made his last stand. As we go past a lonely roadhouse my lift says 'All the truckies go in there, sheila with every meal.'

'How much is a meal?'

'Don't know. Never bought one, not like that...' Pause. 'They've got about a dozen waitresses and when you get your meal you're given a room number.'

At Tintaldra we stop at a pub for a drink and a man rushes in after us saying there's about to be a murder. A 'New Australian' is chasing a woman round his car with a pistol.

'These hot-head I-talians, I don't know,' says a boozy old lady. 'We'd better inform the police, if you ask me.'

'Better not interfere,' says an English woman behind the bar, then turning to me, 'Where are you from?'

'England.'

'Yes, but whereabouts?'

'Sussex, where are you?'

'Nottingham, I've been here fifty-three years but I'm still a pommie. Where are you going?'

'I don't know. Sydney.'

234

'I'll see if I can get you a lift along the track. Eddie, are you going to Albury? Take this lad, would you?'

Towards dusk, outside Albury, I slip down a bank into a field to fix up my mosquito net and sleep under it until the dew begins to seep through to my feet towards morning. Then I get up and walk back into the town to get some maps at the Mobilgas. I think I'll go into the Snowy Mountains to Thredbo, the 'Alpine Village'. A couple from Sydney, on holiday in their Holden, pick me up and I sit beside them on the front seat, feeling dirty.

'Of course, Thredbo has been completely opened up by New Australians,' says the woman. 'They can take the cold you see and they love skiing.' Mrs Australia on her immigrants from that mysterious waste-land 'Overseas'.

I spend one night in Thredbo at an Austrian Ski Lodge. There are bearskins on the beds and Lieder songs and wiener-schnitzel, but no snow and no skiing. I move on up the Murray River Valley with its occasional yellow poplar trees glowing out on the ashy hillside like sucked lime drops.

Now Sydney is within reach I seem to quicken my stride, or perhaps my will has started to take a hand in matters and I am beginning to transmit a sense of urgency through my hitching thumb. The last of many Jehovah's Witnesses takes me a few millimetres nearer home. Then an entire wedding stops and takes me on as a mascot, a sort of sweep-substitute, a symbol of endurance, or perhaps of their own generosity. I sit in the back of a big car next to the bridesmaids, who are dressed in pink and have dappled arms and legs and first perms. They turn off before Sydney and I take a bus into town.

VI – PACIFIC–ATLANTIC

Blue Peter

I thought she must be one of the passengers. Visitors were leaving the ship and she had no handbag. She wore black and red. Black hair and red, mediaeval-looking shoes, stitched from a single piece of leather. I felt like going up and saying 'thank God for you', but I thought there would be plenty of time later. We were sailing from Sydney to Marseilles. We would be eight weeks together. For the moment I was certain she would not go ashore. It seemed very important. I watched out of the corner of my eye and she stayed where she was, sitting behind me on a step, watching the people on the quay as they reached out for the streamers.

The streamer-seller was walking up and down the deck. Conditions were ideal for him. There was a strong wind and most of the streamers broke before they reached the sad, uplifted hands forced to be frivolous at the last minute. Already there were big bundles of them round the feet of the wavers, or blowing over and over, becoming litter.

I looked around for the girl. She was standing beside me, her hair blowing away from her white face. I turned back to my friends and waved happily. The boat began to back away from the quay, wrenching at the paper anchors till they broke and blew back in our faces. A few more streamers were thrown but they landed in the water like damp squibs. We had sailed. The Blue Peter was run down. The girl was gone. I walked about the ship, vaguely looking for her and exploring. She didn't come to lunch or dinner, so I assumed she was eating in her cabin or sleeping. My own cabin was empty. Three empty bunks. I sat in it and felt I knew it all too well. This was the steel box that was going to float me across the Pacific and the Atlantic.

In the morning seasickness began. I didn't retch, I just lay on my back with the sickness in my brain like bad news. I lay like that for a day, well enough to eat, but not to get up, so that in the evening I was told that meals wouldn't be brought any more. If you're sick, you're sick enough not to eat the meals they bring. So they stop bringing them. Nobody else was feeling at all sick I was told. I lay back, feeling the triumph of the invertebrate in me. I was a mindless bug. I saw myself sprawled on a specimen sheet, with a pin through my stomach and a short indictment of my loathsome nature written underneath. Why must my homecomings always be tempered with a death wish?

Once I went to the Tourist Bar for some brandy. There was a French boy in there showing round some photographs. I looked over someone's shoulder and saw that they were of the girl I had seen the day before. As soon as I recognized her I knew she wasn't on board and felt sad, but relieved. The boy was saying how he'd stowed away in her cabin on the way to Australia from Tahiti, but hadn't been allowed to go ashore. He was at the moment being repatriated to Tahiti and everyone thought it very fine and wanted to buy him drinks.

Back in my cabin I spoke for the first time with Saïd, the negro cabin boy. He was exactly like Joyce Carey's *Mister Johnson*. He shook me boldly by the hand and said what terrible French I spoke. He wanted to know where I came from and whether my country was independent yet, like his own Madagascar.

'Ah, so Australia is governed by Australians then? That is

very good for them. Much better. Not by Queen Elizabeth then?'

One or two days went by. The screws throbbed behind steel walls. The pressure piled up round my iron box, and it began to get hotter. I was no longer seasick, only vaguely liverish and the ideal conditions for writing which a ship is supposed to afford did nothing to help. There seemed to be nothing more off-putting than the sarcastic-looking green notebook and pen lying within easy reach.

Except possibly a pen and notebook which were out of reach.

I would sit down in front of the three-way mirror and try to screw up my courage by writing out lots of brave resolutions for myself, blackening the page with example-eggs. 'Finish this notebook by Tahiti,' I would put. Now what is that? It sounds like someone knitting a jersey.

The jersey remained unfinished and we arrived at our first port: Noumea, New Caledonia.

I had the telephone number of an architect who lived there, so I rang him up and he said he would meet me in some hotel that evening. I went to the beach and fell with relief into the turquoise Pacific.

For anyone who has dreamt of negresses in red underwear, this is the place. They were sun-bathing all along the beach. I watched two come out of the water all shining wet, their hair tied up in orange handkerchiefs. They threw themselves down in the sand, which immediately clung to their legs and shoulders. Then they got up and stalked off to buy drinks. I walked down the beach with one of the French officers from the boat. At one end, in the shade of a tree, were two French girls. They were lying on their tummies and they didn't look up immediately. One of them had a little line of hair running down her back into her bikini. I said something about holidays to them. Annie and Claudine, a Tahitian. But no, they were not on holiday, their fathers worked here with the administration. At this point, Jean, my officer friend, moved in on my opening and my French was left behind. As for the evening, they could not come out and it seemed strange after Australia to hear that they were never allowed out alone. I heard later that the Australians who come here on holiday can never believe the strictness they find and that they have won themselves a bad name for their disbelief. It was easy to imagine the equation in the mind of the average Aussie tourist. French port = French women = the Folies Bergeres = a challenge to any red-blooded Australian, with the result that they are regarded much as the Americans used to be in Europe: just rich enough not to be chucked out. For some reason it constantly annoyed me to see waiters laughing up their sleeves at this joke they were all so sure of.

In the evening I had a drink with my architect in a hotel bar. He invited me to a Rotary Club meeting in two days time and said he hoped I enjoyed my stay. This was standard treatment from a 'Caledonian' apparently. They value their privacy and resent intruders, especially the vulgar 'Metropolitans' who come here with opinions from France on how the colony should be run.

Later I went to the Tivoli Dance Hall with Jean. It was full of sailors and Foreign Legionnaires and girls of all colours and shapes. I danced with a rather prim-looking girl and for lack of anything better to say, said she had a face out of the 18th century, but she was not amused and I had to sit the next one out with an old Melanesian 'indigene' selling stale sandwiches. She sat down beside me and said she wanted to kiss me.

Everywhere one looks in Noumea one notices the women. They seem more vividly drawn creatures than their menfolk. It is even the women who wear the pads here. On Saturday evenings they play cricket together in the setting sun at the Noumea Cricket Club: Melanesians, with their dark skins and crinkly brown hair, Polynesians with pale skin and straight black hair. Wherever I went it was the women, children and grandmothers alike, who caught the eye and lent the island its flavour.

On the day we were due to leave I went to the Rotary Club meeting. I think the motion of the day was 'Road Safety', but after the magnificent lunch of sea-urchins, and tournedos Rossini, the urgency of it was rather lost. One man did suggest that natives with dark skins should carry something white with them when walking along the black roads at night, but that was about as far as they got.

New Hebrides

E.II.R. R.F. 6d. 2fr. Condominium. That is the inscription on a stamp I bought in the New Hebrides, our next archipelago. 'So much nicer than the French ones from Tahiti, don't you think?' said the woman behind the desk, 'they're so big there's no room to write on the post-cards.' Impossible though it seems, these islands are ruled simultaneously by France and England and the rivalry is almost Napoleonic. It has been so since 1902 when the two countries took over from Spain and someone first made the joke of 'Pandemonium'.

Two ways of life survive, if not flourish, in the same town, in the same street and occasionally even in the same household. There are two languages, two pidgin languages, two currencies, two police forces – with two different uniforms, and two systems of justice, with separate courts. The intent is barely cordial.

Cohabitation seems to have an exaggerating effect upon each country's weaknesses. Here are the French simulating their famous two-faced egalité with the natives to get them to think that they could all one day be French. Here are the last colonial Britons in all their starch-shorted integrity, all their so-much-and-no-more sense of what's what, all their insularity.

The British Residence is even situated on the only isle in Vila Harbour: a birthday cake among the trees, where Mr A. Wilkie, the rather short Resident Commissioner, peacefully awaits his knighthood. Visitors to the island by invitation only, when the residential launch comes to pick you up at the wharf. Appropriately enough, the French Residence is on the mainland, a fine old Spanish villa on a hill, and when a visiting ship passes between island and mainland, etiquette requires that the two national flags be flown, the tricolour towards the mainland and the Union Jack towards the island.

The flags on the residency roofs were recently the subject of a whole chain of acrimonious chits which fluttered back and forth for a few days between the two houses. By God knows what furtive midnight measuring someone had divined the flag on the island to be two feet higher than the flag on the hill. The British were obliged to step down – their flag was coldly lowered to the exact height of its rival.

There is no such thing as *laisser-faire*. All dispatches to Europe are invariably sent in code lest vital intelligence fall into enemy hands. One telegram between plotting British officials was recently signed ' . . . eat this, yours, Peter.'

The two countries meet only at the Tennis Club when one of them holds an open night, and in the Joint Court, when one of them commits an offence against the other. Foreigners settling in the islands have to decide on arrival to which country's laws they are to be subject. But if the case is inter-racial, it is heard in the Joint Court, where a unique amalgamation of justice is administered.

The Joint Court itself is a formidable old crumbling palace left over from the Spanish régime. Within preside two judges, one English, one French, and between them is an empty chair, supposedly for the President of the Court, a dignitary traditionally appointed by the King of Spain. But since there hasn't been a king in Spain since 1936, neither has there been a president of the Joint Court. So the chair remains empty, and 'yes, we don't have a president at the moment actually . . .' people say, as of a tiresome, but unavoidable delay.

An interesting character I met while looking around the place was the court's cleaner, a man called Simon, a native of Malekula Island, who had just been released after serving a life sentence for murder. He had been chosen by his tribe to carry out some kind of vendetta against a neighbouring tribe. Lumbered with the shortest straw, he had set out into the jungle with his banana knife and knocked off the wrong man. He returned in triumph, expecting the outstretched arms of welcome, only to find that his tribe had got cold feet and decided to leave him to it. He was soon picked up by the police and locked up in the white-washed prison behind Vila.

Simon, as he soon insisted upon being christened, was a model prisoner, and when he had been there a few years his gaolers began to relax their vigilance. They would let him go for a swim or to the pictures if he wanted to. Once his old employer on the plantation came to see him and found him in the company of a young girl. 'You must go now,' said Simon to her, 'I have to speak with my old boss.' Obediently the girl let herself out. Then Simon spent half an hour with his visitor and insisted on walking him back to his house in the town afterwards.

He is now thought to be the only known murderer in the entire employ of the Foreign Office. He laughs at the lingering interest of his tribe in the primitive Cargo Cults.

These cults began in New Guinea, long ago before the war and were brought to the New Hebrides by Jon Frum. This was a mysterious, half-mythical little man with bleached hair and a blue coat with shining buttons, who used to appear to the inhabitants of Tanna island in the flickering light of their campfires, while they were slightly sozzled on *kava*.

The gospel of this self-appointed prophet is a lesson to anyone who takes for granted the 'cargoes' which are delivered to him daily by the milkman, the postman and the butcher. His dreams show up our comfortable lives with feats of imagination that would astonish the best science fiction writers.

Like many other people from isolated communities finding their voice for the first time, he wanted to know where everything came from, and what it had to do with him. The shouting white man came from another island. That was easily explained. But did his supplies come from the same source? Magic was taken for granted, so with a little of the wishful thinking endemic in these islands, it was not long before he came to the conclusion that the beautiful cargoes he saw so eagerly commandeered at port and airport were meant for the original inhabitants of the island.

Some said Jon Frum lived in a volcano, which would one day erupt, joining all the islands together and making them rich. Others said he was king of America, a white negro who would come and drive out the white man and replace the hated pound that they never seemed to have enough of with Jon Frum's currency, printed with the head of a coconut. Some of this new money actually appeared, and they thought that if they all boycotted British currency, the Europeans would be obliged to use their own and would slowly slip from power. They accordingly began an orgy of spending in European shops in order to get rid of the stuff. Some even hurled their long-hoarded savings into the sea. One man came into town with £100 worth of gold sovereigns which had not been seen since 1912, when they had been paid to all the chiefs who accepted the authority of the new government.

The policy of Jon Frum was not entirely negative though. As a purely temporary measure, to stave off famine till the good ship Lollipop sailed in, he promoted gardening. He also laid out a great road from one of the villages down to the shore at the place where the cargo was supposed to arrive. One white man living near this spot was even obliged to move house lest he turn back the freighter when it arrived. When the road was completed, he organized gangs to clear a vast area of jungle in case the goods were delivered by one of the great cargo-birds they had seen. He even constructed a pathetic land-locked aeroplane which he left on the airstrip as a decoy.

Patiently they waited, but no plane and no ship came. Instead, an army of Americans came. But not to deliver them in the way they hoped. The Pacific war was on. It was a great moment for the cargo cultists. Another phenomenon to be cheerfully reasoned out to their ultimate good. An opportunity was soon given to them. One day a native watching the landings of GI's noticed that one of them was black. At first he thought it must be another islander, then he noticed that the stranger was strong and tall and that he had chewing gum and cigarettes like the other Americans. He was a spy. He was a prophet of the great army of black Americans which Jon Frum was going to deliver them with.

The good news spread round the islands like fire. It was soon well-known that the negro came from a great brother nation to their own and that a black army was on its way from America to drive out the white man and – somehow – make them all rich.

They adapted an American flag to be their own, and they waited, more or less happily and more or less rebelliously. But no army came with their salvation.

During the years which followed the Jon Frum legend was slowly changed, dissipated and modified. Now it was Jon Frum's son who would go to America to seek the king, or his sons were coming from America, or his sons had now taken over and were both setting out to find a king. The defeat of their hopes lead them to a belief in invisible things. Jon Frum and his sons were said to be invisible to whites and women. The air was also full of invisible aeroplanes belong to J.F.

Since the early days of the cult, its high priests had never been afraid of varying, even contradicting their gospel. But never did anything they give out have anything in it of the puritan, or the mediaeval-European 'asceticism' advertised for them so fervently by the missionaries awaiting a saviour of their own. Rather gaiety and equality seem to have accom-

panied their hopes. They did occasionally stem their dis-
appointments by boycotting the dull, misguided missionary
schools, or by throwing off the absurd mother-hubbards the
missionaries got them to wear and marrying everyone in sight.
But they can hardly be blamed for that. One of them made the
very shrewd observation that the kinfolk of the missionaries
in business and government seemed to live by yet another
moral code. Their own alternative doesn't seem so bad. 'It
was rather an emphasis on purity of heart and freedom of self
expression', says Peter Worsley in his book on the cults, 'to
such an extent that the sexual act was to take place in public,
since there was no shame in it; even irregular liaisons should
be open affairs. Husbands should show no jealousy, for this
would disturb the state of harmony which the cult was trying
to establish.'

One could perhaps understand them, their bewilderment at
our ways, the conclusions they arrived at, by having the
civilization of a stray planet suddenly revealed to one and
being asked to relate it to one's own way of life.

Next day we woke in Santo, another port on another island in
the New Hebrides. I looked out of my porthole and saw a
steaming jungle literally overhanging the roofs of the town
like a tangled forelock. The jungle was the colour of moss,
or seaweed, and it came right down to the quay from the hills.
It seemed to be forcing its settlers back into the ocean. This
was an island which allowed the sea no part of it, not even a
beach. It seemed to be trailing its tendrils straight into the water.

I went ashore. It was mid-morning and there was no one
about. Only the whirr of cicadas and a big coconut crab walking
down a palm tree. I walked up the road, trying to find a shop
to buy some bread. It was a long, disjointed, unintentional
township, spread along about two miles of surprisingly good
bitumen. There were one or two stores lying hopefully open,
but no one inside to do business. I wondered why we had come

249

here, what France required of this backwater. A Landrover appeared. One of the ship's officers was driving and he asked me if I wanted to see the Japanese fishing village. He said it was the only thing worth seeing. I got in and we drove a few miles through the trees to another part of the coast.

Suddenly there were Japanese everywhere. Pale little men dressed in furs, running in and out of a large building in the humid midday. The building turned out to be a freezing plant. The men were transferring tuna fish from it into a little white ship flying the Japanese flag. I could see them working inside with the breath freezing in front of their faces. Each man had a longshoreman's hook which he swung into the flank of a tuna, heaving it on to a conveyor belt which travelled away towards the ship. The fish swarmed along this belt, glassily cold-dry and hard as rocks. Their eyes were frozen open and their tails sometimes snapped off, leaving jagged edges. All along the belt men with heavy gloves had to keep the fish moving by hitting them with Karate-like blows of the hand. The fish made a clattering noise as they went, then a crash as they landed at the feet of the last Japanese, who hitched them into the ship's refrigerated hold with his hook.

We stood about, staring at the giant, hurtling fish for a while. Then we decided to go swimming. I didn't expect to find anything more than a breach in the jungle big enough for a human to slip into the water, but someone had heard tell of an actual beach with the astonishing name of the Santo Water Ski Club. It turned out to be a ghost-lido, not long abandoned but already rotting back into the jungle, whence it was no doubt wrested. The shower hut had fallen on its side and the diving board had fallen into the water. There was even a shute pointing despondently into the sand. It was impossible anymore to imagine defiant colonials carving out a Pacific Riviera for themselves. Even the white sand was littered with the poorest kind of beachcombings. Coconut shells, fish bones, leaves, old dead crabs. There was a smell of sea-rot and the warm water was covered with a fine film of plankton. It was so salty that everyone bobbed about like corks on the surface. There was a very old Swede from the first class who lay in the water quite motionless with his head and stomach and toes well above the surface.

I forced myself down to the sea-bed and picked up a beautiful shell, like a little flat saucer with a star traced upon it. Even in the water one didn't feel cool though. There wasn't a hot sun, only a humid cloud hanging over the island, blurring the horizon.

In the evening we went to a little dance hall in the town. There was a round bar with a Tahitian band inside it, and Tahitian barmaids, pouring constantly. The band hadn't started playing yet, but the whole of our Italian crew and French staff were already there waiting for the first note before they jumped up, those who were not too drunk, and stumbled over to where a few girls were sitting by the door. I jumped up too, but when my catch stood up she only came up to my first rib. So we sat down and talked. She was a dark-skinned girl with very big eyes and a crew-cut. She drank whisky and we talked in pidgin French about pop stars, and cannibals. Then she said she would come to England with me. But at about eleven her brother came over and said it was time she came home. In the morning our ship sailed for Tahiti.

Tahiti

Some people blossom on board ship. They quickly find themselves at home, with an unfamiliar sense of leadership on their hands and plenty of unsuspecting followers to practise on. Others spend weeks, like prisoners of war, discovering unrealized talents, stitching fantastic fancy dress costumes out of thin air, or writing diaries. Within a day of leaving the New Hebrides for Tahiti I was a chess-playing fungus. All I could do was lose at chess while thinking of all the notes I could be taking of amusing fellow passengers. I felt disinterested in where I was going, nostalgic, hungover, guilt-ridden.

It wasn't sea-sickness any more, but a sea malaise. I was sick of the throbbing noise behind bulkheads, the inevitable ship shape: hollowed out, curved, rounded off, and the sea smell of melting galvanised iron, grease, linoleum and garlic.

A friendly woman called Hilda Bracknell told me I needed to take some exercise, quoits or something, but I simply didn't have her steely will power, or her craving for exhaustion. I even felt no enthusiasm for the one or two Tahitian girls whom the waiters were always fussing round. I knew they were beautiful and I rather liked them, but there just seemed no time like tomorrow for getting to know them. In a way I was lucky, because the segregation of the sexes in the tourist class had some people jumping overboard with frustration. A first-class passenger might feel within his rights asking the steward if there was a spare cabin anywhere, but not a tourist. Tourist class passengers simply DO NOT HAVE SEX.

They were lucky if they even ate on board the *Oceanien*. Meals were disgusting, but at least they formed a common meeting ground for abuse. Our mistress of ceremonies in this field was a tiny lady from Gravesend who called the waiters back ceaselessly to complain about the food and service, each time as wide-eyed and astonished as before.

Unfortunately this was not the only kind of speech she had time for. She was also a chatterbox of the advancing variety. She was one of those women with kind expressions on their faces who come very close up to you and then tell you about the occasion on which they came nearest to being murdered. For Glenda, this had been her marriage. If there was one snippet of information which had really done its time before the mast on this voyage, it was that Glenda's marriage had been 'unconsummated'. I believe I was one of the last people she told, and I was fool enough to show interest. From that moment on she sought me out wherever I went, her mouth poised for speech, an upraised finger pinning the moment in time. It might as well have held a cutlass, and if there had been a plank handy, I would gladly have walked it. When I caught sight of the red steeple of Papeete church, raised above the trees on Tahiti, I made up my mind to go inside on landing and say my prayers.

Within ten minutes of stepping down at Papeete, capital of Tahiti, I felt life creeping into my fingers again. The pavement slid once beneath my feet and came to rest. I ran my eyes lovingly over the square buildings rising at the beautiful angle of 90° to the flat, steady land. At a café on the port called Café Vaima, I settled down to enjoy the details of free-

253

range living, like a newly released prisoner. A Gitane crackled happily between my fingers and a coffee brought back forgotten hungers.

From my table I watched an old Chinese woman in faded blue pyjamas, hanging up onions on a little foodstall, outlined against the ocean. Her busy hands and pale colouring contrasted strongly with the flowered prints of the Tahitian girls, flying by on Mobilettes. They turned their heads towards the cafés, narrowly missing cars. A legionnaire raised his glass to one and she waved her flag of black hair in his direction. Near me in the café two Tahitian girls were sitting on the arms of a legionnaire's chair, their arms round his shoulders. Another girl passed a French boy in the road and pretended to butt him with her knee. She crossed the road and got into a Renault that was waiting for her, kissed the grey-haired man who was driving, and they disappeared. Wherever I looked, white man, brown girl seemed to be the pattern. Except at the table next to mine where two short-nosed Frenchmen leant towards an attractive French woman, and each other. Everything was sleepy and sensual, like a village resisting a siesta. A chestnut stood in its black shadow. Cinzano sunshades. Kodakolor. Two ships at berth: the *Karimata*, the *Oceanien*, and far behind them, where the coral lagoon spilled into the ocean, a thin, white crest, moving forever leftwards.

I walked along the harbour and came upon the alien shape of a French warship, parked like a taxi, close up against the lawn of the promenade. Its storm-grey rose cold and European out of the South Sea blue ink. I could smell the hostile hot steel and iron oxide.

Nearby was the Messageries Maritimes office and I went in, thinking I might try to disembark and catch the next ship on. There was frigid air-conditioning and long motionless queues in front of empty desks, so I left. At least the offices on shore are not hypocritical about their services at sea.

Further on there was Quins Bar, the roughest corner of the South Seas. I raised my camera and a morsel of spit flew up from the mouth of one of the girls standing in the saloon-style doorway and was immortalized on my film. The girls in 'Quins' are supposed to be able to swear in every language in the world, but this one obviously reckoned I was German: she may have learnt her vocabulary from some of the German Foreign Legionnaires stationed on the island. The Legion's second speaking language and first singing language has always been German.

All the bars in town were open and had been since ten in the morning. But the little red-steepled church in the middle of the town was locked up with broken windows. The shops too were open, each with an attentive, withdrawn Chinese behind the counter. In the first one I went into there were postcards for sale of lovely, bare-breasted Tahitian girls. It seemed to sum up relations between the two races: clever, Chinese merchants exploiting idle, sensual Tahitians. I learnt later that day that it is the Chinese girls too, with their cool intelligence and pale, unpurchaseable skins, who attract the rich foreigners and handsome legionnaires. The Tahitian girls are too easy and slothful for them. They drink too much beer and go about in a haze, till their brief, fantastic youth is over and they have to quit the nightlife and assume their responsibilities in the country.

Papeete seemed too much geared to its nightlife and slightly hungover, so I hired a Mobilette and set off to explore the island.

I was soon in a tunnel of leaves, with bright hibiscus blooms hung in it like lanterns. They looked like floppy tissue-paper hats out of crackers. Nearby, but out of sight, was the sea, flashing the reflected sun in my eyes as it found gaps in the branches.

The tunnel ended and I went past several 'Tahitian Village' hotels, with varnished woodwork protruding in all directions and imitation thatch. Then a school, advertised with 'Ecole. $2+2=4$.'

Every few miles there was a little white church with a red tin roof and graceful steeple. Twelve churches in all: one for each 'commune', and round the churches a few leaf-roofed houses, catamarans on end against trees, clothes lines of faded pareous (the Tahitian sarongs) and always children.

Once away from Papeete, I noticed that everyone looked either older or younger than the people in town. There were old men on verandahs and old women looking after hoards of various-coloured children. I passed one old man pushing two little boys in a wheelbarrow. One had black hair, the other blond. It seemed to be the duty of the old folk to look after their children's babies while their children were trying to have more in town. Between the age of sixteen and thirty the young try to glimpse what they can of the outside world as relayed to them by visitors, before their youth is over and the ships have all sailed. It must be the unique sadness of an island like Tahiti, thousands of miles from its nearest continent, that those who live there may never see more of the country that rules them than the images brought them by their rulers. Perhaps the hardness and hedonism in many of them is the result of being forever reminded of their isolation and hope-lessness by the foreigners returning home.

I cruised on round the 52-mile circuit. A speed of 15 mph gives the eye's camera about perfect exposure time for a strange country, but the photographs do take a second to develop. It is what an actor calls a 'take'. I was just riding out of one village when I caught sight of a drink stall beside the road, and a bored girl behind it. I turned round and went back. The girl was sitting reading a novel. She stood up and I bought a Pepsi Cola and a week-old little tart of perhaps bread-fruit, which stuck to the roof of my mouth. I said some-thing about the village and we went on talking across the counter for about two hours. She told me she was half Chinese and that a hundred years ago her family had been forcibly transported by the French from Indo-China to work in the new cotton fields of Tahiti. The Polynesians could never be made to work very hard and France's supply of cotton from America had been cut off by the civil war. She told me that all Tahitians had French nationality and that every young man was given a chance to visit France for two years when he did his military service. But the Chinese Tahitians were still looked upon as aliens and some, including part of her own family, were soon to be repatriated to Vietnam.

Later I met her mother and grandmother, who had once been to Hollywood. She had been a make-up artist and known Clark Gable when he made the first *Mutiny on the Bounty*. I drank coconut milk with them, took photographs of their children and when I got the chance, asked the girl to come out with me that evening. I don't know how I thought I was going to get her back to Papeete. We were twenty miles into the country and my bike had only a luggage rack. It was also beginning to get dark and I had no lamp. It was an impossible invitation, but I was miserable when she refused. She said Chinese girls never went dancing in Papeete. She was not allowed out at night and only went to town once a week with her brother. She had to stay and look after the house. I said I would never see her again and prepared to take off into the gathering night on my Mobilette, when a little voice called after me 'Je crois que vous me devez . . . ' I had forgotten to pay her for the tart and the drink.

It is hard to imagine the Pacific Ocean being small-minded, but when it gets rough the waves are crooked and petty and they throw a boat about like a plastic duck.

On the ferry from Tahiti to Moorea the locals were making hideous faces as they tried to smoke and talk off their sea-sickness. The lagoon was like an ice-rink, but once we came through the gap in the reef the ocean took its revenge. Lagoon and ocean, ice-rink and sea. And you could see the contrast continued between the two islands. Moorea is only ten miles from Tahiti, but utterly different in shape and mood. Tahiti is a pillowy, pastoral down. Moorea is the shot of Bali-Hai in South Pacific. It is wild and mountainous and the crags are circled with black smoke-rings which cast steep shadows down the mountain sides. The island seems to be much more part of the Pacific than Tahiti, which lies at a becalmed mooring, untouched by the storms over Moorea.

There was one other European on the ferry, an artist called Pierre Heyman. I had met him briefly when we were lifting our bikes aboard. He had a bag of paints with him and some old English magazines under his arm, so I asked him if I could have a look at one. In the first one I looked at was a poem of Voznesensky:

'Along a parabola life, like a rocket flies,
Mainly in darkness, now and then on a rainbow.
Red-headed bohemian Gauguin the painter
Started out life as a prosperous stockbroker.
In order to get to the Louvre from Montmartre
He made a detour all through Java, Sumatra,
Tahiti, the isles of Marquesas . . . '

I showed it to him and he said he didn't like 'Red-headed bohemian Gauguin the painter.' Gauguin, anyway, was raven, he said. Then he pointed back towards Tahiti and showed me where the painter used to ride his horse along the coast into Papeete. He was a Swede and had lived in Tahiti most of his life. He said he was going to Moorea to repair a painting he had done in the chapel there thirty years before. It was a trip full of memories for him. So much had happened and changed since those days. He said Papeete had been completely ruined. There was now a self-conscious hunt for pleasure and peace, where before it had been a way of living. The war, the tourist trade and finally the jet airport had completed the decline. He thought there would soon have to be a crusade against tourist trafficking, just as there once was against the slave trade. For every tourist who came to the place took away a little piece of it as a souvenir, till in the end there would be nothing left of it to rob, except what other tourists had left behind.

Soon we were in Captain Cook's Bay, held to be the most lovely corner of the whole Pacific. We stopped briefly at the landing stage of a new American hotel, while the young American manager, in red swimming trunks, collected a pig and a couple of Tamourré dancers for his Tahitian Feast that night. The quay was crowded with little children and one or two adolescent girls pining for Papeete and the arms of some handsome legionnaire. One twisted her naked body at me under its strip of garish print. A refrigerator was eased ashore and we moved on.

The bay was really marvellous and I couldn't help wishing Captain Cook had left a flag behind him with his name. It is long and turns a corner, cutting off sight of the sea. All round are palms and beaches and catamarans and above two crags like spiked lawns change colour as the shadows slip down their sides. One was in sunlight and cast its shadow upon the other. We went ashore and my Swedish friend introduced me to a hotelier friend of his called Annie. Annie brought us breakfast and told us she was just getting ready to go to the Ashram at Pondicherry in India in order to lose some weight. I began to sense that quite soon someone would ask me what my plans were for passing the night, so I asked what beach would be best for me to sleep on and was immediately offered not only a bed, but a whole chalet to sleep in. They were having a little 'off season' and all the chalets were empty. Nobody seemed to mind. It was as if they were grabbing a little peace before the tourist trade finally broke over Tahiti and Moorea, as surely it must. Talk was of the good old days. Pierre was remembering how he had met Annie way back in one of the 'thirties years, when he had been painting a Madonna behind the altar of the church during the morning and Annie's portrait in the afternoon. She had been thin and even-tempered in those days. Pierre told how a young girl had watched him painting in the church. She had just sat there all through the mornings, staring at his face till his hand had begun to shake and he was obliged to go home. Nowadays the girls were not so excited about their white daddies. They had come to realize that their own skins were more beautiful.

Later in the day Pierre and I went to inspect the chapel on our bikes. It was a tiny, pink and white thing on the side of the bay. The shutters were closed and the door was locked, so we went to look for the padré in a house nearby. This was not locked. All the doors and windows were wide open, but the padré was not there. We walked in and there was a notebook lying open on the kitchen table with a child's drawing of a flower in it. We went out and climbed through a window into the church. Behind the altar was his reredos of a Tahitian Christ. Pierre told me that the painting had been unpopular for some time after it was done, because the people of the island could not understand why he had given Christ a brown skin and Mary a red kerchief round her head like their own women. They said they knew very well that Christ was a white man and that the picture was a mockery of both their own race and of Christ himself.

Pierre said he would have to stand on the altar to repair the painting, but he couldn't do anything without the padré being there to remove the altar cloth. We went back to the hotel and found Annie and her sons and friends all dressed as Indians for a farewell party. We had curry by candlelight, served by a bare-footed Tahitian girl, then a swim in the bay afterwards. There were crazy lime-coloured fireflies, going off like fireworks for the night birds and a vast traveller's tree, spreading its plumes over us and against the dark blue sky. As our bodies came out of the water, they were momentarily a greenish silver as the phosphorus streamed off us into the quick-silver sea.

La folie Anglaise

Next day the *Oceanien* was flying the Blue Peter and at five o'clock a bell rang on board, signalling our departure. It was not sad. Too many people were laughing and crying and waving to ward off their home-sickness. The whole of Papeete seemed to have left their shops and bars to see us off. There were more people there than on the quay at Sydney, but instead of streamers, it was necklaces of shells and garlands of flowers they threw to one another.

We had taken on a lot of Tahitians and their necks were completely hidden under huge collars of seashells and hibiscus. I circled about taking pictures of them as they leant over the rail throwing back their necklaces like broken promises. In the middle of the crowd below was a little knot of white-clad nuns, their white faces like snowdrops among the tulips. People who had never met and would never meet were waving and blowing passionate kisses to one another.

Most of the new passengers were 'metropolitan' civil servants returning to France with their Tahitian wives and girl friends. But there were also some young Tahitian boys leaving home for the first time. Since 1958, all eighteen-year-olds have had to do two years military training in France. It is all part of de Gaulle's plan for integration and assimilation. After two years the young men return to their island completely Gallicized and Tahiti is a little more part of France than it was before. So far the results have been sad. The young men come home dissatisfied and uncertain. They no longer feel part of Tahiti and yet they know that they can never be true Europeans.

There was one Tahitian on board who was making the journey to France for the second time. He had been to France on National Service and while he was there he had married a French girl. The girl wanted to go back to Tahiti with him, so when he came out of the army he took her there and they tried to settle down. Things soon began to go wrong. He found he couldn't make as much money as the Frenchmen living on the island and yet they found that they spent most of their time with the French, trying to keep up, but succeeding only in alienating both their Tahitian and French friends. In the end they decided to give France another try. They had scraped together the cash and booked a passage on the *Oceanien*.

There was no separation of the two races on board, as there might have been on an English ship. Perhaps that was why, being English, I was given a French family to share my cabin. It was the end of my isolation. Maître Pompier Toulemonde et Fils had come to stay. Madame Toulemonde was on the other side of the boat in the Women's Quarters, but soon after we sailed she came round to introduce herself and help her husband unpack. As soon as she knew I spoke French she started to pour out her heart to me. For two years in Tahiti she had had to put up with Madame So-and-So and her daughter and now she found herself sharing a cabin with them on the way home. It was too much. She added that there was some terrible island girl who kept combing her scurf about everywhere and speaking to men in the doorway. Also there was no room for her clothes in the wardrobe and one of the women had already left some dirty knickers in the bathroom.

'Well, you'd better move into our spare bunk,' I said jokingly.

'Oh thank you, thank you,' she said. 'I was so hoping you would understand. You are too kind.' A minute later the bunk was unfolded from the wall and that night we had the only openly mixed Tourist cabin on board.

I took it as a bad sign. The cabin was already tiny and there is something much more voluminous about women than men. It is to do with their bottles and a tendency to put up clothes lines. I was immediately sure that Madame Toulemonde would always be in the bathroom washing out her husband's under-clothes and ranging them over the bath-tub. She had already set a phalanx of ointments and pill boxes against the three-sided mirror, making it a one-sided mirror. Her husband seemed almost as dismayed as I was and shrugged his shoulders at me as she stooped over their young son, who was suffering from sea-sickness. She was in the process of administering a suppository to him. He gave a sudden yelp as it was plunged home, and burst into tears. I went up on deck and walked around looking for someone to grumble to. But I soon got used to the idea and in the end it turned out for the best. Madame Toulemonde was so grateful for my unconditional surrender that she decided to look after me from the start. She seemed to never cease washing and ironing for me and bringing me back pieces of fruit and cheese from her table because she thought I was too thin. She would sit and look at me as I ate to see the effect of it on me. She had big round eyes which blinked when she agreed with you or laughed, and when she said 'no' she always held up one finger and shook it briefly. She was a real Marseillaise and never stopped chatting and roaring with laughter at her own jokes.

I might have really got to like the Toulemondes, but for one thing. This was a sea-shell which they kept in the soap dish in the bathroom. It was very large and lifeless and every time I leant over to clean my teeth I smelt its powerful cat stench. I am usually rather fiery about such things, but my previous concessions and sea-sickness made me phlegmatic and all I did was ask after it from time to time. I naturally assumed that it was a rare specimen, but Monsieur soon told me that no, it was not particularly rare, but extremely venomous, that is to say 'mortelle', highly dangerous. Once I suggested boiling it in water so that the animal would melt and run out. But they had already thought of that and decided that it would spoil the colour. I got to know it well over the weeks that followed. It actually had a big crack in it and was not at all beautiful. I believe it wielded some strange power over its benefactors. I may even have come under its influence myself during the weeks which followed.

One day I went to the cabin after lunch and found the door locked. I knocked and then crept off feeling rather stupid. After that it was accepted that I stay on deck a couple of hours at that time of day. I used to take up a pad and a pen and try to write home. It was usually no good. I would just lie there, my mind as empty as the clear blue sky, knowing that one day, some day, it would all have to be described, but grateful that I felt unable to do it at the time.

I believe I shall be writing home about this trip for the rest of my life. I think I may easily develop a mania to be heard out and may well be seen, years from now, still recollecting, like an old white hunter, shadowy images to an empty fireplace, far into the night.

Life on board the *Oceanien* was like some terrible bed-sitting-room marriage. Almost everything formed grounds for divorce: the conch in the bathroom, the bad food, the way the waiters threw down the plates then completely disappeared, because they had gone to sea for adventure and were sick of finding themselves waiting all the time, the peeling, yelling Australians, the cynical French, the argumentative, prick-proud Germans, the lolling sea, the timelessness. I was either in a stupor or furious. Life was like an uneasy sleep constantly interrupted by the drunk friends of one's flat-mate stumbling over one's inert body in the middle of the night. There was nowhere to go to escape. All one could do was remain anonymous and go to the commissaire every day at three o'clock to make deflated complaints about the service and food. What a clever move to have a special complaining time! The idea has unpleasant memories of queueing up to be punished. We expect you to come, it says, being foreigners you won't understand, so you'd better all come together and get it over with. But by the time an hour had elapsed after lunch one was either asleep or pacified.

I once made the fatal error of calling one waiter a cretin and from then on I was the villain. Later in the trip someone got so angry with him he challenged him to a fight in the next port, but it never came off.

At 4 o'clock every afternoon there were taped concerts in the First Class Music Room and I used to creep in there to read in the air-conditioned salon. But there was one woman in there who resented my tourist ears on her First Class music. She had a huge book which she was always marking and when I entered the saloon she would lift pointed steel eyes in my direction, knit me a little and drop me where I stood. I always waved a smile as a white flag, but she never relented and in the end I grew to admire her as one admires a cliff or a crater. I admired her loneliness, for she never smiled or spoke much, even when the Australians played with her little girls by the swimming pool. She seemed to display more energy and intelligence on her own than all the other enthusiasts playing quoits and deck golf and scrabble around her. She was like Queen Victoria.

Energy of any kind for anything was hard to conserve from the hours and hours of unpolarized sunshine which fell every day upon the deck, melting the very muscles in one's fingers. There was no escape. Even the cabins were constantly wobbling with the brilliant, reflected light from the sea. It was like being a desert reptile without any eyelids.

Just an hour on deck was enough to turn everyone a shade darker – redder, browner or blacker – each day and most people concentrated their attention without much subtlety to this end.

We had crossed the International Dateline and the waiters were even more mutinous because they were working an eight day week.

To mark the occasion there was to be a Fancy Dress Ball. 'Travestis Recommandés' said the invitation, so six of us dressed up as CND beachcombers with placards saying 'Save Tahiti from the Bomb' and 'Non à de Gaulle' – the reverse of the most common propaganda slogan to be found in the French Pacific. When the time came to go into the party we discovered that we were the only ones to have dressed up, so our entry was more like a cabaret act and as a cabaret it fell rather flat. It was another case of 'La folie Anglaise' the French passengers were saying in their neat, round-shouldered suits and dresses, having never for a moment considered wearing anything else. 'Ils font ça sur les bateaux anglais', said one woman sitting near us, excusing the lunatics. Another, sitting not far off, had made a small concession to the occasion by pinning one of the artificial orchids from the tourist bar to her bun, à la Tahitienne. It was worn in such a way that the large phallic stamen seemed to be poking out of her ear, which we all took to be the 'travesti' of the evening.

All of us were soon outshone by a host of little vahinés who came swaying on to the floor in grass skirts and shell necklaces to dance an exciting Tamourré. This is a modernized version of the old Hula Hula. Instead of going round and round, as with a hula hoop, the hips flick from side to side, faster and faster as the dance progresses. In the euphemisms of a brochure 'The Tamourré is a dance designed to quicken the heartbeats of the menfolk.' Nowadays 'menfolk' get away with all kinds of things ordinary men go to prison for.

Only one of the dancers was not Tahitian. This was the beautiful young daughter of a French fonctionnaire returning home from Tahiti. I had admired her across the deck for more than a week, but had only spoken to her the day before at Bingo, and hadn't expected to find her so young. She was sixteen, but her parents had obviously zealously protected her from Tahitian ways during the four years she'd lived there and she had a tantalizing innocence. On the dance floor, among the Tahitian girls, she was all at sea. I suppose her parents must have jollied her into it but she was terribly shy and embarrassed at the hot rhythms and absurd necklaces, with the result that she looked completely naked and thereby memorable. It was the sort of traumatic experience parents let their children in for out of sheer goodwill, unknowingly hastening their own dispensability.

There was a small Scottish contingent among the First Class passengers, who for some reason took objection to the sexy dancing. They voiced their opinions and kept craning their scrawny old necks upwards and away from it all to glimpse an eclipse of the moon which was going on prettily enough, if somewhat inevitably, overhead. But it was the eclipse which was eclipsed in the end.

Next day, the Tahitian men and women were strumming and laughing as usual in their corner of the deck. But as the days took us further from Tahiti, their hibiscus garlands and their lilting songs seemed to grow more feeble and to fade. Soon they were to be subdued and Westernized, perhaps forever.

Last islands

One morning we sighted Coco's Island, an extraordinary eruption of cliffs and jungle, not part of any archipelago. It was the first land for nearly two weeks. Everyone was very excited and even the helmsman seemed to steer unnecessarily close. There was a story on people's lips that two Frenchmen had landed there recently in search of the legendary Coco's gold and that only one had arrived back in France afterwards. Another story was that the island had an English king who was angling for membership in the UN. From the ship all one could see was steep jungle and a white ribbon of water falling from a great height into the splashing sea.

As we passed by, porpoises came out to greet us. They came quite close up to the ship and swam alongside in pairs leaping out of the water in twin arches and grinning at us with their friendly old faces. There must have been sixty or seventy bouncing out of the water at a time. Strange birds followed us for a while, too. Big bony creatures with long beaks, albatrosses perhaps. But they didn't settle on the ship. Perhaps it is harder than it looks, or perhaps they had an idea that the birds on the planet we were going to were more up to date genetically than them. They seemed strangely prehistoric in design, like harpies, or pterodactyls, or aborigines. Soon they banked noisily and loped away back to their ocean lair.

As we went slowly past it, the island seemed to flow away in the opposite direction, defying us to call it a landmark in the timeless space of the ocean. The next day we sighted Darien. 'Balboa this evening,' I wrote on a postcard, 'get out my atlas. West end of the canal. Only one more ocean, my darlings.'

Beatalic sounds again from a transistor. America! Everyone on deck.

Little steam engines with cogs for wheels were tugging our ship through the locks of the canal. The Atlantic is a quarter mile higher than the Pacific. Slowly we were pumped up into the Caribbean. Lodged there in the middle of the land, the ship suddenly looked enormous and for the first time significant.

Soon we came out into a lake before the next canal. Binoculars and cameras probed the shapeless jungle. The ugly green clogged the shores like camouflage thrown over a tank. Away to the right was Darien. At Balboa we went ashore. The ground rocked to a standstill under my feet and seemed to press hard against my footsteps as I walked. Two American checkpoints inside the docks, then no more white faces to be seen in the crowded, rollicking, sea-faring street scenes of Balboa.

The Panama Canal is an American Zone and anti-American. School children are always running down the American flag and running up their own. But I didn't once ask the way without someone getting to his feet from the roadside and pointing it out with a smile. No doubt the Communists are driving home their warheads on shop-floors somewhere, but as elsewhere, all the really serious dissent seemed to be going on in the press. The foreign press at that. In an evening of shopping and night clubs it wasn't apparent.

Here too it was the women who wore the plumage. Basketed or willowy, their curls separated by half a dozen partings and tied up with ribbon, they subdued even their bright surroundings with their humanity. Anyway, how could any real woman be a Communist? Rubbery and numerous, they were infinitely preferable to the phonily sophisticated, basically coarse Tahitians.

American bars too, attracted with their sticks of nervous neon: spearheads of the Re-Conquistadores, the great Spanish American Adventure in reverse. One of the English girls from the ship unwisely dropped behind when we wandered through this area and an Indian tried to snatch her handbag. Being a true-blue Joan Hunter Dunn, she hung on and a furious tug of war took place. The cunning bastard managed to turn the bag upside down, but only a lipstick fell out, which he scooped up in a flash and made off with like a jackdaw.

Balboa was untameable. There was a sort of carnival under the skin at all hours. But in a single night one couldn't hope to locate it.

While I had been sipping night life, the Toulemondes had been buying stuffed baby alligators to sell in Marseilles. Next morning the cabin was crawling with them: vicious, varnished creatures which stood on their feet and fixed you with beady eyes. What a menagerie!

Next stop Curaçao, and very pi by comparison. A sunny, barren, bourgeois free-port, it is colourful, but its colours are of paint and products rather than nature. Dutch design seems to lend itself naturally to the lights of the Caribbean. The Burgomasters' houses along the harbour are painted thickly in greens and yellows and reds like a Dutch panto-mime. Across the harbour is a pontoon bridge which opens to let ships into the largest port in the Caribbean.

Most of the day I spent shopping. I hadn't got any presents for anyone and here in places like 'King Solomon's Mines' – Curaçao has many Jews and the oldest synagogue in the Western Hemisphere – were goods from every country I'd been to. At last I could clutter myself up a bit. The worst thing about travelling is the luggage. The problem is seldom where to go next, but how to get there with a suitcase of ornamental daggers on your hands. Sadly, that problem was over for me. I was a tourist again and all I had to do was carry my souvenirs back to the ship.

Saïd, the Madagascan cabin-boy, did no shopping while we were at Curaçao. He had friends there apparently, for in the morning he was complaining proudly to his passengers of a terrible back-ache, his punishment for too much love-making.

Another night's voyage and we were in the last port. Fort de France, Martinique.

It was the day of the annual bicycle race round the island: Le Tour Martinique. There was the kind of patriotic hysteria in the air countries normally reserve for their Independence Day. In the Bar des Allies a radio chattered about the race's progress on the other side of the island. In the main square huge crowds jostled the gendarmes at the winning post. Above, balconies teetered on the verge of collapse under the weight of whole households. The year before one had fallen.

I let a potent rum 'planter' tour my veins, then I teetered happily round the fine old French town with its peeling shutters, ornate balconies and little sunny squares jigging with school children. In the Place Florentine was a faded Palais de Justice with the blue lettering of 'Liberté, Egalité, Fraternité' irreverently half-hidden under a great wisteria. I walked through the seedy old cathedral where white-clad school-girls were kneeling two by two in the confessionals, with the dim shadow of a white confessor between them, turning first to one, then to the other. And I wondered what there could possibly be to dredge those little hearts of.

In the Place Fabien there was a bistro called Chez Anna, run by a Dutchman and his negress wife, Anna. The Dutch seem to be scattered as far as the English across the earth, but not as far as the Scottish. I had something to eat and a very ancient Canadian came over to talk to me. He said he was a new arrival and didn't know anyone yet. At 80, he'd decided to go and live in a warmer place, but he hadn't realized Martinique was French, and he couldn't speak the language. He said he was sure it hadn't always been French. Then, on top of that, a Social Security officer had just informed him that as a Protestant his marriage wasn't valid in Martinique. He'd been to see the bishop, but there was nothing to be done. A wicked smile spread over his face.

'Perhaps God sent me here on purpose,' he said, 'and I'll be able to get rid of the old bitch at last. All these years I've put up with her, but it's not too late yet. I always wanted hundreds of kids, but she couldn't have any. Miss Baron, her name was when I met her. I should have taken the tip. But I've still got life in me . . . ' He told me he'd run away to Canada from Liverpool in 1902. His brother still lived in Sussex, but he couldn't remember what he looked like. He took out a card and wrote his address on it for me. I turned the card over and it said 'Membership of the British Israel Society'. I asked him what it was and he got very excited and said it was an association of people who believed that England was Israel, the Promised Land – that the Jews only came from one tribe, Judah. All the others were in England and they could prove that the Queen was directly descended from David. Her throne was the throne of David, he said. It was all in the Bible. Even the British Empire was prophesied there and its fall was our fall from grace, due to the spread of atheism. He got out a booklet and I read:

'Until the time arrives when Jesus Christ shall reign in Person, the right to occupy the Throne of David has been conferred by Divine promise on earthly descendants of David. Accordingly the throne must be functioning on earth today among some section of the descendants of ancient Israel.

'The only earthly throne which could possibly qualify as the

Throne of David is that *now* occupied by a monarch of the British Royal House.'

The old chap was nodding to himself, dreaming perhaps of leaving his poor old wife to lead a tribe of children home to Jerusalem in England's green and pleasant land.

I left him drinking a planter and walked back to the quay. There was the pulsating ship smell again: oiled rope and iron oxide, but above the sound of the ventilators came the beat of a calypso. I went on board and a man asked me if I was a passenger. He wanted to see my passport. An exhibition of Martinique dancing was going on for the people on board and plenty of natives who had never seen it before had crowded on to the ship.

In the middle of the deck a cock-fight of colour was flashing and weaving in the spotlight. Mazurka, quadrillo, minuetto, beguine. Four girls, a negress, a mulatress, a quadroon and an octoroon and four men were demonstrating the Caribbean versions of these lovely dances, exported by the French during the last century, but long ago forgotten by them at home. At the end we were also given a completely indigenous dance, still banned in Fort de France, but not in the banana fields outside. This was a love-making dance. The girls fluttered their bottoms in the way of the men's gyrating loins, then whisked them away at the last moment, with a flick of pleated skirts. The final step of the dance, as in real life, was made by the women. They approached the men, face on this time, and made a little jump on to their outstretched thighs. 'It has to be done,' said one of them in English to the audience, and at that moment the lights went out.

My own pigeon

The Atlantic swell: the water slapped and banged about the swimming pool, occasionally streaming across the deck. The passengers lifted their feet and let it flow under their deck chairs without looking up. I knew them all so well. I knew the shirts and change of shirt of everyone on board. I knew them out of the corner of my eye. I knew their footsteps, voices, ankles, even their shadows. I could tell who was blocking my sun without opening my eyes. Yet I hardly knew anyone's name and less people knew mine than anyone's on board. I think I was referred to vaguely as 'the student', or, earlier on, as 'the seasick student', for by the time I recovered people had, mercifully, thought better of their first light-headed sociability and returned to normal. After all the heartfelt mixing of nationalities that had gone on in the Pacific, the different countries had drawn their frontiers across their chosen parts of the deck and that was that.

Once upon a time the initials POSH against the name of a passenger travelling on a British ship ensured he be given a cabin on the *port* side going *out* and on the *starboard* coming *home*, to avoid the midday sun. Today the word 'posh' means something more ridiculous and on the *Oceanien*, at any rate, it was the French who ranged themselves down the shady side of the ship, while the English grilled in the sun.

I think everyone was bored. The two-month journey, the

longest left in the world, was out of time with people's lives and they felt wasteful, wasted. A few Germans who had briefly emigrated to Australia to avoid their draft, sweated at quoits. A Dutch couple, separated at night by Tourist Class regulations, made it up to each other during the day with passionate ping-pong sessions. An Austrian used to yodel at dinner, then fall drunkenly off his chair backwards so that two sulky-faced French waiters had to carry him to his cabin. A little red Englishman in shorts and built-up shoes kept up a running commentary on matters, rather like Jimmy Clitheroe, but, like the conch in my bathroom, the trip had gone too far. People were cracking. 'I can't believe I'm really going home,' they would say. But were we really going anywhere? The day of arrival in the far-off harbour was like a mirage: the trotting horseman in the shallow water, who seemed to be approaching but never got any closer. The water we passed through one day looked much like that we passed through the next. We had only time to tell us that it was not and why should one have believed that? Time needs landmarks, but we had only the waves.

In fact, most people were not deceived, but there were some who slipped into a kind of malaise which might have been a symptom of the most widespread unhappiness in any part of the world. For nowadays, unless one is the inhabitant of an undiscovered island it is impossible to be at any one place at any one time. One's imagination has been dispersed about the globe, so that one is always more or less dissatisfied, more or less on the move, more or less dependent on new things to reassure one of life. Remove them, create an illusion of movement without its proof, you get disbelief, apathy.

The bearded American, Bill Collins, wasn't apathetic. He was one of the last people to surrender to the voyage and he never surrendered to the ship's staff. To the last minute he was perfecting his manifesto and petition to be handed to Messageries Maritimes in Paris. With great charm and a fast,

276

priest-like voice, he had got every passenger on board – and one or two of the crew besides – to sign their names to a diatribe it had taken us weeks to compose.

Bill had already been travelling two years and was showing no homing tendencies. He had walked all over South-East Asia: from Bangkok up to Burma, from Sarawak into Borneo, where he'd stayed in the native long houses and been offered a girl in every one, each anxious to pass on some of his lovely white blood to the next generation. Yet he had no desire to record any of it. 'I've got a memory, haven't I? And how could I ever forget that kind of thing?' Perhaps it is only writers who forget what things are like and have to invent and remind themselves with notes all the time. Bill had an almost fanatical allegiance to the present, for he saw things as they were and not how best they would strike the folk back home, as I did. Perhaps he never thought of his absence lengthening like a shadow there, or rather shortening like a shadow and disappearing. He knew you couldn't be in two places at once and there was no point trying. But how did he convince himself? If I hadn't been in two places at once I could never have left home. Being my own remote controller was what made it possible. I had to see more, go further, not to let myself down at home. I was my own pigeon, homing to its conscience and critic.

Sometimes I imagined myself already there. Aeroplanes, with their instant arrivals in far places, leave the spirit cowering in disbelief. But the *Oceanien* had moved so slowly through time I found myself no longer thinking as a foreigner. Hearing the extraordinary voice of the BBC again, I realized I had re-orientated to that powerful illusion of a club that is England for the expatriate. To cockney humour, Speaker's Corner, Woolworth's, Soho, the Thames, the parks. To Jack Demanio, Edmundo Ros, Housewife's Choice. To 'Bristol Rovers 2, Nottingham Forest nil'. To Osbert Lancaster, pantomimes and Private Eye. To knowing the reason for finding all the shops

277

closed in the Edgware Road on a Thursday afternoon. To the Edgware Road even, though I wouldn't have believed it. To damp autumn evenings with the sodium lamps deadening the flesh of skinny secretaries with hair like green smoke. To the sound of diesel taxis drawing up outside at night and to their single orange signs in the distance after parties. To being anonymous in the streets. To being asked the way and knowing it. To no longer being absurd and wrong when I complained. To a servility so subtle it is really politeness. To chance meetings, telephone calls, dates. To No. 14 buses, mewses, evening papers, Indian restaurants, buskers, the Everyman. To Victoria Station, the Brighton Belle, the Battersea Power Station. To bricks. To Brighton: the white helmets of the policeman in summer, the Pavilion, the lanes, the piers, the penny in the slot machine of the execution of Mary Queen of Scots, the Aquarium, the Ice Rink, the smell of fishing boats on the shingle in winter, tar and multitudes in summer and the summer-flowering beatniks hating it. Hugh Williams at The Theatre Royal and the drive home afterwards to where everything is still exactly the same: the yellow sofa, the Campari, the smoke in the window blurring the view of the downs, the Copenhagen china, the Sunday papers, the smell of cooking and my father saying 'I put two bottles of Hugel in the fridge...'

Like a gradually surfacing bathysphere, the boat had re-conditioned me to former days. Yet I had a sinking suspicion that wasn't the end of it. You travel, you return, people ask you what it was like and the real trip begins as you start wondering ... pulling in the runaway spools, peering after the memory which recedes like a star, faster than the speed of its light reaches out to you.

Rain pearled the sea: damp, windy, land rain. Tomorrow we would be in Marseilles and I would go ashore there from the same little steel cabin I had gone ashore from at Tahiti. Somehow it still seemed unlikely, or already passed. It is a quality of ships that they seem to be outward, not homeward, bound. Trains take one home, but ships adventure on. Or else hang back from their ports like fickle women, or broken elevators, hovering tantalizingly over the target, fostering mirages. Then one day, quite without warning, they come alongside the strange new world, indifferent as prostitutes to your relief.

About the Author

HUGO WILLIAMS was born in Windsor in 1942, grew up in Sussex, and now lives in north London. He has published eight volumes of poetry: *Symptoms of Loss* (1965); *Sugar Daddy* (1970); *Some Sweet Day* (1975); *Love-Life* (1979); *Writing Home* (1985); *Selected Poems* (1989); *Self-Portrait with a Slide* (1990); and *Dock Leaves* (1995). In addition to *All the Time in the World*, which was originally published in 1966, his other books include a travel narrative entitled *No Particular Place to Go* (1981), and *Freelancing* (1995) a collection of columns written for the *Times Literary Supplement*.